AFTER THE GOOD FRIDAY AG
ANALYSING POLITICAL CF...
IN NORTHERN IRELAND

CONTRIBUTORS TO THIS VOLUME

Professor Paul Arthur, Professor of Politics, University of Ulster

Arthur Aughey, Senior Lecturer in Politics, University of Ulster

Bernadette C. Hayes, Professor of Sociology, The Queen's University of Belfast

Ian McAllister, Professor of Politics, and Director, Research School of Social Sciences, Australian National University

Christopher McCrudden, Professor of Human Rights Law in the University of Oxford

Joseph Ruane, Senior Lecturer in Sociology, University College Cork

Jennifer Todd, Senior Lecturer in Politics, University College Dublin

AFTER THE GOOD FRIDAY AGREEMENT

Analysing Political Change
In Northern Ireland

edited by
Joseph Ruane and
Jennifer Todd

University College Dublin Press
Preas Choláiste Ollscoile Bhaile Átha Cliath

First published 1999 by University College Dublin Press
Newman House, St Stephen's Green, Dublin 2

ISBN 1 900621 26 6

Cataloguing in Publication data available from the British Library

Index by Helen Litton
Typset in 10/12 Sabon and Palatino by Elaine Shiels, Bantry, Co. Cork, Ireland
Printed in Ireland by Colour Books, Dublin

CONTENTS

Acknowledgements   vi

Preface   vii

1 The Belfast Agreement: Context, content, consequences
   Joseph Ruane and Jennifer Todd   1

2 Ethnonationalism, public opinion and the Good Friday
   Agreement
   Bernadette C. Hayes and Ian McAllister   30

3 Nationalism, republicanism and the Good Friday Agreement
   Jennifer Todd   49

4 'Quiet diplomacy and personal conversation'. Track Two
   diplomacy and the search for a settlement in Northern Ireland
   Paul Arthur   71

5 Equality and the Good Friday Agreement
   Christopher McCrudden   96

6 A new beginning? The prospects for a politics of civility in
   Northern Ireland
   Arthur Aughey   122

7 The end of (Irish) history? Three readings of the current
   conjuncture
   Joseph Ruane   145

Appendix: The Agreement reached in the Multi-Party Negotiations   171

Bibliography   202

Index   214

ACKNOWLEDGEMENTS

The editors wish to acknowledge the role of the Department of Politics, University College Dublin, where some of these chapters were initially presented as guest seminars; the British Council for funding some of these seminars; participants in the seminars, particularly Mark Crystal, Allan Leonard, Claire Mitchell, Muiris MacCarthaigh and Conor Scott; many others for informal briefings and discussions; Barbara Mennell of UCD Press; and Jonathan Harvey who helped prepare the manuscript for publication.

PREFACE

Joseph Ruane and Jennifer Todd

The Agreement reached in the Multi-Party Negotiations – to give it its official title – or, variously, the Good Friday Agreement or the Belfast Agreement, was reached on 10 April 1998. It was endorsed at referendums in both Irish jurisdictions the following month. It was a momentous occasion. Since the fall of the Sunningdale Agreement in 1974, the British and Irish governments had sought a settlement that would have cross-community support and would bring a permanent end to violence. For 24 years it had eluded them. Now, it seemed, it had been achieved, based on a compromise not simply between unionism and nationalism but between loyalism and republicanism, and promising a permanent cessation of violence. At referendum, the settlement secured the support of a large majority in the North (71%) and an overwhelming majority in the South (94%). Even among its unionist opponents in Northern Ireland, its significance was recognised.

In the immediate aftermath of the Agreement, widely divergent interpretations were put forward by commentators and politicians alike. Some saw it as a new dawn that would transform relationships not simply in Northern Ireland, but throughout Ireland and between the two islands. Others declared it to be fundamentally flawed, with a hidden price-tag which 'will only be reckoned when the music stops' (McCartney, 1998). Some hailed it as a good day for the union; others saw it as a victory for nationalism and a step on the way to dismantling the union. Some saw it as a historic compromise between two historic blocs who would remain unchanged by it; others saw it as a transformative process which would soon bring far-reaching cultural, institutional and – in time – constitutional change.

Amidst the extremes of optimism and pessimism the most informed voices tempered hope with caution. The party leaders who negotiated it stressed that it would work only if people applied their mind and will to make it work; it was described as 'a new beginning', 'an historic opportunity', 'a great opportunity', 'a start . . . [to] . . . the healing process'. The most authoritative, neutral observer of the peace process, the talks chairman, Senator George Mitchell, warned that the Agreement might not still be in existence in eighteen months' time and commented on the complete lack of trust, 'a presumption of bad faith', between unionists and republicans (Fletcher, 1998).

In the months that followed, the need for caution was borne out as unionists and nationalists disagreed over the interpretation of key clauses of the Agreement. Its implementation would be uneven. Progress would be rapid in matters which were totally in the control of the governments (elections to the new Assembly, legislation to establish the new institutions, prisoner releases), slower where the agreement of the Northern political parties was required, and on key issues (in particular decommissioning and the formation of the executive) at a snail's pace.

More than a year after the signing of the Agreement, there is now some distance from the emotion, excitement and partisanship of its birth. It is possible to view the Agreement in a more reflective and analytical way and to understand better the context out of which it emerged, the forces which shaped it, the extent to which it has addressed the under-lying conflict and what must be done if it is to succeed in this task. These are the central themes of this book. At the same time, the book cannot offer a final judgement on the significance of the Agreement. As this book goes to press, it remains unclear if the Agreement will survive its second year or emerge from it in fully operational form. But the chapters can and do point to the underlying conditions which work for the success of the Agreement, the clauses which are central to it, the ways in which they can be implemented and the tendencies and processes which threaten successful implementation. It is here that social scientific analysis can inform political action.

The book draws together scholars from the fields of politics, sociology and law, and the articles are written from a variety of theoretical and methodological perspectives. The authors draw on theories of ethnonatio-nalism and of ideology, theories of the (relative) autonomy of the political and the possibilities and processes of conflict resolution, of mainstreaming equality, and of modernity and postmodernity. The research methods used include the statistical analysis of survey data, documentary analysis and participant observation. The mode of argument ranges from the normative to the historico-sociological. The unity of the book derives from its focused subject matter and the concern to bring the insights of the social sciences to bear on it.

In chapter 1, Ruane and Todd contextualise the Agreement. They describe its background, its provisions, its political logic and the difficulties experienced in implementing it. More generally, through this detailed analysis, they delineate the limits of political autonomy: the Good Friday Agreement shows the transformative potential of elite negotiation and compromise and institutional innovation, but also its limits in the face of communal division. The chapter draws attention to a paradox: the conflict that the Agreement promises to resolve may prevent it from functioning as anticipated.

Chapters 2–4 focus on changes in political attitudes, identities, ideologies and practices which made the Agreement possible, and which may also set limits to its successful functioning. Bernadette Hayes and Ian McAllister (chapter 2) chart changes in political attitudes and identities in the wider population over the past decade. After a period of seeming moderation in the mid-1990s, they show the emergence of 'strong pro-state' and 'strong counter-state' groups and provide evidence of increasing communal polarisation. At the same time, new forms of intra-communal divisions are being created. These changes are manifested in public attitudes to the Agreement, particularly in oppositions which centre as much on the social as on the political implications of the Agreement.

Jennifer Todd (chapter 3) examines the processes of ideological reconstruction which have taken place within nationalism and republicanism over the past generation. Reconstruction has opened the possibility of negotiation and compromise with unionism. But the space for compromise is narrow. The Agreement offers the potential to sediment the changes in nationalist and republican ideology, but the difficulties in its implementation also threaten to disconfirm and destabilise the ideological changes in republicanism.

Paul Arthur (chapter 4) examines the contribution of Track 2 diplomacy to the process of negotiation which led to a settlement. He focuses on two issues: the role of Track 2 diplomacy in the US decision to grant a visa to Gerry Adams in 1994; its role in developing among the political elite in Northern Ireland a capacity to work together and negotiate on practical issues. That capacity was further enhanced in the multi-party talks process.

Chapters 5–6 deal with two core aspects of the Agreement on which its success will depend. Christopher McCrudden (chapter 5) looks at the equality agenda. He shows how the Agreement picks up on a wider trend – internationally and in the history of fair employment legislation in Northern Ireland – towards 'mainstreaming' equality. He examines the politics that surrounded the insertion of equality provisions into the Agreement and into the subsequent legislation, and the prospects for their full implementation.

Arthur Aughey (chapter 6) focuses on the normative principles on which the successful functioning of the Agreement will depend. He argues that the Agreement has not, need not and should not bring a convergence of substantive aims. The aim should be a 'politics of civility' – an acceptance by all of the rules of the political game and a willingness to abide by them. This will require in turn establishing the (relative) autonomy of the political realm from the different, antagonistic, logic of communal conflict.

In a final chapter (chapter 7) Joseph Ruane interrelates a socio-historical theory of the emergence and reproduction of conflict in Northern Ireland with more general theories of modernity and post-modernity to analyse the current conjuncture and the possibility of a lasting settlement. He offers three contrasting readings of the conjuncture before suggesting that the most appropriate model may be one which views each reading as a partial approximation to a complex and contradictory reality.

As always in matters to do with Northern Ireland, there are problems of nomenclature. Individual authors and chapters vary in their naming of the Agreement as the 'Good Friday' or 'Belfast' Agreement. We have not attempt to enforce uniformity in this matter; nor indeed did we observe it ourselves.

1

THE BELFAST AGREEMENT: CONTEXT, CONTENT, CONSEQUENCES

Joseph Ruane and Jennifer Todd

INTRODUCTION

The Belfast Agreement was once famously described as 'Sunningdale for slow learners'. It is the second cross-community settlement to be put into place since the political crisis began in Northern Ireland 30 years ago. The Sunningdale Agreement of 1973 was the first, and it lasted only eight months. The Belfast Agreement is still in place, well over a year after it was signed, although its implementation has been slow and crisis-ridden. The central thrust of the two agreements is the same – nationalist acceptance of the present constitutional position of Northern Ireland within the United Kingdom in return for power-sharing within Northern Ireland and links between North and South. In other respects, however, the comparison is misleading. The two agreements differ in important points of constitutional and institutional detail. The Belfast Agreement offers a fuller recognition of the right of the people of Northern Ireland to determine their constitutional future. It is much more inclusive of the range of political opinion and more supportive of equality and human rights. Crucially, it offers something which Sunningdale could not: a complete end to political violence. These differences reflect profound differences in the contexts of the two agreements which give a different significance to superficially similar elements.

The Sunningdale Agreement was introduced less than two years after Stormont had been prorogued, and the social structures and many of the institutional practices of that period were still in place. The unionist position was still strong and their political expectations were high: for many, anything less than majority rule was unacceptable. But there was also real fear of long term British intentions. Northern Ireland's industrial economy was still intact; many unionists believed that an independent Northern Ireland was viable. Catholics' sense of grievance at their treatment during the Stormont years was acute. The IRA was convinced that it could force a British withdrawal; Protestant paramilitaries had mobilised in large numbers; violence was intense and indiscriminate. Nationalist sentiment in the Republic – only a year after Bloody Sunday – was strong. Unionists did not accept that the government of the Republic had any role in the search for a solution; the British government was at best ambivalent about granting it such a role. There was little or no international involvement – the conflict was seen as a matter internal to the United Kingdom.

The situation has changed, profoundly and irreversibly, in the years since Sunningdale. The demographic balance of Protestant to Catholic has altered from 63:37 in 1971 to 58:42 in 1991 (Kennedy, 1994, p. 9). The nationalist vote has grown from under 20 per cent of the total in the 1969 Stormont elections to nearly 40 per cent in the 1998 Assembly elections. Catholics are a stronger presence in the institutions of state. Substantial economic inequality remains between the two communities, but less than before, and comprehensive fair employment legislation is now in place. The economy of Northern Ireland has de-industrialised and is now highly dependent on the British state. Culturally Northern Ireland has become more integrated into the UK, and the terms of public discourse that once privileged unionists are now more even-handed. Nationalists have a new sense of political capacity and cultural self-confidence; unionists feel vulnerable and are conscious of decline. The Anglo-Irish Agreement of 1985 gave the Republic a role in the affairs of Northern Ireland as of right; Southern nationalism is now more liberal and more pluralist. Since the late 1970s, the international influence on the conflict has increased: from 1977, US Presidents have played an increasingly important role in the search for a settlement; the European Union has been an important model and resource. Crucially, republicans have concluded that they cannot achieve their goals by violence and, with the major loyalist paramilitary organisations, seek a negotiated settlement.

The Belfast Agreement has been made possible by these changes and is itself an attempt to harness the possibilities in the new situation. Its constitutional guarantees are given in a context of a continuing unionist majority and a rising nationalist vote. Its equality and human rights legislation builds on a series of measures which, beginning with the fair employment legislation of 1976, has led to a substantial improvement in the Catholic position. Its consociational structures are proposed in the context of an increasingly bi-national approach to the conflict. Proposals for North–South bodies are made in the context of a more pluralist nationalism in the South, a deepening involvement by the Irish state in the search for a solution to the conflict, and of European Union cross-border cooperation. The promise of industrial investment following the implementation of the Agreement has real meaning in the context of a de-industrialised economy. The prospects for peace, stability and reconciliation are infinitely greater with the commitment by paramilitaries on both sides to a negotiated settlement.

Even in this new, more favourable context, the success of the Agreement is far from guaranteed. The political regulation of communal conflicts is a complex and delicate affair. Negotiated settlements are at best a mixture of compromise and fudge which leaves no side entirely satisfied. They reflect – more or less crudely – the balance of communal and state power at the time they are negotiated. But their implementation may alter the balance of power and may do so in ways that limit their effectiveness. They may enjoy cross-community support at the level of general principle, but fail to secure agreement at the point of practical implementation. They are above all political interventions, whose success depends on conditions outside the political domain.

These points raise a general question with real practical import: the autonomy of, and limits to, political action in conditions of communal conflict. There has been much general debate on the autonomy of politics in relation to social structure (Evans et al, 1985; Hall, 1985). The literature on conflict regulation is similarly divided between perspectives which emphasise political institutions, organisation and leadership, and those which emphasise the social and communal conditions of conflict and conflict regulation (see, for example, Sisk, 1996). The division is echoed in studies of Northern Ireland. For example, Dunn (1995, pp. 6–7) and Irwin (1998) give primacy to the communal level, while political scientists tend to see politics as the motor of progress (McGarry and O'Leary, 1990; McGarry and O'Leary, 1995; Pollak, 1993). Elsewhere we have stressed both the importance of the political and the constraints which structural conditions impose on it (Ruane and Todd, 1996, chapters 5, 11).

The Agreement, reached in a context of continuing division, shows the power of the political in one respect: the capacity of elite political skills, will and determination to forge an agreement against the odds. But the difficulties experienced so far in implementing that agreement show that the limits to political progress can soon be reached. Political will, pressure and contingency can bring elite agreement on political institutions. But where the institutions need wider party and communal support to function, that support may not be forthcoming. This is not, on our view, to be attributed simply to a failure of party leadership; it is the product of the interplay between political leadership and structurally defined, conflicting communal interests.

Are the structural, communal and political conditions now in place for a peaceful settlement to the conflict in Northern Ireland? It is too soon to say. The desire for a settlement is not in question; nor is the willingness to compromise. Moreover, so much progress has been made towards a settlement – the Downing Street Declaration, the paramilitary ceasefires, the multi-party negotiations, the Agreement itself, the referendums, the formation of the Assembly, the enactment of the new legislation, prisoner releases – that it seems impossible that it could end in failure. But there are still powerful forces dividing the communities and pushing them into competition and conflict (Ruane and Todd, 1996); and it is salutary to bear in mind that in tandem with the political progress has gone an intensifying sectarianism.

In this chapter we look at the changes in conditions and circumstances which led to the Agreement. We examine its content and analyse its political logic – how it defines the conflict and proposes to regulate it. We discuss the difficulties encountered in implementing it and ask whether it adequately addresses the conditions of conflict. We conclude by pointing to the issues which must be tackled if the Agreement is to fulfil its potential.

BACKGROUND TO THE AGREEMENT

The political crisis of the past three decades in Northern Ireland has deep historical and structural roots (Ruane and Todd 1996, chapter 2; Ruane, this volume, p. 147 ff.). At one level, it is simply the latest phase in an unfolding set of relationships between Protestants and Catholics in Ireland and the British state. These relationships, which are now centuries old, have constituted and reconstituted Irish (and now Northern Irish) Protestants and Catholics as communities with sharply opposed interests, identities and strategic options. Conflict has been more or less continuous, but it has unfolded in alternating phases of low and high intensity. The past 30 years have been one such high intensity phase.

The conditions for such intensity are above all structural: on the one hand, a set of general conditions predisposing towards conflict, on the other the conditions for a particularly intense struggle for power between the communities (Ruane, this volume, p. 156 ff.). We may see the crisis of 1969 as a product of the change in the balance of power which took place in the decades after 1921; and we may see the conflicts and political developments of the past three decades – the succession of (mostly failed) political initiatives, the programmes of political and social reform, the strategic manoeuvres of the governments, political parties and paramilitaries – as a complex process in and through which the new communal power balance was at once consolidated and confirmed. As this happened, the conditions for a settlement began to emerge. They were grasped in a new political initiative.

The initiative came from the republican movement. It was a response to several factors. One was the military stalemate which had emerged between the IRA and the security forces. If the IRA had proven that it could not be defeated, the British government had proven that it could not be forced to withdraw from Northern Ireland. And the IRA's campaign came at a price to its supporters: it meant, on the one hand, harassment by the security forces, attacks by loyalists and the constant tension of living in a 'war situation'; on the other hand, it imposed a definite limit on the development of a wider political base. It also carried a political risk: if the moral tolerance of republican opinion was stretched too far, support both for the campaign and for the political objectives would fall away. Public reaction to the atrocity at Enniskillen on Remembrance Day, 1987, raised that prospect in an acute way.

The practical and political limits of the armed campaign directed the attention of the republican leadership to alternatives. Here the Anglo-Irish Agreement (AIA) of 1985 was critical. The AIA for the first time recognised the Irish government as a representative of Northern nationalists and gave it what the then Taoiseach, Garret FitzGerald, called a 'more than consultative' role in policy-making on Northern Ireland. In return, there was a reiteration of Irish state recognition of the right of the majority in Northern Ireland to determine its constitutional status as part of the United Kingdom or of a united Ireland, and a pledge of closer security cooperation. Republicans publicly denounced the Agreement as a betrayal of Irish nationalism and a setback to the achievement of Irish unity. But the more politically minded were impressed. It showed what could be achieved by the combined forces of peaceful, constitutional nationalism – the Irish government, the Social Democratic and Labour Party (SDLP) and the pressures of influential Irish-Americans through the US government.

Other developments reinforced the view that republican objectives might be achieved quicker and with less cost by constitutional means than by violence. One was the growing strength of the nationalist community, in particular the growth in the Catholic proportion of the population, their stronger position in the economy and the rise in the overall nationalist/republican vote. This pointed to the potential strength of an alliance of constitutional nationalists and republicans throughout Ireland and in the US. The condition of any such alliance, however, would be an abandonment of the armed struggle. The first step towards that began in the spring of 1988 with talks between Sinn Féin and the SDLP. The talks ended inconclusively, but a beginning had been made.

Meanwhile unionists were beginning to re-evaluate their strategy. The Anglo-Irish Agreement had been a profound and traumatic setback for unionism. The two main unionist parties, the Ulster Unionist Party (UUP) and the Democratic Unionist Party (DUP), made strenuous efforts to bring it down; there were boycotts of Northern Ireland ministers, mass mobilisations of protesters, appeals to the courts and to the Crown, and threats of an armed campaign. But the efforts proved futile and after two years of protest the UUP and DUP began the difficult task of trying to remove it by negotiation.

This prepared the way for a series of multi-party talks between the British and Irish governments and the Northern constitutional parties between 1991 and 1993 (see Bew and Gillespie, 1993). The talks were important less for their outcome – they led to no agreement – than for the consensus that emerged about negotiation procedures and the conditions for a settlement. First, and perhaps most important, the unionist parties accepted that the Irish government had a central and proactive role to play. Second, there was agreement on the need for a three-stranded agenda: Strand 1 concerned issues internal to Northern Ireland; Strand 2 dealt with issues concerning North–South relations; Strand 3 addressed issues pertaining to British–Irish relations. Third, the principle was accepted that 'nothing was agreed until everything was agreed'. Fourth, the talks were chaired by independent international figures.

During the period of inter-party talks the republican initiative of 1988 was sidelined but did not come to an end. Contacts between John Hume and Gerry Adams continued; there was also contact between the Irish government and republicans, and between the British government and both Sinn Féin and the IRA. When the inter-party talks finally ended without agreement, the republican initiative – now described as the 'peace process' – returned to centre stage. Progress was rapid, with agreement between John Hume and Gerry Adams on the basis for a joint nationalist–republican approach to a settlement (see Todd, this volume, p. 57 ff.), and a major statement by the two governments on 10 December 1993 – the Downing Street Declaration (DSD) – setting out the general principles on which a settlement might be reached (see Ruane and Todd, 1996, chapter 11).

The DSD, whose terms were negotiated not simply with nationalists and republicans but with unionists and loyalists, marked a decisive shift in the analysis of the conflict and in the approach to it. It located the roots of the conflict in a historical process on the island of Ireland which primarily affected the people of Ireland, North and South (paragraphs 1, 2); it reaffirmed the British government's lack of 'selfish strategic or economic interest' in Northern Ireland and its intent to promote agreement on the island (paragraph 4); it affirmed a (revised) notion of national self-determination (paragraphs 4, 5) which was conjoined with an Irish acceptance of the need for consent of all significant groups to a constitutional settlement (paragraphs 5, 6, 7); and it pledged change in both parts of the island (paragraphs 6, 7, 9) in an attempt to undo the causes of conflict (paragraph 1). Any progress towards this would, however, require an IRA ceasefire.

An IRA ceasefire was declared the following August after months of clarification between Sinn Féin and the British government about the details of the DSD. A loyalist ceasefire followed six weeks later. In February 1995 the two governments sketched out in some detail their proposals for a constitutional and institutional settlement: the Joint Framework Document. The proposals, which emphasised North–South harmonisation and integration, were forcefully rejected by unionists. They had been suspicious of the peace process from the outset; they were now extremely anxious at the direction it was taking. James Molyneaux resigned as leader of the UUP and the party elected as his successor the candidate who, at the time, appeared the most hard-line – David Trimble.

Meanwhile political progress was blocked by the British requirement that the IRA must decommission its weapons before Sinn Féin (SF) could enter multi-party talks. The stalling of the process, and the suspicion that the British government was not serious about it, eventually led the IRA to return to violence in February 1996. The renewal of the IRA campaign led to a quickening of the political process. In May 1996 elections took place with a dual purpose – to provide representatives for a Northern Ireland Forum and to designate the parties which could participate in negotiations (Elliott, 1997). The unionist vote splintered with the UUP gaining less than half of the total unionist vote. Within the nationalist bloc, the SDLP continued to represent the majority (58 per cent) but the SF vote grew to 42 per cent. Negotiations began the following month between the parties who had attained a minimum representation at the elections. SF was excluded because of the continuing IRA armed campaign.

In the event, the Forum was boycotted by nationalist representatives and the multi-party talks failed to break the political deadlock. On the nationalist and Irish government side, the general view echoed that of a government adviser that talks were 'not worth a penny candle' without Sinn Féin. However, Conservative Party dependence on UUP votes in the House of Commons ruled out any British initiative that did not have UUP support. And unionists, both UUP and DUP, refused to negotiate with SF without prior decommissioning.

The situation altered dramatically in June 1997 with the Labour Party's return to power in Britain with a huge majority. The new government was determined to re-start the peace process and to involve Sinn Féin in negotiations. The condition of prior IRA decommissioning was waived and it was stated that SF would be admitted to a new round of talks in September if a ceasefire took place some weeks earlier. The IRA renewed its ceasefire on 20 July. Doubts continued, however, about unionist participation. Two unionist parties – the DUP and United Kingdom Unionist Party (UKUP), representing nearly 43 per cent of the unionist electorate at the Forum elections – refused to participate in talks with SF prior to IRA decommissioning. However, the UUP (46 per cent of the unionist electorate at the Forum elections) and the Progressive Unionist Party (PUP) and Ulster Democratic Party (UDP) (small parties with just over 10 per cent of the unionist vote and with links to the loyalist paramilitaries) participated. This fulfilled the requirements for cross-community participation – over 50 per cent of nationalists and unionists – and it made talks possible.

The UUP decision was a calculated response to two factors. One was the steady erosion of the unionist position under direct rule – their loss of control of the Northern economy, the continued shift in the demographic balance and the growth in nationalist political representation, the marginalisation of some core aspects of their culture (particularly Orange marches). The other was the precedent set by the Anglo-Irish Agreement and the British government's willingness to do a deal with nationalists over the heads of unionists. Whereas the DUP prepared to dig in its heels all the more, David Trimble was convinced that unionists should 'bring the fight' to nationalists, participate in talks, and ensure that unionist interests were protected in any settlement.

The changing conditions in Northern Ireland gave (almost) all parties a strategic interest in entering negotiations. Wider changes enhanced those interests and gave a favourable context for successful negotiations. The 1990s were a decade of exceptional change in the Republic (see Crotty and Schmitt, 1998). The decade began with the resignation of Charles Haughey – the *bête noire* of unionism – as leader of Fianna Fáil and Taoiseach; he was followed by two moderate nationalist figures, Albert Reynolds and Bertie Ahern. The economy began a period of rapid and sustained expansion; the Catholic church experienced substantial erosion in its moral authority; under Mary Robinson's presidency, there was an increasing emphasis on cultural pluralism. The effect of these changes was to moderate unionist aversion to the South and suspicion that the South was trying to manoeuvre unionists into a united Ireland against their will.

Changes in Britain also played a role. The return of New Labour to power in 1997 after 18 years of Conservative rule marked a sea-change in British politics. Constitutional referendums prepared the way for Scottish and Welsh devolution, facilitating further constitutional experimentation and opening up the potential for new understandings of the union, both in Britain and with respect to Northern Ireland. Separate arrangements could now be made for Northern Ireland without making it appear wholly anomalous in the UK context and, in unionist fears, a candidate for ultimate expulsion from the UK. Also, while the overwhelming Labour majority in the House of Commons meant that the government in power in Britain was no longer dependent on UUP votes, the prime minister Tony Blair declared his very strong personal commitment to the union. Meanwhile nationalists saw in the rise of Scottish nationalism another route to the dissolution of the union.

The European and wider global context was also important. The late 1980s and early 1990s saw a new surge in European integration, which further decreased the emphasis on national sovereignty and gave a new impetus to cross-border cooperation. Proposals for North–South links could be presented, not as a first step to Irish unity, but as simply an application of the European principle of cross-border cooperation in the British–Irish context. The birth of a 'new world order' was consistent with increasing US interest in 'soft diplomacy' (see Arthur, this volume, pp. 71–95). It indirectly facilitated the peace processes in South Africa and the Middle East which have served as models in Northern Ireland, particularly for republicans.

In short, the circumstances in which the negotiations began were more conducive to a settlement than at any time in the past. But there was plenty of evidence that conflict was continuing, not least in the intensifying confrontations surrounding Orange marches, particularly at Drumcree. As the multi-party talks began, commentators and participants alike were far from convinced that a settlement would follow.

THE TALKS PROCESS

Sinn Féin entered the multi-party negotiations in September 1997: immediately afterwards the DUP and the UKUP left. The remaining participants were the UUP, PUP and UDP, the SDLP, the Alliance Party (APNI) and two small parties, the Northern Ireland Women's Coalition (NIWC) and the Labour Party. The talks were chaired by Senator George Mitchell, General John de Chastelain, and the Finnish ex-Prime Minister Harry Holkerri.

The format and agenda were remarkably similar to the multiparty talks of 1991–3. They followed the now familiar three-stranded formula: Strand 1 dealt with internal Northern Ireland institutions, Strand 2 with North–South relations, and Strand 3 with East–West relations. Other issues, like the equality agenda (see McCrudden, this volume, pp. 96–121), policing and prisoner releases, were included in or dealt with on the margins of Strand 1. Decommissioning was to be dealt with by an Independent International Commission on Decommissioning, chaired by General John de Chastelain, which met parallel to the talks process. Constitutional issues were to form part of a new inter-governmental agreement, to be endorsed by the parties and incorporated into the multi-party Agreement.

Discussions progressed by the principle of 'sufficient consensus' – the support of a majority of unionists and of nationalists (as measured by support in the Forum elections). The UUP needed PUP or UDP support for a unionist majority. The SDLP was sufficient to make up a majority of nationalists but in practice the governments considered SF support as crucial to the success of any agreement. The principle that 'nothing was agreed until everything was agreed' was adopted: the settlement was to be a package, with bargains and trade-offs between strands and agendas. The hardest bargaining would be left until the end when a package was finally put together.

In the initial months the parties presented widely divergent views and aims. On Strand 1, the UUP, SDLP and the minor parties agreed on the desirability of a devolved assembly; SF was totally opposed on the grounds that it would stabilise Northern Ireland as a regional entity and reinforce unionist dominance as the majority in the region. The SDLP and the UUP were divided on the form and terms of reference of an assembly. The UUP were resolutely opposed to an executive with collective cabinet responsibility in case this meant taking collective responsibility for policy with Sinn Féin. They favoured instead an assembly which worked through committees, with each party taking committee chairmanships in proportion to their numbers. The SDLP favoured an assembly with strong legislative powers and scope and a strong executive. Mechanisms for protecting minority rights were also in contention as was the relation of the Assembly to the North–South bodies under discussion in Strand 2.

There were further wide divisions on Strand 2. The central nationalist demand was for North–South bodies with wide ranging functions (SF wished them to include policing and the courts), constituted by acts of the British and Irish parliaments, with substantial ('executive') powers, a permanent and proactive administrative staff and a dynamic for expansion on the model of EU institutions. In contrast, the UUP was adamantly against any form of North–South cooperation whose effect might be to integrate North and South or weaken the union with Britain. They proposed voluntary cooperation in bodies constituted by the Irish parliament and the Northern Assembly (which could then veto their development) and conceived as part of wider British–Irish relations. Implementation would be through already existing institutions, North and South, or at most through new cross-border – rather than all-island – bodies. The SDLP and UUP, but not SF, agreed that the bodies should be 'accountable' to the Assembly, but there was disagreement on how close this account-ability should be. A North–South parliamentary tier was also suggested by the Irish government.

On East–West relations, a central concern of unionists had long been to abolish or replace the Anglo-Irish Agreement. They proposed that British–Irish cooperation and institutions not be confined to Northern Ireland but should be applicable to all of Britain. They suggested a 'Council of the Isles' which included Northern Ireland as an equal partner with the other constituent parts of the UK and with the Irish state. Nationalists saw the continuation of some form of intergovernmental conference as essential, both to ensure continued Irish influence in such areas as policing and security and as a fall-back mechanism should the Assembly fail to function as envisaged.

There was little evidence of serious engagement in the early months of the talks, still less substantial negotiations. Then and later the UUP refused to talk directly to SF. Outside the talks process tension was high, further raised by a series of murders over the Christmas and New Year period. The first steps towards serious negotiations began in January 1998 with the publication by the two governments of a short position paper – 'Propositions on Heads of Agreement' – setting out in broad outline their proposals for a settlement. Its thrust was very different from the 1995 joint Framework Document, appearing to prioritise the Northern Ireland and British Isles dimensions over the Irish dimension. It used the term 'equity' rather than the stronger term 'equality' (see McCrudden, this volume, p. 104); it proposed a limited number of North–South 'implementation bodies' that would be accountable to the Assembly; and it proposed a council composed of representatives of the British and Irish governments, the Northern Ireland administration and the devolved institutions in Scotland and Wales. The document suggested a tilt towards unionism. It was warmly welcomed by unionists and produced serious disquiet among nationalists.

Discussions now became more focused, although progress was inter-rupted by crises. Both the UDP and SF were briefly expelled on the grounds that their associated paramilitaries were in breach of the cease fire. However, there was now serious engagement and in late March George Mitchell set a deadline of 9 April for the conclusion of the talks. As the talks moved into their final stages, the differences remained stark and breakdown was widely predicted. During the final two weeks, the Irish and British governments failed to reach agreement and the Irish government, the unionist parties, and SF publicly stated incompatible 'bottom line' positions. Days before the deadline, the chairman, George Mitchell, presented a draft agreement to the parties that was roundly rejected both by the UUP and by the Alliance party because of the range of proposed North–South bodies and their accountability to the Assembly (Mitchell 1998). The crisis brought the British Prime Minister and Irish Taoiseach hurriedly to Belfast. Intensive negotiations followed on the structure of the Assembly, the executive and the North–South bodies.

In the final two days, the talks took on a quality of high drama. Participants speak of all-night meetings, exhausted negotiators, pressure by the Prime Minister and Taoiseach, consultations with paramilitaries, phone calls to key participants from President Clinton and constant redrafting to accommodate the most important parties (Mallie, 1999). Unionist disquiet grew as the package emerged, and focused on the issue of decommissioning. The UUP demanded decommissioning prior to SF's entry into the executive. SF rejected this and reached agreement with Tony Blair on a form of words that did not require it. On the morning of Good Friday, 10 April, when the official deadline for an end to the talks had already passed, the UUP was still deeply divided. The crisis was finally resolved by a fudge: the Agreement did not require decommissioning, but the British Prime Minister wrote a letter to David Trimble to confirm his understanding that it should begin once the Agreement was signed. This did not satisfy all members of the party and a senior negotiator, Jeffrey Donaldson, left the building before the Agreement was signed.

Agreement was finally reached on the afternoon of Good Friday, 10 April. All parties signed, except SF who agreed to bring it to their party members. The text of the Agreement did not resolve all the outstanding issues, but in many ways it was a triumph of the political process. From beginning to end the negotiations were skilfully chaired. The political resources of the two states were mobilised. British and Irish politicians, advisers and civil servants worked full time on successive drafts. At the very end, the experience, negotiating skills and (among some of the parties) trust built up over the previous months paid off. Bargains were struck. Compromise forms of wording were found. When it appeared that agreement might not be reached, it was secured by the personal interventions of the political leaders, Prime Minister Tony Blair, An Taoiseach Bertie Ahern and President Bill Clinton. The final plenary session announcing agreement was an emotional affair. It seemed that the political logjam had finally been broken.

In the six weeks that followed, the driving role of political elites was again clear. Sinn Féin leaders secured endorsement of the Agreement among their supporters. Unionists were divided but David Trimble and the pro-Agreement Unionists kept control of the UUP. The referendum campaign was carefully managed to ensure a strong majority yes vote: the final event of the campaign – a major U2 concert in the grounds of Stormont where David Trimble and John Hume came on stage with Bono – is said to have swung wavering unionists. In the South, Fianna Fáil won overwhelming support for the constitutional changes. The two referendums were ratified – with a positive vote of 71 per cent in the North and 94 per cent in the South – on 22 May 1998.

THE TERMS OF THE AGREEMENT

The Agreement Reached in the Multi-Party Negotiations, to give the Agreement its official title, is a detailed and complex document. Unlike the joint government statements which preceded it (the DSD of 1993 and the Framework Document of 1995) there is little new in its first principles: the Declaration of Support pledges partnership, equality and mutual respect, exclusively democratic and peaceful means, a spirit of concord. The body of the text consists of detailed, practical institutional arrangements negotiated by the parties under the following headings: constitutional issues; Strands 1, 2 and 3; rights, safeguards and equality of opportunity; decommissioning; security; policing and justice; prisoners; validation implementation and review; with an annex detailing the agreement between the British and Irish governments.

On constitutional issues, the Agreement recognises the right of a majority of people in Northern Ireland to choose between the union and a united Ireland, and pledges legislation to make possible a united Ireland if a majority so chooses. It reproduces much of the text of DSD (paragraph 4) with its emphasis on the Irish locus of the conflict and the right to Irish self-determination. It adds to this a formal recognition that the present status of Northern Ireland as part of the United Kingdom reflects the wish of a majority in Northern Ireland. It pledges changes in UK legislation and an amendment to the Irish constitution to reflect these principles.

In the British context, these changes involve the repeal of the Government of Ireland Act 1920. A declaration will be incorporated in British legislation that Northern Ireland remains part of the United Kingdom and shall not cease to be so without the consent of a majority of the people of Northern Ireland voting in a poll. Provisions for such border polls (at intervals of no less than seven years) are also incorporated in British legislation. In turn the Irish government pledges to put proposed constitutional changes to referendum. Some of these changes (to Article 29) are designed to prevent constitutional challenge to the powers of North–South bodies. The politically important changes are to

Articles 2 and 3 of the constitution. Article 2 is reformulated to replace the definition of the Irish national territory with a definition of the Irish nation, in which all people born on the island of Ireland have the right of membership. Article 3 is reformulated to restate the national aspiration to Irish unity while respecting the principle of consent.

In Strand 1, the Agreement provides for an Assembly elected by PR–STV with legislative devolution in areas presently dealt with by the Northern Ireland departments (roughly the internal affairs of Northern Ireland with the exception of policing and security-related issues). Policing may later be devolved to the Assembly. Assembly members must declare themselves either unionist, nationalist or other, and for key decisions either parallel consent or weighted majority cross-community support will be required.

A first minister and deputy first minister (with identical powers) will be elected by parallel consent, thus in practice ensuring that a moderate unionist and moderate nationalist hold the post whatever the strength of the more extreme parties in the Assembly. In addition there is an executive of up to ten ministers, appointed proportionate to party strength in the Assembly (by the d'Hondt system), which will function without collective cabinet responsibility. The holding of executive posts is conditional on affirmation of a pledge of office, which includes commitment to exclusively peaceful and democratic means, commitment to the principle of equality and cooperation with colleagues. The Assembly will exist in 'shadow' form without powers until it approves the North–South Council and implementation bodies.

In Strand 2, a North–South Ministerial Council is to be constituted by legislation in Westminster and the Dáil. It is to come into existence within six months of the election of the Assembly, and its existence and the Assembly's existence are to be mutually interdependent. It is to function by agreement, while pledging (in a partial echo of the AIA) to make 'determined efforts to overcome any disagreements' (Strand two, paragraph 5 ii). It is to involve at least six new cross-border or all-island implementation bodies and a permanent secretariat. Its remit is to involve areas of mutual interest to North and South. The Council, and through it the implementation bodies, are to be broadly accountable to the Assembly, but there is to be some room for autonomy within the 'defined authority' (Strand 2, paragraph 6, cf Strand 1, paragraph 24) of those attending. The North–South Ministerial Council and the Northern Ireland Assembly are 'mutually interdependent, and . . . one cannot successfully function without the other' (Strand 2, paragraph 13).

In Strand 3, the Agreement provides for a British–Irish Council – composed primarily of representatives of the Northern Irish, Welsh and

Scottish Assemblies and the British and Irish governments. The Council is legally enabled to set up modes of cooperation parallel to North–South cooperation but is not required to do so. In addition, the Agreement proposes a continuing role for an intergovernmental conference with a permanent secretariat whose remit includes non-devolved matters relating to Northern Ireland, including security and policing. Decisions will be by agreement and, as in the Anglo-Irish Agreement, the governments will make 'determined efforts to resolve disagreements between them' (Strand 3, British–Irish Intergovernmental Conference, paragraph 4). It is explicitly stated that this implies no derogation from sovereignty by either government. Representatives from the Northern Ireland executive will be involved in the meetings but their status is not that of the governments: there is no requirement that the governments make 'determined efforts to resolve disagreements' with them.

On 'rights, safeguards and equality of opportunity', the parties to the Agreement affirm their commitment to a set of human and civil rights. The British government pledges to incorporate the European Convention on Human Rights into Northern Ireland legislation and to create a statutory obligation on all public authorities to carry out their functions with due regard to promote equality of opportunity (McCrudden, this volume, p. 106 ff.). A new Northern Ireland Human Rights Commission is to be set up with advisory, review, research, publicity, watchdog and legal functions, and an Equality Commission is to be set up. The Irish government pledges legislation to ensure protection of human rights (at least equivalent to that in Northern Ireland), employment equality and equal status. There is a pledge of support for organisations involved in reconciliation, a pledge by the British government to pursue policies for sustained economic growth in Northern Ireland and for promoting social inclusion in its jurisdiction, including new regional and economic development strategies, measures on employment equality, and promotion of the Irish language.

On decommissioning, the parties pledge 'to use any influence they may have, to work to achieve the decommissioning of all paramilitary arms within two years following endorsement in referendums North and South of the agreement and in the context of the implementation of the overall settlement' (paragraph 3). In a separate section, the British government pledges – in the context of 'the development of a peaceful environment' – to reduce the numbers of armed forces in Northern Ireland, to remove security installations and emergency powers. On policing, the Agreement proposes a Commission on Policing to report on police reform. It has an international input, a wide and reforming remit and a limited time scale (to complete its report by autumn 1999). A review of the criminal justice system in Northern Ireland is also promised. On prisoners, both governments promise accelerated releases of appropriate categories of prisoners (to be completed within two years).

The Agreement between the British and Irish governments, appended to the Multi-Party Agreement, is explicitly a replacement of the Anglo-Irish Agreement. It contains identical material to that covered under constitutional issues (see above). This is the first time that the Irish government has formally recognised that the present status of Northern Ireland as part of the United Kingdom reflects the wish of a majority in Northern Ireland. The Agreement comes into effect only when the relevant constitutional amendments have been approved in referendum and the relevant legislation (including the repeal of the Government of Ireland Act and legislation to establish the North–South Council and implementation bodies, the British–Irish Council and British–Irish intergovernmental conference) has been enacted.

As a package, the Belfast Agreement has consociational elements in the powers and protections it gives to the two communities. But it goes beyond consociationalism in a number of its elements: in the strong egalitarian and liberal thrust of the document; in the proportional representation on the executive which in principle allows non-communal parties into power; in the provision for a Civic Forum; in granting the Irish government an input into policy through the British–Irish conference; in the North–South Council which is explicitly made co-dependent with the Assembly; in the (weaker) British–Irish Council; and in the provisions for constitutional change. O'Leary (1999) points to confederal and even federal aspects to some of these provisions.

The Agreement is a highly complex, well-crafted document that combines general principles with detailed and innovative institutional provisions. Its preparation drew on the store of general political and constitutional knowledge, but it was targeted to the specific nature of the conflict in Northern Ireland. The question now is whether it will work. To answer this question, we have to look beyond the formal provisions of the Agreement to its political logic: the manner in which it proposes to address the core issues in conflict.

THE LOGIC OF THE AGREEMENT

The Agreement addresses the conflict at two distinct, though related, levels. On the one hand, it is a political deal, an elaborate mechanism for the sharing of power, designed to allow two communities with conflicting interests, aspirations and allegiances to coexist with justice and without violence. On the other hand, it is a framework within which the underlying conditions of conflict can be addressed by some form of transformative social process. These goals divide the participants: unionists have been concerned to secure a deal; nationalists have in mind an open-ended process. The Agreement tries to offer both.

As a political deal, it addresses three aspects of the conflict. First, it addresses the conflict of communal interests – in particular, the interest of Protestants in the union, and the interest of Catholics in equality. Second, it addresses the problem of legitimacy – the fact that to date no political system has been able to win the allegiance of both nationalists and unionists. Third, it addresses the problem of the future – the danger that changes in the demographic and political balance in Northern Ireland will lead to future crises. As a framework for addressing the deeper roots of division, its goal is to generate and channel wide-ranging social changes to secure reconciliation within Northern Ireland and on the island of Ireland. We examine each aspect in turn.

The conflict in Northern Ireland has been intense and uncompromising because each community believes that its vital interests are at stake (Ruane and Todd, 1996). For Protestants, these interests are twofold: first, the preservation of their dominant economic, political and cultural position within Northern Ireland; second, the maintenance of the union of Great Britain and Northern Ireland. For Protestants, these interests are interdependent: the best guarantee of their position in Northern Ireland (and, more especially, on the island of Ireland) is Northern Ireland's continued membership of the UK; maintaining their position in Northern Ireland is the best way of securing the union. Catholic interests centre in the first instance on remedying inequality – not just material, but also cultural and national. Irish unity is an important goal for many Northern Catholics, but for most it is not the most pressing issue (Hayes and McAllister, this volume, pp. 45–6). Even republicans, who have stressed the importance of unity, have as often been motivated by the 'irreformability' of the Northern state; more recently they have reversed the argument – equality within Northern Ireland is the first step on the road to unity.

These interests conflict because any reduction in the extent of inequality threatens to weaken the Protestant position. Increased economic equality would bring Catholics additional material resources. Increased cultural equality would strengthen Catholic cultural self-confidence, change the public culture of Northern Ireland, the perception of its place within the United Kingdom and the value of each community's cultural capital. National equality would involve the formal equality of Irishness and Britishness in Northern Ireland and, arguably, joint British and Irish authority. The net effect would be to change the balance of power between Protestant and Catholic in ways that could eventually undermine the union. The Agreement attempts to reconcile these conflicting interests by putting the union on a firmer basis while guaranteeing full equality to Catholics and nationalists within Northern Ireland.

The Agreement establishes that the constitutional status of Northern Ireland is to be determined by the wishes of a majority of its citizens. Formally this is similar to previous government assurances. Substantially, however, it represents a firmer basis for the union for several reasons. First, it was the fruit of direct negotiations between unionists and the government of the Republic and to that extent has stronger moral force; previous assurances by the Irish government were made as part of intergovernmental agreements. Second, the assurances were coupled with a commitment to remove the clauses in the Republic's constitution claiming jurisdiction over the island of Ireland as a whole. Third, the Agreement includes a recognition (by the Irish government as well as the British) that the present status of Northern Ireland as part of the United Kingdom reflects the wish of a majority in Northern Ireland – for the first time, therefore, the Irish government has formally recognised the legitimacy of British rule in Northern Ireland. Fourth, while the establishment of new North–South bodies might be seen as an infringement of Northern Ireland's place within the Union, this is balanced in some degree by the formation of a British–Irish Council. Finally, it was made clear in the negotiations that there was no question of the British government becoming a 'persuader' for Irish unity. Indeed, Tony Blair made clear his strong personal commitment to the union and his belief that it will be still there several generations from now.

If the Agreement gives Protestants the security of the union, it challenges their position within Northern Ireland. The Agreement includes a range of ambitious measures, not simply to eliminate discrimination or unequal treatment, but to establish substantive equality between the two communities. They include a system of voting in the Assembly involving a combination of parallel consent and weighted majorities; a power-sharing executive; a first minister and deputy first minister with identical powers elected so as to ensure that one will be unionist and the other nationalist; a pledge of office which includes commitment to the principle of equality; a North–South Ministerial Council with a permanent secretariat that counterbalances in some degree Northern Ireland's integration into the union; a battery of measures to ensure respect for human rights, parity of esteem, equality of treatment and movement towards equality of condition; promise of reform of the police to enable full participation of Catholics within it; the implication that there will be modifications to the ritual and ceremonial activity of the state to take account of the fact that Northern Ireland is made up of people with different national identities and aspirations (section on Rights, Safeguards and Equality of Opportunity, subsection on Human Rights, paragraph 4., subsection on Economic, Social and Cultural Issues, paragraph 5).

In this sense the Agreement gives strong protection to both communities within the union. Can unionists now be secure without dominance? Can nationalists now be equal without constitutional change? The answer to both questions is yes, but only in part. The Agreement moderates the potential for conflict but does not eliminate it. Under the Agreement, Northern Ireland remains part of the UK only as long as the majority so wish. Protestants have either to maintain their demographic and political majority or to persuade Catholics to support the union. If the demographic gap continues to narrow, and the strategy of conciliating Catholics brings no immediate results, the Protestant sense of vulnerability will return. On the other side, it is clear that while the Agreement is a major advance in the achievement of equality for Catholics, strictly speaking it offers not equality but the possibility of achieving it. If its achievement is likely to narrow the demographic gap still more – as seems likely – it will have to be struggled for, and will pit Protestant against Catholic as in the past.

If the conflict over interests explains the persistence of the conflict, the conflict over legitimacy explains its totalising character, the tendency for each particular disagreement to become generalised into a defence of or attack on the state (cf. Wright, 1987). The failure of the institutions set up in 1921 to achieve legitimacy among the Catholic community was a key factor in the conflictual dynamic of the Northern state during the Stormont period. It intensified Protestant fears about the security and permanence of the Northern state, and was used to justify their harsh treatment of Catholics. This in turn further intensified the Catholic sense of grievance; not alone were they being harshly treated, but this was being done through institutions which they considered illegitimate. When Catholics eventually mobilised to press for civil rights, Protestants saw their campaign as an attack on the state itself; and republicans seized the opportunity to make it just that (Ruane and Todd, 1998b). Not just civil rights marches, but conflicts over particular institutions of state (from police to prisons) and symbolic practices (from Orange marches to political violence) quickly escalate to become conflicts over legitimacy of the state.

In Northern Ireland the sense of legitimacy of the state is grounded in part, but only in part, on conflicting national identities and allegiances; the sense of justice, of democratic rights, of liberty, of equality, of corruption or honesty, and of family tradition are all also relevant and resonate with wider communal perceptions of inequality or insecurity (cf Ruane and Todd, 1996, chapters 4, 5). There are three dimensions in dispute: the legitimacy of Northern Ireland as a separate political entity, of its union with Britain, and of the mode of government there. Nationalist and unionist opinion has been polarised on all three dimensions, in each case for a range of reasons, with nationalism being of decreasing importance as one moves from the legitimacy of the political entity to the legitimacy of the mode of government.

The Agreement sets out to create a new institutionalisation of legitimacy which both nationalists and unionists can accept, and which is conferred with democratic legitimacy in the subsequent referenda. It does not attempt to justify the original partition of Ireland. Instead it deals with contemporary Northern Ireland. Whatever its provenance, Northern Ireland has existed for more than 70 years and this gives it the right to determine its own future (Mansergh, 1996; Kennedy, 1998). The constitutional status of Northern Ireland is, therefore, to be determined by a majority of its citizens. If they choose to remain part of the United Kingdom, British rule in Northern Ireland is fully legitimate. To that extent the Agreement endorses unionist views concerning the legitimacy of Northern Ireland as a political entity and of British rule there (Bew, 1998; Trimble, 1998).

On the other hand, the Agreement falls short of meeting unionists' claims. First, it makes British sovereignty and the union dependent on the will of a majority in Northern Ireland, not – as some unionists wished – an unbreakable point of principle. Second, the self-determination of the people of Northern Ireland is treated as part of the self-determination of the Irish people as a whole; and if Northern Ireland leaves the union its only option is unity with the rest of Ireland – there is no provision for an independent Northern Ireland. Third, the Agreement formally recognises the separate constitutional aspirations of nationalists, acknowledges their right to pursue these by peaceful means, forbids discrimination against them on political grounds, and establishes North–South bodies (on which unionist ministers appointed to the executive are obliged to serve) to provide greater island-wide integration and to give expression to their island-wide identity. Finally, and to the outrage of many unionists, the early release of republican prisoners as part of the settlement implicitly gives a measure of post-hoc legitimacy to their campaign of violence.

Furthermore, while the Agreement makes the will of the majority the determinant of Northern Ireland's constitutional status, this principle does not apply to its mode of governance. Here legitimacy depends upon cross-community agreement and the norms of justice and fairness. Moreover, the mechanisms for establishing the legitimacy of Northern Ireland's constitutional position and of its mode of governance are part of the same package; this implies that recognition of the legitimacy of Northern Ireland as a political entity is contingent on the justice and fairness of its governing institutions. This linking could prove significant in the future. If it turns out that, despite all the provisions of the Agreement, Northern Ireland does not and cannot function in an egalitarian manner, the question of its constitutional legitimacy and legitimacy as a political entity will again come sharply into question. Indeed for many republicans, these issues have never disappeared (cf Todd, this volume, p. 66 ff.)

Conflict in Northern Ireland has also been motivated by concern over demographic and political change: in the past this produced unionist discrimination and intimidation; today, local patterns of demographic change provoke bitter sectarian conflict. The Agreement addresses this issue by setting down a clear procedure whereby the will of a majority of the population of Northern Ireland can be assessed and the constitutional status of Northern Ireland changed. Moreover the envisaged administrative and economic integration of the two parts of Ireland through the North–South Council and implementation bodies will allow constitutional change to take place without administrative or economic disruption. In the meantime, the provision for proportionality and power-sharing ensures that changes in the demographic and political shape of Northern Ireland are immediately reflected at the level of government, thus avoiding pressures for change building up and precipitating a further crisis. As change occurs, the power-sharing and equality provisions which now benefit the Catholic minority will be available to Protestants should they become a minority. Finally, the Agreement contains provision for a greatly increased concern with human and minority rights in the Republic; this, in addition to the moral weight of the Agreement, ensures that, in the event of Irish unity, provision would be made to accommodate the interests and concerns of the Republic's new Ulster Protestant minority.

Future demographic and political trends are debated among experts (for trends up to the present, see Kennedy, 1994) and it is not certain that a Catholic, much less a nationalist, majority will come about in the short term. Nor, should a majority vote for Irish unity, is it clear that all sections of the Protestant community would respect their choice. Moreover, the provisions of the Agreement do not tackle local level sectarianism (cf below). But, for the moment, the terms of the Agreement suggest that it is a flexible and adaptable instrument capable of accommodating change both of a gradual and radical kind. The provisions for change strengthen the perception that the Agreement is genuinely even-handed between the communities. As such they form part of the argument for the legitimacy of the new settlement and the new institutions.

The Agreement goes a considerable way to contain conflict. As we have seen, it leaves aspects of the conflict of interests and of legitimacy untouched, while other issues in conflict may re-emerge as the Agreement is implemented. But the Agreement is also conceived as a framework for more far-reaching long-term change that will address the deeper roots of division. The radical changes promised in the Agreement – a shared experience of governing, equality, a rights culture, the end of the 'prison culture', decommissioning and demilitarisation, harmonisation and convergence of both parts of the island, multiple and overlapping contacts between different parts of the two islands – can be expected to produce changes in attitudes, identities and even aspirations. It will take some time before the dynamic effects of the Agreement become clear. Two questions can be posed now. First, is there anything about the terms of the Agreement which might prevent the deeper problems being addressed? Second, could the Agreement find itself in a Catch-22 situation where to address the deeper sources of conflict it must first come into effect, while the conflicts may be such as to prevent it ever coming fully into effect?

As far as the first question is concerned, much depends on the causes of the conflict. On one view – that the conflict is at base an ethnic one, which can neither be deconstructed nor transcended – there is no point in trying to address the deeper problems; the most that can be done is to devise institutions that contain and manage conflict as peacefully as possible (Darby, 1997). But the architects of the Agreement, particularly on the nationalist side, are seeking more. The document speaks of 'a new beginning', the 'achievement of reconciliation, tolerance, and mutual trust', 'partnership, equality and mutual respect' (Declaration of Support). Political leaders and commentators alike have spoken of the Agreement as a first step in a 'healing process' which will lead to a coming together of the two communities in Northern Ireland, North and South and the peoples of Britain and Ireland, in a spirit of harmony and good will.

It is not spelled out precisely how this is to happen and unionists and nationalists envisage the process differently. Moreover, some critics have argued that the terms of the Agreement are profoundly ill-suited to the purpose; that by institutionalising communal division at the political level, they reinforce it (McCann, 1999). For example, the requirement that Assembly members register as 'nationalist, unionist or other', and the provision for parallel consent and weighted majority decisions, work against those who wish to develop issue-based rather than communal politics. The architects and supporters of the Agreement acknowledge the problem, but see it as a necessary concomitant of meeting vital communal interests, one which is essential now, but may not be in the future.

Moreover, as pointed out above, the Agreement combines this element of communal protection with other mechanisms which can potentially break down rigid divisions – the strong guarantees of equality and rights, the Civic Forum, and the provision for voices other than simply the communal ones.

There is, however, a further and immediate problem: what if the depth and intensity of the conflict, which the Agreement is meant to contain and ultimately to resolve, prevent it ever being fully implemented or operating in the way intended? Here there is a real danger and it is already evident in the controversies surrounding decommissioning, reform of the police, marches and other human rights issues. These issues, which the Agreement left to commissions precisely because of their complexity and divisiveness, are already threatening its smooth implementation. They are issues which very potently symbolise and bring to the fore those general aspects of the communal conflict that the Agreement has not (yet) tackled – they relate directly to the long term interests of both communities and symbolically raise the issues of the past and present legitimacy of Northern Ireland.

They also tap into personal feelings and memories of pain, loss, intimidation and humiliation, forged in the heat of violent struggle. The Agreement did not – and could not – dissipate those feelings or memories; for many, particularly those who had suffered irreparable loss, the Agreement rendered them all the more acute, isolating them from those who could now enjoy the peace. The implementation of the Agreement demands that each community give political respect to, and place its political trust in, those who have been responsible for the most painful of its feelings and memories and who – to add further to their distress – continue to affirm the justice of their cause and the rightness of their actions, not least in their views on decommissioning, policing and marches.

If it was simply a matter of emotions, this problem might ease as time passes and peace holds. But the emotions are reinforced by the logic of the conflict. Questions of communal interest and legitimacy are at stake and still to be fought for in the issues of decommissioning, policing and marches. Whether the battles will de-rail the Agreement before it can begin to work on the deeper sources of division and conflict, or whether the gradual implementation of the Agreement can help resolve these outstanding issues remains in the balance.

IMPLEMENTING THE AGREEMENT, APRIL 1998–JULY 1999

Over a year after the Agreement was signed and ratified by referendums, how much progress has been made in its implementation? Progress has been uneven, far advanced in some areas, but blocked at crucial points. On the positive side, the Assembly elections took place in June 1998. (The SDLP consolidated its share of the vote at 22 per cent and topped the poll for the first time, while SF increased its share of the vote to 17.6 per cent. The pro-Agreement unionists won a majority of the unionist votes and seats, although the UUP vote fell to only 21 per cent, while the DUP vote was consolidated at 18 per cent.) The first and deputy first ministers – David Trimble and Seamus Mallon – were elected without delay. The number and character of ministries in the executive and the composition of North–South bodies were the subject of further negotiation and were only agreed in January 1999.

The Northern Ireland Act 1998 set in place the major provisions of the Agreement on equality (see McCrudden, this volume, p. 113 ff.). The Human Rights Commission was appointed in January 1999, and the Equality Commission in the summer of 1999. Prisoner releases have been swift and steady: within six months of the Agreement, half of the qualifying 400 prisoners had been released. A Police Commission has been set up and has taken submissions; it is due to report in autumn 1999. The British government have made some progress in demilitarising the society: troops have been withdrawn to barracks, some troops (a small proportion of the total) have been withdrawn from Northern Ireland, some (not all) army bases have been dismantled. The Independent International Commission on Decommissioning has been meeting and Sinn Féin's Martin McGuinness has been working with it. Strong support for the Irish language is now part of the brief of one of the North–South implementation bodies.

At another level, progress has been almost non-existent: an executive has still to be formed; the North–South Council has not come into existence; and the Assembly remains in shadow mode. In January 1999, on the basis that all the constitutional and institutional provisions were now in place, the British government published its agenda for the transfer of powers to take place on 10 March. On that date, the British–Irish Agreement Act passed through the British parliament and the Irish Dáil. However there was no transfer of powers. Neither the executive nor the North–South Council and its implementation bodies yet exists (July 1999) and the Assembly remains without powers. Pending full implementation of the Agreement, the constitutional changes agreed at referendum have yet to become part of the Irish Constitution.

Conflict over a single issue is holding up the process: the decommissioning of IRA weapons. SF's vote entitles it to two seats on the executive. The UUP refuses to enter an executive with SF without at least the beginning of IRA decommissioning. SF argues that this breaches the terms of the Agreement which state simply that the parties must do all in their power to achieve decommissioning within two years (May 2000), and that office-holders must pledge their commitment to non-violence. SF declares its commitment to both of these principles, and argues that any attempt to make decommissioning a condition of its entry into the executive constitutes a renegotiation of the Agreement. Besides, it does not have weapons to decommission: that is a matter for the IRA which makes up its own mind. For its part, the IRA has given conflicting signals, including the claim that it will not decommission under any circumstances.

Unionists respond that while decommissioning may not be a precise precondition for setting up the new institutions, it is an 'obligation'. At the very least decommissioning should happen concurrently with SF's entry into the executive. The UUP argues that democracy cannot function if one party to government can back its demands with the implicit threat of a 'private army'. If SF accepts the legitimacy of the new political institutions, surely then decommissioning should now begin? If SF and the IRA are truly committed to democracy and non-violence and progress is being made on all aspects of the Agreement, this demands similar progress on decommissioning. SF replies that the UUP's attempt to breach the terms of the Agreement indicates their lack of commitment to it and, ultimately, their resistance to sharing power with nationalists.

The first step by the two governments to break the impasse was taken on 1 April 1999. The joint Hillsborough Declaration stated that decommissioning was not a precondition, but it was an 'obligation'. Executive members were to be nominated immediately, but they would not take up office until some arms had been put 'beyond use' on a voluntary basis. This was to happen in the following four weeks. Powers would then be devolved to the executive. Unionists had reservations about aspects of the declaration but on balance supported it; republicans rejected it as inconsistent with the terms of the Agreement. Further negotiations at Downing Street six weeks later led to a revised package: the executive was to be set up immediately, with the final transfer of devolved powers to follow shortly (and no later than 30 June). This did not depend on prior decommissioning and the commitment to eventual decommissioning appeared no stronger than in the Agreement itself. When David Trimble brought the package to the UUP, its members rejected it outright.

Intensive negotiations in the final week of June failed to reach agreement among all the parties. The two governments, therefore, set out their policy which they declared to be their final statement on the matter. Their document – 'The Way Forward' – committed the British government to set up the executive on 15 July with devolution of powers by 18 July; decommissioning was to be completed by May 2000; the (unwritten) understanding was that it would begin by the autumn. In the event of unionists or republicans failing to fulfil their responsibilities – entry into the executive, decommissioning – the Agreement would be suspended. This document implied a stronger commitment by SF to ensure IRA decommissioning by May 2000 and the governments added the 'failsafe' mechanism that the working of the Agreement would be suspended if this did not occur. The proposal, however, failed to win UUP support. When the d'Hondt mechanism to form the executive was triggered in the Assembly on 15 July, the UUP did not attend, and an executive with cross-community support could not be formed. In the light of this failure, Seamus Mallon resigned as Deputy First Minister and called on David Trimble to do likewise – in the event he did not. A process of review of the Agreement has begun in a further attempt to resolve the issue. All-party talks, reviewing the Agreement with reference to the issues in dispute, will take place in September 1999 under the chairmanship of George Mitchell.

However it is resolved, the decommissioning issue reveals much about the possibilities and limits of the peace process as a whole. Interest is involved: for unionists to secure decommissioning; for republicans to avoid leaving their community defenceless in face of loyalist attacks. For both unionists and republicans, however, decommissioning is a matter of meaning as much as practicality. Both sides are well aware that the weapons and explosives yielded could be replaced, some without difficulty. But for unionists, decommissioning would establish in a public and universally acknowledged way the legitimacy of Northern Ireland and British rule. It would be a sign of the normalisation of politics, of the stability of the new institutions. It would be an assurance that democratic politics could now proceed without the implicit or explicit threat of violence, that republicans had truly renounced their past and were committed to democracy and the rule of law. It would ensure too that the standing and weight of each party would now depend solely on its electoral support. The day when a minority party would be able, through the threat of violence, to shape the political agenda would be over.

For republicans too, the meaning of decommissioning is crucial. It appears that most – not all – republicans are committed to a totally peaceful strategy. But it is extremely important to republican identity and pride that they were undefeated: that the struggle was not lost with the ceasefire but continues in a new, peaceful phase. The central imperative for republican politics after the Agreement has been to integrate the peaceful political strategy of the leadership with the sense of the grass roots that their struggle was worthwhile and is continuing, albeit in new forms (see Todd, this volume, p. 60 ff.). This makes decommissioning a potent symbolic issue. If carried out under any form of duress, decommissioning would symbolise an act of surrender and acceptance of defeat, and an implicit admission of the illegitimacy of the armed struggle of the past. If decommissioning is to take place, it must be carefully managed. It must be a free choice concomitant with the disarming of the other participants. Above all, it has to be done in a way which does not undermine the unity and morale of the republican movement and its capacity to continue the struggle.

The decommissioning issue, then, feeds on the remaining conflicts of interest and legitimacy which have been side-stepped, not resolved, by the Agreement. It potently symbolises the conflicting unionist and republican perspectives on the Agreement: unionists want decommissioning as a symbol of the stabilisation of Northern Ireland, republicans can accept it only as a part of the transformation of Northern Ireland that will pave the way to a united Ireland. Decommissioning has become an early test of the conflicting interpretations of the Agreement: whether it stabilises or transforms the union. If it is resolved, other such issues remain in the wings, in particular the reform of the RUC and the regulation of Orange marches. Neither of these issues was resolved in the Agreement itself. As each arises, it will test the parties to and the institutions of the Agreement: whether or not the potential for compromise has increased and the conflict-generating capacity of these issues decreased since the Agreement.

The continuing conflict over the character and trajectory of politics in Northern Ireland reflects deeper communal oppositions. One of the purposes of the Agreement was to stabilise the political arena, and to insulate it from communal conflict and concerns (cf Aughey, this volume, p. 139 ff.). Is there any sign of this happening? And has there been sufficient communal and cultural change to allow for such a political development? Thus far the process of change has been at best uneven.

On the positive side, the Agreement has set in motion an administrative dynamic, whereby civil servants on both sides of the border have become committed to the new direction of policy. There are reports of improvements in relationships between the pro-Agreement parties, particularly between the UUP and SDLP. The UUP has now held direct talks with SF. There are also reports of a firm bond of mutual respect between David Trimble as leader of the UUP and the Taoiseach, Bertie Ahern. In 'civil society' the initiation of the Civic Forum augments the positive role that business leaders and NGOs have already played in the peace process. In other respects, institutional innovation (e.g. in the school system, in cross-community networks) remains slow. The potential effects of the Human Rights Commission and Equality Commission are radical but that is for the long term.

In the sphere of community relations, there is little evidence of progress and few reasons for optimism. On core issues, as Hayes and McAllister (this volume, pp. 45–7) show, public attitudes remain polarised. The signing of the Agreement curtailed but did not eliminate organised paramilitary violence. Sectarian attacks have continued. Some of the worst atrocities of the Troubles have occurred since the Agreement: the murder of the three Quinn children in July 1998; the Omagh bomb of August 1998; the murder of lawyer Rosemary Nelson in March 1999. Paramilitary policing since the Agreement has resulted in many horrific injuries and deaths which have been increasingly publicised. As a result of public and political pressure, IRA punishment beatings ceased from the beginning of 1999. Reports of IRA intimidation of republicans opposed to the Good Friday Agreement have continued to appear.

Meanwhile disturbances and violence associated with Orange marches have continued since the Agreement. For example, between 6 a.m. 4 July 1998 and 6 a.m. 8 July 1998 the RUC reported 1430 public disorder incidents, including 437 attacks on the security forces, 44 RUC officers injured, 412 petrol bombings, 137 hijacked vehicles, 73 houses damaged (*The Irish Times*, 9 July 1998). In some areas, there were concentrated attacks on Catholic homes, businesses and churches, culminating in the murder of the three Quinn brothers. In July 1998, 141 families (including 50 RUC) had to be rehoused following the Drumcree crisis (*The Irish Times*, 24 July 1998). From July to September 1998, there were nightly loyalist protests in Portadown and between July 1998 and March 1999 there were 150 loyalist demonstrations in Portadown. There are reports of a deliberate campaign to force all Catholics and couples in mixed marriages out of Carrickfergus, Dunmurry and Derriaghy (*The Irish Times*, 3 July 1999).

If the Agreement signalled a degree of elite convergence, the wider public has not yet followed. Given this continuing polarisation, we must ask, are there fundamental weaknesses in the Agreement? Perhaps its compromise did not touch the real interests of the communities? This is the view of unionist and republican opponents of the Agreement, and, for different reasons, of those who argue that it actually intensifies sectarian conflict. We have argued above, however, that the Agreement does go a considerable way to address the real conflicts. Perhaps, then, either unionists or republicans are not yet ready to enter wholeheartedly into a political agreement? However, the political leadership on each side does seem genuinely to want an agreement. Is it then a problem of the limits of the political process? This type of politically crafted agreement may require benign structural conditions and a degree of popular support which may not yet be available.

It might be argued that the more appropriate model remains that of government imposition of reforms and institutions which can continue to act on the conditions of conflict to a point where both communities and leaders are motivated to negotiate. While there may indeed be some truth to this view, after the Agreement one can no longer dismiss the possibility or importance of a negotiated settlement. Indeed the Agreement has provided the context for far-reaching government initiatives: on equality, human rights, police reform and prisoner releases. If the present crisis over the formation of the executive is not resolved, it may be necessary to move back to an administrative-led approach to the conflict. Indeed some of the provisions of the Agreement may be integrated into such an approach. But the loss, in terms of legitimacy, democratic backing and potential for longer-term conflict resolution, would indeed be great.

What has to be achieved is precisely a balance between progress at the political level and progress in undoing the conditions of communal conflict: the creation of 'a politics of civility' while changing the conditions which generate a tendency to return to 'incivility' (Aughey, this volume, pp. 122–44). Both the gains made by the Belfast Agreement and its problems illustrate the central paradox in Northern Ireland: a political settlement is necessary to address the wider communal division, but that division sets limits to the viability of even the most imaginative political settlement.

2

ETHNONATIONALISM, PUBLIC OPINION AND THE GOOD FRIDAY AGREEMENT

Bernadette C. Hayes and Ian McAllister[1]

INTRODUCTION

Ever since the term was first coined by Walker Connor in the 1960s, ethnonationalism has been a major explanation for political conflict in ethnically divided societies (Connor, 1972, 1978, 1993). The predictions of economic modernisation theorists such as Deutsch (1953) and Nairn (1973, 1996) that widespread material affluence and mass communications would reduce ethnic political conflict have found little empirical support; recent history has shown that ethnic conflict is as likely to occur in advanced societies such as Canada or Switzerland as it is in less economically developed societies such as Sri Lanka or Indonesia. The persistence of ethnic conflict has also confounded those assimilationists who placed their faith in the modernising influence of the nation state. The disintegration of the former communist nation states of Eastern Europe has demonstrated the weakness of the nation state in resolving such conflicts (Smith, 1996). Connor's prediction that ethnonationalism would outlive communism has proved particularly apt.

With only about one in 10 of today's states being defined as ethnically homogeneous (Haymes, 1997), the political consequences of ethnonationalism are potentially widespread, deep-seated and intractable. Ethnonationalism has already challenged the stability of the international system that emerged during the latter half of the Cold War, and led to disintegration and major upheaval across large parts of Europe, the Middle East and Asia (Gurr and Harff, 1994). What appears to differentiate the fate of many ethnic conflicts is the key role of political elites in trying to defuse them. Political elites can influence the direction and content of collective memory as it evolves (Gillis, 1996) and moderate the political goals and expectations that accompany it. Such elite intervention has been particularly effective in Canada, Switzerland and Belgium, and recently elites played a major role in managing the relatively peaceful break-up of Czechoslovakia (Linder, 1994). Equally, elites have been less effective in many other conflicts.

The 1998 Northern Ireland ('Good Friday') Agreement is an example of elite intervention designed to resolve ethnonationalist conflict. For the first time in Northern Ireland's long and troubled history, representatives from the two religious communities came together to endorse one of the most difficult and far-reaching agreements that has ever been proposed as a solution to the conflict. On 22 May 1998, the Northern Ireland Agreement was formally ratified by an overwhelming majority of citizens. The scale of the endorsement – 71 per cent for and 29 per cent against – appeared definitive. Yet, no sooner had the result been declared than the unionist politicians who had opposed the Agreement claimed that a majority of the unionist electorate had voted against it. Such claims were eventually shown to be false by opinion polls. However, although a majority in both communities had voted in favour of the Agreement, only a bare majority of Protestants (51 per cent) had done so (see Hayes and McAllister, 1998).[2]

The primary purpose of the Agreement is to establish political institutions that will reconcile the two communities of Northern Ireland in a lasting political accommodation, providing recognition for differing identities, traditions and heritages. But to what extent was the Good Friday Agreement an elite-driven accommodation, with little popular support (and therefore legitimacy) across the society? Did popular support for the Good Friday Agreement signal the beginning of a new political era of mutual toleration in Northern Ireland? Or was its passage merely designed to mask continuing and deeply felt ethnonationalist divisions? We address these questions mainly using the 1998 Northern Ireland Referendum and Election Survey.[3]

ETHNONATIONALISM AND THE NORTHERN IRELAND CONFLICT

Perhaps more than any other modern society, Northern Ireland has been subjected to the gamut of theories that have been advanced to explain communal conflict.[4] Academic research on the subject has moved through several phases, often in parallel or slightly ahead of policy initiatives. The first phase of research, which commenced before the present conflict began, emphasised political and economic inequality as a source of the conflict. This view was exemplified in its most extreme form by the views of Terence O'Neill, a moderate Unionist prime minister during the 1960s, who believed that 'if you give Roman Catholics a good job and a good house, they will live like Protestants' (quoted in Rose, 1971, p. 301). But it was also an approach that found favour with the British government, which moved to secure the political and legal rights of the Catholic minority through such measures as anti-discrimination legislation.

The second phase, which can be traced to the early 1970s, viewed Northern Ireland as an ethnic conflict rooted in colonialism, albeit with religious and economic overtones, involving a dominant and a subordinate group. This approach stressed the comparative dimension, setting it in the context of similar conflicts in South Africa, the Lebanon or Algeria (Wright, 1987). The policy consequence of this approach was to develop a statebuilding process so as to ensure the full political participation of both communities at the executive level of government. The high point was the creation of the power-sharing executive in 1974, which collapsed after just four months in office; these statebuilding attempts effectively ended with the failure of the Assembly in 1984 (O'Leary, Elliott, and Wilford, 1988).

Since the early 1980s, there has been an emerging academic consensus that the conflict is essentially ethnonationalist in origin. As McGarry and O'Leary (1995, p. 356) put it, 'the crucial endogenous cause of the conflict has been the presence of two competitive ethnonationalist communities within the same territory'. This was a view that resonated with many observers of the conflict, who had identified the differing collective memories of the two communities, and its political conse-quences, as a major source of conflict (see, for example, Whyte, 1990). At a policy level, this interpretation also found favour with the British and Irish governments, which saw Northern Ireland as a regional conflict with international implications; as a consequence, it could only be solved within the context of an agreement between Britain and the Irish Republic, both acting as honest brokers. This approach was ultimately reflected in the 1985 Anglo-Irish Agreement, but the concept of identity and the need to give it political expression also underpins the Good Friday Agreement.

Ethnonationalism in Northern Ireland is fuelled, perhaps more than in any other society, by its multi-faceted and complex nature. It is much more than a simplistic clash between Protestants and Catholics, those with a British versus an Irish identity, or unionists and nationalists, or even those who support the link with Britain versus those who wish to see both parts of the island of Ireland reunited. Rather, it is rooted in significant intra- as well as inter-community differences based not only on differences in ethnic and national identity but also on conflicting views concerning the very legitimacy of the state and its boundaries. At a conceptual level, according to Ruane and Todd (1996), it is reinforced by three 'sociocultural dimensions of conflict' – religion (Catholicism versus various strands of Protestantism); ethnicity (Gaelic-Irish versus English and Scottish); and colonialism (native versus settler). At a practical level, ethnonationalism is reinforced by the primary agents of socialisation that are to be found in any modern society: parents, family, education, and social networks.

Much of the ethnic conflict in modern society arises because of the lack of congruence between ethnic identity, national identity, and the state. Although these three terms are often used interchangeably, they are very different concepts. Ethnic identity refers to the collective memory and consciousness which is shared by a group, and is passed from generation to generation through childhood socialisation (Gillis, 1996). It is often reinforced by an ascriptive characteristic (such as language, religion, race, or ancestry), but shared symbols and a common history and traditions also serve to underpin it. Not all of those who share an ethnic identity seek the same national goals; for example, ethnic Armenians or Kurds may regard themselves as such but may differ in the national identities that they assume, some Armenians seeing their national identity as Russian, some Kurds as Turkish.

There is an even greater potential incongruence between ethnic and national identities and the state. Although the term nation state is often used as a synonym for the state,[5] few states are ethnically or nationally homogenous. The state refers to the political institutions which exercise legitimate, authoritative control over an agreed territory. In many instances, the territory over which the state exercises control is contested – as is the case in Northern Ireland – and as a consequence the legitimacy of the state is put in question. In many other cases what is regarded as a state is often more akin to a 'quasi-state', using Jackson's (1990) term, where the control that is exercised by the authorities is weak or non-binding. Often such quasi-states have emerged from the collapse of larger national states or empires, the states of the former Yugoslavia being a good contemporary example.

Based on these three dimensions of ethnic identity, national identity and state preferences, we can devise a four-fold typology (Table 1). Those whose identities correspond to the state and to its ethnonational configuration on all three dimensions can be regarded as strongly pro-state: their ethnicity and national identity are in accord, and these in turn cohere with their view of the territorial boundaries of the state. Protestants who see themselves as British, describe themselves as unionist and support the British link would be classified as strongly pro-state in this typology.

Divergence on ethnic and/or national identity would result in individuals who are weakly pro-state in their outlook. For example, individuals who see themselves as British and wish to retain the link with Britain, but who were not unionist, would fall into this category.

TABLE 1. A Typology of Ethnonationalist Political Attitudes

Type of identity			Political attitude
Ethnic	National	State	Outcome
Same	Same	Same	Strong pro-state
Same/different	Same/different	Same	Weak pro-state
Same/different	Same/different	Different	Weak counter-state
Different	Different	Different	Strong counter-state

The third and fourth categories in Table 1 are both counter-state in their political attitudes. The obverse of being strongly pro-state is to be counter-state, by displaying opinions diametrically opposed to the prevailing political arrangements. Catholics who identify as Irish and nationalist, and who support Irish unity as a territorial arrangement for the state, would be regarded as strongly counter-state. Their weaker counterparts would be those who share less definitive views about ethnic or national identity, but who adhere to the essential state goal of ending the link with Britain.

Applying this fourfold typology to Northern Ireland during the past decade shows that, as we would expect, those who favour the state are more numerous than those who oppose it (Figure 1).[6] However, those who hold their pro-state beliefs more strongly have been increasing, peaking at 36 per cent in 1998 and outnumbering their weak counter-parts for the first time. During the decade for which survey data are available, strong pro-state respondents have increased by nine percentage points. With the exception of the mid-1990s, counter-state respondents have varied little over the decade; in the 1998 survey they numbered three out of every 10 respondents, almost equally divided between weak and strong in their views. Most notable over the period is the decline in the strength of the pro-state groups in the mid-1990s, which coincides with the IRA ceasefire of August 1994 to February 1996, the visit of President Clinton in November 1995, and the beginning of all-party talks in 1996.

FIGURE 1. Trends in Ethnonationalism

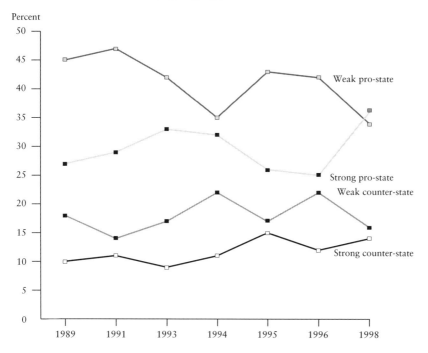

Sources: Northern Ireland Social Attitudes Survey, 1989, 1991, 1993–6; Northern Ireland Election Survey, 1998

In general, Protestants are more pro-state in their views than Catholics are counter-state (Table 2). Strongly pro-state Protestants outnumbered their weaker counterparts throughout the decade, most notably in the most recent survey conducted in mid-1998; at this time six out of every 10 Protestants were strongly pro-state, compared to around one in three who were weakly pro-state. Catholic ethnonationalist opinion has been more evenly distributed across the categories, with a significant minority – up to four in every 10 – expressing weak pro-state opinions. In parallel with changes in the Protestant community, opinions became more polarised in 1998, and 42 per cent were strongly counter-state, the largest proportion recorded over the course of the time period.

Ethnonationalism is the most promising theoretical explanation for the Northern Ireland conflict. Ethnonationalism does not cause conflict or instability in and of itself; rather, when ethnic and national identity are out of alignment, the potential for ethnic conflict exists. By stressing a clash of identity as a cause of the conflict, this explanation highlights the roots of the problem in primary socialisation and in the way in which a variety of social agencies help to reinforce and sustain it. The extension of ethnonationalism to the state provides a further link in the causal sequence which brings political identities into conflict. When ethno-nationalism lacks a political expression, there is potential for it to be mobilised as a political force. In Northern Ireland, that mobilisation has occurred at several points during the course of the past two centuries, but most particularly since the start of the present Troubles in 1968.

TABLE 2. Religious Differences in Ethnonationalism, 1989–98

| | Percentages | | | | | | |
	1989	1991	1993	1994	1995	1996	1998
Protestants							
Strong pro-state	50	49	54	57	49	47	60
Weak pro-state	45	46	38	35	43	43	34
Weak counter-state	4	5	7	8	8	10	6
Strong counter-state	0.1	0	0.1	0	0	1	0
Catholics							
Strong pro-state	0	0.2	0	1	0	0.3	1
Weak pro-state	35	39	40	27	36	38	27
Weak counter-state	39	28	32	41	26	33	30
Strong counter-state	26	33	28	31	37	30	42

Sources: Northern Ireland Social Attitudes Survey, 1989, 1991, 1993–6; Northern Ireland Election Survey, 1998.

ETHNIC, NATIONAL AND STATE IDENTITY

To many outsiders, the conflict in Northern Ireland appears to reflect an archaic struggle between two groups identified by religious labels – Protestants and Catholics. While there is no doubt that religious affili-ation serves as an important boundary-marker in identifying the two protagonists, the conflict cannot be reduced to religious terms. Religious behaviour and religious belief play little part in defining the substance of the conflict, despite the attention that religious symbols receive in popular interpretations of the conflict and in the mass media (McAllister, 1982). Rather, as O'Leary and McGarry (1993) suggest, the conflict in Northern Ireland can best be understood in terms of a dispute over two contested national identities, unionism versus nationalism, and it is these two differing interpretations of ethnonational identity which lie at the heart of the present conflict.

This is not to suggest that the conflict is totally bipolar. Both within and between these two opposing ethnonationalistic traditions – British-unionism versus Irish-nationalism – there are also important differences not only in terms of religious affiliation but also state identity.[7] Not all Protestants perceive themselves as British or adopt a unionist label. And even among those who see themselves as British, a notable minority do not describe themselves as unionist. Similarly, neither do all Catholics identify themselves as nationalist and claim a territorial identity with the rest of Ireland. In Northern Ireland, religious affiliation, ethnic identity, national identity and territorial allegiance are all intertwined in a complex way. It is these interlocking facets that not only provide the ethno-nationalistic basis of the conflict but also give rise to its reinforcing and recurring nature.

Current empirical evidence supports this view. In 1998, although almost eight out of every 10 Protestants saw themselves as British, one in five used a different description (Table 3). Furthermore, there is some evi-

TABLE 3. Religion and Ethnic and National Identity, 1989–98

| | Percentages | | | | | | |
	1989	1991	1993	1994	1995	1996	1998
			(Ethnic Identity)				
Protestants							
British	69	66	69	70	67	60	78
Other	28	32	29	27	29	34	21
Irish	3	2	1	3	5	6	2
Catholics							
British	10	10	12	9	11	10	11
Other	30	28	27	29	26	32	25
Irish	60	62	61	69	63	58	65
			(National Identity)				
Protestants							
Unionist	71	73	76	77	75	73	76
Neither	28	27	24	23	25	26	23
Nationalist	0.2	0.2	0.1	0.0	0.1	1	1
Catholics							
Unionist	1	1	1	1	1	0.3	1
Neither	59	48	59	45	49	52	33
Nationalist	40	51	40	54	51	47	66

Sources: Northern Ireland Social Attitudes Survey, 1989, 1991, 1993–6; Northern Ireland Election Survey, 1998.

dence to suggest that this endorsement of a British identity by Protestants is a relatively recent phenomenon. In fact, with the one exception of 1998, throughout the previous decade the number of Protestants who perceived themselves as British has never exceeded 70 percentage points. And, although only a tiny minority of Protestants rejected a British identity in favour of an Irish label – 6 per cent or less across all the survey years – a significant minority, even as high as a third in some cases, did so in favour of a Northern Irish, Ulster, British–Irish, or some other ethnic identity.

Among Catholics, intra-community differences in ethnic identity are even more marked. In 1998, just under two-thirds of Catholics identified themselves as Irish, as compared to 25 per cent as other and 11 per cent as British, and these divisions have remained relatively stable through time. Since 1989, the proportion of Catholics who see themselves as Irish has not deviated more than seven percentage points, ranging from its lowest level of 58 per cent in 1996 to its highest level of 65 per cent in 1998. More importantly, however, among those who do not claim an Irish identity there is a sizeable minority – approximately one in 10 across all of the survey years – who are willing to cross traditionally expected allegiances and claim a British identity. Thus, at least as far as the Catholic adult population is concerned, there is some empirical evidence to suggest that, for a significant minority of individuals at least, religious affiliation and ethnic identity are by no means coterminous.

A similar result is found when intra-religious differences in national identity are considered. Contrary to popular stereotypes, not all Protestants claim a unionist identity. While the large majority of Protestants do so (in excess of 70 per cent over the last decade) there is also a significant minority, approximately one-quarter across all survey years, who reject both a unionist and nationalist label and adopt an intermediate position. Catholics are also divided in relation to this issue. Prior to 1998, approximately half the Catholic population rejected a nationalist label in favour of an intermediate position. While the proportion who claimed a nationalist identity increased dramatically to 66 per cent in 1998, a third of Catholics still do not claim a nationalist identity. However, perhaps the most striking, though expected, finding, is the marked unwillingness – less than one per cent across all survey years – of either the Protestant or Catholic population to cross traditionally established allegiances and claim either a nationalist or unionist identity.

The relationship between ethnic and national identity is also far from clear-cut (Table 4). In 1998 just under one-third of those who regarded themselves as British were unwilling to identify themselves as unionist. Furthermore, this lack of adherence to a unionist identity within the British-identifying population has remained relatively stable through time. Since

1989, the proportion of British identifiers who do not claim a unionist label has not deviated more than eight percentage points, ranging from its highest level of 40 per cent in 1989 to its lowest level of 32 per cent in 1998. This is not the case, however, when the Irish-nationalist population is considered. Contrary to earlier years when only around a half of all individuals who saw themselves as Irish were also likely to claim a nationalist label, in 1998 a dramatic shift in opinion occurred. Currently, not only do three quarters of Irish identifiers also endorse a nationalist label, but this widespread support reflects a 20 percentage point increase since 1996. In fact, so dramatic is this increase among those who perceive themselves as Irish that the traditionally expected congruency in ethnic and political identity within this group is now greater than that within its equivalent British counterparts.

While various explanations could be offered for this sudden change in national identity among Irish identifiers, the most likely interpretation is the increasing respectability of a 'nationalist' label among the Catholic community as a whole. Contrary to previous connotations, the use of this term is no longer associated with republican sympathisers, for two reasons. First, the use of the terms unionist and nationalist has recently been widely endorsed by both the British and Irish governments as a legitimate way to define the two communities in Northern Ireland. Similarly, it is now commonplace for the SDLP to refer to their own supporters as nationalist (Murray, 1998).[8] Second, the Good Friday Agreement explicitly endorsed the use of this term as a legitimate and acceptable way to identify the aspirations and goals of the Catholic community, consistently using the terms unionist and nationalist to identify the two communities. It is this factor, and the recent respectability in its usage, which we suggest

TABLE 4. The Relationship Between Ethnic and National Identity, 1989–98

| | Percentages | | | | | | |
	1989	1991	1993	1994	1995	1996	1998
British Identity							
Unionist	61	64	67	67	65	62	68
non-unionist	40	36	33	37	35	38	32
Irish Identity							
Nationalist	46	57	49	56	57	55	75
non-nationalist	54	43	52	44	43	45	25

Sources: Northern Ireland Social Attitudes Survey, 1989, 1991, 1993–6; Northern Ireland Election Survey, 1998.

accounts for the dramatic rise in its use among those who define their ethnic identity as Irish.

Finally, when the relationship between ethnic, national, and state identity is considered, further anomalies emerge (Table 5). In contrast to the British, unionist, or British-unionist group who are overwhelming – over 90 per cent in all cases – in their wish to preserve the union with Britain, territorial preferences within the Irish or nationalist community are not as definitive. Although a significant majority within this community – over two-thirds – wish to see Ireland reunited, there is still a notable minority who endorse Northern Ireland's present constitutional status within the United Kingdom. For example, whereas around one-fifth of all Irish or nationalist identifiers wish to retain the union with Britain, the proportion among the Irish-nationalist group, although lower, still accounts for more than one in 10. This is not to deny the lack of support for the maintenance of the union with Britain within these

TABLE 5. The Relationship Between Ethnic, National and State Identity, 1989–98

	Percentages						
	1989	1991	1993	1994	1995	1996	1998
	(Union with Britain)						
British	95	96	95	90	93	91	93
Unionist	97	98	95	95	94	95	94
British-Unionist	99	98	97	96	96	98	96
Irish	25	25	25	22	25	31	16
Nationalist	19	22	16	12	16	18	21
Irish-Nationalist	11	14	13	8	18	15	12
	(United Ireland)						
British	4	4	3	6	6	4	4
Unionist	2	2	2	3	4	4	3
British-Unionist	1	2	2	2	2	2	2
Irish	70	71	71	71	72	61	70
Nationalist	78	74	82	79	81	69	67
Irish-Nationalist	85	83	84	85	86	75	76

Sources: Northern Ireland Social Attitudes Survey, 1989, 1991, 1993–6; Northern Ireland Election Survey, 1998.

groups. Indeed there is evidence to suggest that at least as far as those who perceive themselves as Irish are concerned, support for the union is in decline. For example, whereas around a quarter of Irish identifiers across all survey years but one were willing to endorse the maintenance of the union with Britain, in 1998 this proportion dropped to its lowest level, at just 16 per cent.

THE GOOD FRIDAY AGREEMENT

The Good Friday Agreement is based on the principle of providing full expression for differing identities – what the Agreement terms 'parity of esteem'. In practice, this means the recognition of the political rights of both communities in Northern Ireland, and the right to express those rights in political institutions. In addition to establishing basic principles, the Agreement organises the institutional arrangements into three strands. Strand one involves the election of an Assembly in Northern Ireland with a power-sharing executive; decisions of the Assembly require a majority of both unionist and nationalist representatives before they can be passed. The second strand creates a North–South Ministerial Council to bring together ministers from the Irish Republic and Northern Ireland. Strand three creates a British–Irish Council bringing together representatives from all parts of the British Isles. Other parts of the Agreement stipulate the decommissioning of weapons, the release of paramilitary prisoners, and an inquiry into policing in Northern Ireland.[9]

Each of the three strands represents a trade-off between unionist and nationalist aspirations. In return for nationalist demands for the creation of cross-border bodies, nationalists and republicans endorsed the unionist desire for a return to devolved government and the creation of an elected assembly. To make the creation of cross-border bodies more acceptable to unionists, the north-south dimension was complemented by an east-west dimension via the establishment of a British–Irish Council. For nationalists, in return, the elected assembly would be based on the principle of proportionality with a power-sharing executive composed of all groups within the assembly, chosen by the d'Hondt procedure.

The most significant compromises were achieved on the constitutional position of Northern Ireland. For unionists there was, for the first time, a formal recognition provided by both the British and Irish governments as to Northern Ireland's current constitutional status within the United Kingdom. Furthermore, this recognition was accompanied by a commitment by the Irish government to amend articles 2 and 3 of the Irish constitution and thereby abandon its formal territorial claim to Northern Ireland. To accommodate nationalist aspirations this formal recognition of Northern Ireland's constitutional status within the United Kingdom was officially qualified in terms of majority consent. In other words, the constitutional position of Northern Ireland was a matter for future negotiation, its status to be maintained or modified through the exercise of popular sovereignty by its electorate via a referendum.

These compromises were not equally acceptable to all unionists and nationalists alike. No sooner had the Agreement been signed than significant divisions began to emerge, particularly within the mainstream unionist groups. In addition to those unionists (mainly Democratic and UK Unionists) who had opposed agreement of any kind almost from the very beginning of the negotiations, significant opposition to the Agreement also began to emerge among many Ulster Unionists. The major point of friction which surfaced almost immediately after the Agreement was signed was not so much over constitutional matters, which had already been debated intensely during the negotiations, but rather over the issues of decommissioning by the paramilitaries, reform of the Royal Ulster Constabulary, and the accelerated release of paramilitary prisoners.

For many Unionists, the concession to Sinn Féin and the two loyalist fringe parties, the Progressive Unionist Party and Ulster Democratic Party, to introduce a phased early prisoner release programme was unacceptable. This scheme would see all prisoners released within two years and many released within the first six months. Although acceptance for the scheme was based on strict guidelines, and confined to those prisoners affiliated with organisations that had established and maintained an unequivocal ceasefire, this failed to ameliorate unionist concerns. Many unionists reacted with horror to the thought of the release of individuals who although convicted of murdering offences might, in some cases, be released after having served less than a three year sentence. But disquiet over the prisoner release scheme was not just confined to the unionist community. Concern also began to emerge among nationalists, particularly when they realised that prisoners found guilty of sectarian murders would also be eligible for early release.

A related issue was the continuing ambiguity over the decommissioning of paramilitary weapons. Despite British assurances to the unionists that the decommissioning of IRA weapons was a necessary precondition to the inclusion of Sinn Féin in government, much confusion continued to surround the issue. Claims and counter-claims abounded as to what exactly was the position of the Agreement in relation to this matter. While republicans as well as political representatives of the paramilitary loyalist organisations adamantly denied that decommissioning was a precondition for their inclusion in government, this was not the interpretation advanced by unionists. For both pro-Agreement and anti-Agreement unionists alike, the immediate surrender of all paramilitary weapons was a necessary prerequisite for the inclusion in government not only of Sinn Féin but also of the loyalist paramilitary organisations. Nationalists adopted a different interpretation: decommissioning remained a necessary but more long-term aspiration, whose eventual success should be seen as a consequence of, rather than a precondition for, access to political office.

Unionist concerns also emerged over the proposed Independent Commission on Policing, a key concession to nationalists. Among even moderate unionists, not only was the latter seen as a mechanism to undermine the RUC, but many also feared that it would be used to pave the way for its eventual disbandment. Nationalists, in contrast, viewed the reform of the RUC as an important step in introducing a new beginning in policing. They envisioned that not only would the recommendations of the commission suggest the establishment of a new police service that would attract support and consent from all sections of the community, but one which would, for the first time, be representative in its religious composition of both communities.

Some anti-Agreement dissenters were also present, although to a much lesser degree, among the nationalist community. While the vast majority of nationalists saw the Agreement as an important step forward to meeting their aspirations and demands, for some nationalists – most notably those within the republican movement – the suggested changes in terms of the establishment of cross-border bodies as well as a power-sharing executive were inadequate. Proponents of this position pointed out that not only did the Agreement fail to deliver a united Ireland, but through its principle of majority consent for any future change in the constitutional position of Northern Ireland, it again reaffirmed the unionist veto. Furthermore, they argued that although the Agreement promised the establishment of an Independent Commission on Policing, it contained no firm commitment to either disband or reform the RUC. Eventually, however, most republicans added their voices to the pro-Agreement camp, no doubt encouraged by the promised prisoner release programme.

ETHNONATIONALISM, PARTY SUPPORT AND THE AGREEMENT

The Agreement therefore raised a range of issues for both communities, and these issues were intimately linked to their ethnonationalist identities. Protestants, in general strongly pro-state, were concerned about measures which would potentially undermine the constitutional position of Northern Ireland within the United Kingdom, particularly the North–South Ministerial Council. They were also concerned about the Agreement's potential for weakening the major institutions on which the state depends for the maintenance of public order. Given their composition and outlook, we would expect those who are strongly pro-state to be least favourable towards any form of political or constitutional change, as well as being opposed to the Good Friday Agreement. Furthermore, these individuals should be more likely to support parties most opposed to the Agreement. Weak pro-state individuals should be moderately supportive of the Agreement, and concentrated among Alliance and (to a lesser extent) SDLP partisans.

Catholics were much more positive towards the Agreement than Protestants, since it presaged a period during which they could agitate for extensive reform of the political system. Not least, the Agreement guaranteed Sinn Féin representation in the executive level of government for the first time in Northern Ireland's history. In general, opponents of the Agreement represented a very small minority of extreme republicans. Both of the counter-state groups should be the strongest supporters of the Agreement; however, we would expect weak counter-state individuals to be more likely to be SDLP supporters, and strong counter-state individuals supporters of Sinn Féin.

FIGURE 2. Ethnonationalism and Party Preference

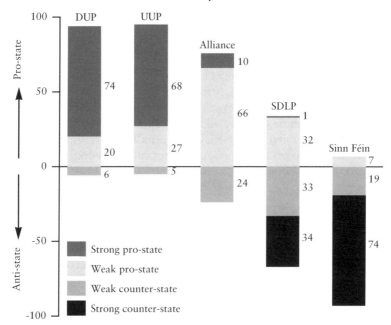

Source: Northern Ireland Election Survey, 1998

The hypotheses with respect to party support are largely confirmed by the results of the 1998 survey (Figure 2). As predicted, strong pro-state beliefs are most prevalent among the unionist parties, although the prediction that they would be concentrated among supporters of Ian Paisley's Democratic Unionist Party – one of the most vociferous opponents of the Agreement – is not supported by the data. As predicted, the majority of Alliance supporters are weakly pro-state, although around one in four are also weakly counter-state. There are substantial differences between the SDLP and Sinn Féin on these attitudes, more so than are found between the two unionist parties. As expected, three quarters of Sinn Féin supporters are strongly counter-state, while SDLP supporters are equally divided between weak pro-state, weak counter-state and strong counter-state.

There is a similarly large polarisation in ethnonationalist views concerning the Good Friday Agreement itself (Table 6). Although the referendum produced a large majority of the population voting yes, just under half of strong pro-state individuals did so. This is in contrast to no less than 98 per cent of strongly counter-state individuals who reported voting in favour of the Agreement. This latter group is also most likely to

TABLE 6. Voting and Support for the Good Friday Agreement

		Percentages			
	All	Strong Pro-State	Weak Pro-State	Weak Counter State	Stong Counter State
Referendum vote					
For the agreement	75	49	79	91	98
Against the agreement	25	51	21	9	2
Degree of support					
Support entirely	16	3	14	25	40
Support as a package	57	45	63	64	58
Not support as a package	19	34	18	10	1
Oppose entirely	8	19	5	1	1
Percieved beneficiaries					
Unionists a lot more	2	2	1	2	5
Unionists a little more	4	1	3	4	11
Unionists/Nationalists equally	53	30	56	69	65
Nationalists a little more	14	17	16	14	12
Nationalists a lot more	27	50	24	11	7

Sources: Northern Ireland Election Survey, 1998.

give the Agreement unequivocal support, although the largest group, 58 per cent, supported it as a package. Exactly half of the strong pro-state group believed that the Agreement benefited nationalists much more than unionists, but a majority in each of the other three groups took the view that it benefited both communities equally. Even two-thirds of the strong counter-state group, composed predominantly of Sinn Féin supporters, took this view, with the remainder equally divided between which community received the most benefit.

Of the eight basic principles underlying the Good Friday Agreement, only four of them receive majority support in each of the four ethno-nationalist groups (Table 7). There is strongest cross-community support for the principle of the decommissioning of paramilitary weapons, which is supported by nine out of 10 of the population, followed by the principle that Northern Ireland should remain part of the United Kingdom based on majority consent, and the establishment of an assembly and power-sharing executive. The widespread cross-community support that exists for the constitutional position of the province subject to majority consent is perhaps surprising, given its centrality to the conflict. However, two factors help to explain why the principle of majority consent attracts such high levels of cross-community support. First, the majority consent principle has been at the core of British policy towards Northern Ireland

TABLE 7. Ethnonationalism and the Good Friday Agreement Proposals

		Percent support			
	All	Strong Pro-State	Weak Pro-State	Weak Counter State	Stong Counter State
Consensus					
Decommissioning	92	95	94	90	83
NI remain part of UK if majority consents	89	98	95	81	66
Establish an assembly	87	79	91	93	93
Power-sharing executive	77	57	83	90	98
Dissensus					
Remove Republic's constitutional claim	69	87	74	53	36
Create North–South bodies	67	40	71	89	93
Commission on RUC future	54	28	54	80	84
Early release of prisoners	19	5	13	37	48

Sources: Northern Ireland Election Survey, 1998.

since 1973, when the first referendum on the constitutional position was held. Since then, it has also been adopted by the Irish Republic. Second, even though many nationalists aspire to Irish unity, there is also wide-spread acceptance of the current constitutional position (Breen, 1996).

Among the four principles which do not attract cross-community support, one, the early release of prisoners, failed to gain a majority in any of the four groups, although the strongly counter-state group just falls short of majority support. Of the remaining three principles, the largest disagreement concerns the future of the police, which finds least support among the two pro-state groups. However, it is also notable that removing the Irish Republic's territorial claim to Northern Ireland is supported by just over one in three of the strongly counter-state group. Both pro-state groups give it strong support since such a change would serve to legitimise the constitutional status quo.

CONCLUSION

Ethnonationalism is not of itself a cause of conflict. Where ethnic and national identities reinforce one another and are given political expression, stability is a more likely outcome than conflict. But in ethnically heterogeneous societies, historical accidents combined with social learning and an artificial nation state provide the prerequisites for ethnic conflict (Smith, 1996). By moderating expectations and political demands, political elites have often been highly effective in defusing inconsistencies between ethnic and national identities and political institutions. But when elites fail, there are major opportunities for the mass political mobilisation of disaffected groups, and for the use of physical force to try and meet expectations (Connor, 1993).

Explanations for the Northern Ireland conflict that have relied on theories of ethnonationalism have advanced our understanding of the problem, as well as providing some practical suggestions for its resolution. The policy implications of ethnonationalism form the basis of the Good Friday Agreement, most notably the principle of parity of esteem which is its centrepiece. In this chapter we have outlined how the relationships between ethnic and national identity on the one hand, and political and state institutions on the other, shape beliefs about the Agreement. Our results suggest more coherence and consistency among the pro-state groupings than the counter-state ones; it is easier to unite supporters around opposition to change and a plea for the status quo, than to unite around a vague and insecure future.

Perhaps most disturbing for the fate of the Good Friday Agreement is the absence of consensual support for its basic principles. Our results show that consensual support exists for just four of the eight principles, and on one of the eight, none of the four groups provide majority support. However, our results also indicate that there are significant variations in ethnic and national identities over time. While these self-identities are learned, they are also subject to change through external events. This appears to have been particularly the case during the 1990s, when the diminution in the intensity of the conflict appears to have moderated outlooks. If the assembly and executive succeed in alleviating the conflict, it is possible that outlooks will slowly change. Equally, if they fail, or if the Agreement itself collapses, it may presage a period in which there is more intense conflict than has been seen in the past.

NOTES

[1] Earlier versions of this chapter were presented at University College Dublin and Nuffield College, Oxford. Our thanks to Anthony Heath, Liam O'Dowd, Joe Ruane and Jennifer Todd for helpful suggestions; the usual disclaimer applies. The data were the 1998 Northern Ireland Referendum and Election Survey. The data was collected by John Curtice, Lizanne Dowds, Geoffrey Evans and Bernadette C. Hayes and funded by the Economic and Social Research Council.

[2] Catholics were overwhelming (99 per cent) in their support for the Agreement, based on an *Irish Times*/Radio Telefís Éireann exit poll.

[3] The Northern Ireland Referendum and Election Survey was funded by the Economic and Social Research Council. It was a nationally representative post-election survey of all adults aged 18 years or older conducted immediately after the Northern Ireland assembly elections in June 1998. Using face-to-face interviews, the survey is based on a randomly selected sample of 948 respondents and has an overall response rate of 71 per cent.

[4] The earliest attempt to summarise and evaluate these theories was undertaken by Darby (1976). The most authoritative account is Whyte (1990).

[5] Perhaps the most prominent contemporary example of this is the United Nations.

[6] The typology was operationalised as follows. Strong pro-state individuals express both a British and unionist identity and want to retain the link with Britain. Weak pro-state individuals want to retain the link with Britain but do not have both a British and unionist identity. Weak counter-state individuals do not wish to retain the union with Britain and do not have both an Irish and nationalist identity. Finally, strong counter-state individuals express both an Irish and nationalist identity and support Irish unity.

[7] See, for example, Ruane and Todd (1992); O'Connor (1993); Trew (1994, 1996); Coulter (1994); Todd (1995); Breen (1996); Duffy and Evans (1997); Shirlow and McGovern (1997); Porter (1998).

[8] Prior to the mid-1980s, SDLP representatives would always refer to the Catholic community as the 'minority community.'

[9] See Wilford (1999) for a comprehensive overview of the terms and conditions of the Agreement.

3

NATIONALISM, REPUBLICANISM AND THE GOOD FRIDAY AGREEMENT

Jennifer Todd

INTRODUCTION

There is no agreement on the character of Irish nationalism and Irish republicanism today, nor on their interrelationship. Are they now satisfied nationalisms, content to work within the new institutions, accepting British sovereignty for the foreseeable future? Or are they nationalisms on the march, intent on further constitutional change? Republicanism in particular is an enigma. Has it simply converted to a gradualist constitutional nationalism? Can it retain its traditional ideological structure and aims while pursuing a peaceful political strategy? Has the Good Friday Agreement and the problems of its implementation strengthened or thrown into crisis the new ideological currents in republicanism? What of nationalist support for the Good Friday Agreement? Is it simply an interim and unsteady compromise with unionism? Or does it mark radical ideological movement which has made a stable settlement possible? On the answers rests the difference between compromise and conflict, violence and peace. On the extent and precise character of the ideological changes depends how the Good Friday Agreement is interpreted. In the longer term, it is the nature of the new nationalisms (and unionisms) which will determine whether or not opposition can be transformed into pluralist coexistence, and, ultimately, whether and how we can move to a situation where politics is no longer structured on competing communal power blocs.

In this chapter I argue that while the Good Friday Agreement was made possible by changes in nationalist and republican (and to a lesser extent unionist) ideologies, the room for compromise between the still sharply oppositional positions was very narrow. The Agreement defined a compromise on this knife-edge and in so doing opened the possibility of further ideological change. As such it was a major turning point, promising an institutionalisation of ideological distinctions which could in turn allow further ideological development. But this depends on the successful implementation of the Agreement, and 'success' here means fulfilling the opposing interests and expectations of the parties. Whether this can be sustained over the long term is still in the balance. If not, the ideological changes may well be reversed. Ideological change remains dependent on benign institutional and structural conditions.

ANALYSING CHANGE IN NATIONALISM: CONCEPTS AND PRINCIPLES

Nationalisms change – in aims, strategies and assumptions. The comparative and theoretical literature provides some of the concepts necessary to make sense of the changes in the Northern Ireland context. A useful starting point is the distinction between classic and liberal nationalism. Classic nationalism, according to McGarry and O'Leary (1995, pp. 13ff.) is a principle of political legitimacy which holds:

1. 'that the nation should be collectively and freely institutionally expressed and ruled by its co-nationals' (the principle that the nation and state should coincide), and

2. 'that the nation must choose how it rules itself' (the principle of self-determination).

In addition, these principles presuppose a notion of a nation distinct from others. Classically, this set of principles was understood in terms of more general political principles: national independence and freedom were the rights of all, and were seen as integrally connected to individual independence and freedom, citizenship and cultural creativity (Alter, 1994, pp. 19–23). In much of the subsequent history of nationalism, the liberal principles were discarded. In the contemporary period, political philosophers and theorists have again focused on the interrelation of liberal and democratic principles and nationalist aims (Miller, 1995; Tamir, 1993). Now, however, the ideals of nation-state coincidence and political self-determination have been revised. Classic nationalism cannot conceptually deal with issues of ethnonational conflict or disputes about the extent of the nation. Nor do classic nineteenth century assumptions provide much guidance for national development in an age of European integration and greater inter-state dependency. Such practical issues have provoked revisions of the classic premises. For example, one form of liberal nationalism focuses on the need for institutional expression of distinct national cultures and identities:

1. the nation should have institutional expression (Tamir, 1993, pp. 70–75).

2. self-determination should be understood as a cultural rather than political goal, aiming at institutional expression of national culture and values (Tamir, 1993, chapter 3).

Another form of liberal nationalism focuses on the political level, arguing that:

1. the nation should have a level of political autonomy (which may fall short of nation-state coincidence) (Miller, 1995, chapter 4),

2. national self-determination is a political value but one that can be satisfied with less than independent statehood (Miller, 1995, chapter 4) ,

Here the conception of a nation distinct from others is maintained, while accepting that there is often overlapping and nesting in national identities (Miller, 1995, p. 46).

The distinction between classic and liberal nationalism is only a starting point for analysis. The concept of liberal nationalism covers a wide variety of political aims and principles. And the abstraction of 'nationalist' premises from wider systems of ideas ignores the way these premises are used in argument and their imbrication with other sets of principles. It is these issues, more than the abstract premises, that are in contention among nationalists and republicans in Ireland today. It is in their interrelations with other premises that liberal nationalist premises either become principles in themselves, applications of other principles or temporary and imperfect steps on the way to classic nationalist aims. It is here, rather than in schematic philosophical arguments, that compromises are or are not made and that seemingly minor distinctions become all important. In studying these processes, the reminder that both classic and contemporary liberal nationalisms have interrelated nationalist premises with liberal and democratic political principles is important. It allows a refocusing of attention from nationalist premises per se (which may be reformulated in the light of new circumstances) to the ideological system as a whole (which gives the limits and possibilities of such reformulation).

In what follows, I treat Irish nationalism and republicanism as *ideological systems* in which nationalist premises are used and combined with others, with some principles given priority and others seen as derivative or second-level principles. Using as data nationalist and republican speeches and statements, I schematise the distinctive ways that nationalists (particularly John Hume) and republicans have ordered their arguments and prioritised their premises. This involves a reconstruction of the logical patterns and priorities in argumentation which are presupposed by the rhetoric of political actors and which can generate the range of ideological expressions. These generative patterns can be called the *structure* of an ideology. Particular forms of ideological expression may or may not be generated from a stable ideological structure. When political actors have developed a distinctive and plausible ideology able to deal successfully with practical problems – John Hume's nationalism is an example – it is relatively easy to reconstruct the underlying structure of the ideology. When an ideology is in process of change and when the political actors are experimenting rhetorically, there may be no single stable structure of ideology, actors themselves may waver between the assumptions of different structures, and analysts can do no more than postulate several equally plausible generative schemes. This appears to be the case with republican ideology at present.

Ideological structures provide a stability of interpretation, a self-confirming perspective. This, typically, is rejected only when situational changes provoke a clear dissonance between ideological categories and social practice (Lustick, 1993, chapter 5). In extreme conditions, change can lead to ideological collapse or conversion (Sahlins, 1981). More often, and particularly for nationalisms where continuity with the past is a constitutive virtue, the ideological changes are presented as changes within a tradition. At the same time, the defining features of the tradition are themselves partially constituted and redefined in the process of ideological change. If traditions limit change, these limits can themselves be stretched in the process of change. This chapter illustrates such a reconstruction of nationalist and republican traditions in Northern Ireland.

Ideological and institutional change are interwoven, hence the importance of the Good Friday Agreement. Institutional change may embody ideological distinctions, provoke ideological dissonances, and provide confirmation of new ideological trends (Lustick, 1993; Sahlins, 1981; Enloe, 1983). Ideologies frame the understanding of institutional options and changes – but at the same time they are dependent on institutional development. To put it simply, the new ideologies are required to prove themselves by achieving strategic successes, by recognising and grasping new institutional opportunities, if they are decisively to win out over the older oppositional ideologies. This chapter traces the dependence of ideological change on particular directions of institutional development. Here we see the fragility of changes in republicanism, which depend on a particular form of implementation of the Good Friday Agreement. Whether this is consistent with continued unionist support for the Agreement is an open question.

THE DISTINCTIVE LIBERAL NATIONALISM
OF JOHN HUME AND THE SDLP

The assumptions of classic nationalism were shaken by events in Northern Ireland in the late 1960s and early 1970s. Northern Catholics were mobilised on civil rights rather than nationalist aims; reform of Northern Ireland – but not a united Ireland – came onto the British political agenda; and the British political system proved not to provide a favourable arena for such reform (Ruane and Todd, 1996, chapters 5, 8). Republicans attempted to force the British government to change its strategy and to create conditions where classic nationalism would be viable. Constitutional nationalists instead responded by ideological change.

In this context, John Hume's ideological innovations were decisive. He, more than any other single individual, developed and fashioned a liberal nationalist discourse which at once provided a practical strategy to deal with contemporary political dilemmas in Northern Ireland, provided long term aims and visions within the nationalist tradition, and, finally, provided a language which made political compromise possible. Hume developed his argument as a practical politician, using the EU and US as models (eg, Hume, 1996, pp. 58–60, 103–4, 111ff., 118ff.); this at once allowed him to show the possibility of change in Northern Ireland and to win international allies for his cause. He sustained his argument through a dual-levelled ideology which had the political virtue of flexibility: it could be more or less nationalist in its demands and aims as the situation and opportunities demanded. Characterisation of this ideology has been difficult because commentators have attempted to fit it into clear nationalist or post-nationalist categories. They have noted the intermixture of post-nationalist with nationalist principles (Longley, 1994; Cunningham, 1997). Hume's ideology is either seen as essentially post-nationalist, albeit with nationalist residues, or as essentially nationalist with a post-nationalist veneer (Kearney, 1997; Longley, 1994). Neither view adequately captures the logical structure of the whole. It is rather necessary to show the distinctive mode of interrelation of nationalist and non-nationalist premises.

The first principles of Hume's ideology are pluralist, egalitarian, dialogic and non-nationalist. He decisively rejected the classic nationalist model of a world of nation states and with it the classic nationalist view that nation and state should coincide, a view he took as irrelevant in an age of European integration and the decreasing importance of state sovereignty (Hume, 1996, pp. 111, 114–15). Instead he emphasised the multiple and interconnected institutional arenas (from the local area to the Irish-American Atlantic community, to the EU) in which interaction now takes place (Hume, 1996, pp. 119–24, 130ff.). He refashioned liberalism's emphasis on consent as the basis of political legitimacy: a legitimate political order must be founded on agreement on the mode of government (Hume, 1996, pp. 93–5, 138). Self-determination remains a central democratic value, but is redefined in non-nationalist and non-majoritarian terms as the process of reaching agreement (on the relevant unit, exercise and end) (Hume, 1986; 1988). Where there is a divided society, such agreement cannot be presupposed or coerced but must be created by inclusivist dialogue (Hume, 1995, pp. 104–5). This dialogue is made possible by institutions which ensure equality and protection of basic rights (Hume, 1996, p. 28). Rights are understood in a broad sense, to include communal and cultural rights so that each core tradition and culture has a right to equal institutional expression, recognition and respect. Agreement is possible, even in the most divided of societies, but only when people move away from closed and oppositional identities. A syncretic, rather than essentialist notion of identity is affirmed, together with a rejection of any oppositional definitions of self and other: diversity is to be accommodated, and difference is seen as a source of strength not weakness (Hume, 1996, pp. 59ff., 133, 142). In short, Hume's first principles are liberal, pluralist and dialogic with an egalitarian edge: this is a form of identity politics, but based on syncretic notions of identity based on multiple, overlapping institutional arenas.

In the second-level application of these principles, liberal nationalist assumptions return. The core – although not the exclusive – identity for one community and tradition in Northern Ireland is an Irish identity. This national identity requires institutional recognition and respect: this requires a movement beyond Northern Ireland to a strong Irish dimension and role for the Irish state in Northern Ireland (New Ireland Forum Report, 1984, sections 4.15, 4.16, 5.2; Hume, 1996, pp. 25ff., 43ff.). This is a necessary prerequisite of a legitimate political order, one to which Catholics as well as Protestants in Northern Ireland can agree; only this allows unionists to express their identity without the 'corruption of exclusivism' (Hume 1996, p. 45). Hume argues that, in the past, the British state has generated conflict in Ireland by giving in to unionist resistance to change (Hume, 1996, pp. 35–40, 84ff.). A settlement must therefore include a British–Irish intergovernmental agreement on the principles of a legitimate settlement and British determination to uphold these principles against unionist or loyalist resistance. At the same time the conflict in Northern Ireland is part of a longer conflict between the peoples on the island of Ireland. A settlement of the Northern Ireland conflict must therefore involve agreement on the island, ratified by simultaneous referendums in both parts of Ireland: this is what Irish self-determination means today

(Hume, 1996, pp. 95, 125). Such a fair settlement which recognises each identity in Northern Ireland and institutionalises equality of respect and human rights, will allow a healing process to start which will begin to overcome communal opposition and allow gradualist evolutionary change (Hume, 1996, p. 28). Irish nationalism will be satisfied by this – a unitary nation state is not necessary in the present global age – and it is a matter for further generations, once political antagonisms are overcome, to decide for themselves where political boundaries will lie in the future.

At this second level, there is a strong sense of Irish national identity, both in the sense of a tradition (largely Catholic) of the oppressed, and in the projection of a broader more federated sense of Irishness which can include Northern Protestants (Hume, 1985). There is a claim that this identity should be institutionally recognised, through the role of the Irish state. There is an argument that the British state must stand up to unionist threats and resistance to change. There is a prioritising of the island of Ireland as the locus of democratic agreement (Hume, 1989). At the same time this is a nationalism that recognises the equal rights of other nationalisms, which is framed within an overarching liberal-pluralist set of principles, and which – once its minimum conditions are met – sees future change as evolutionary, gradualist and consensual.

Hume's central ideological achievement was to distinguish the two levels of ideology in his political discourse and rhetoric. In one sense this is a rediscovery of the classic nationalist tradition which combined liberalism and nationalism. But it is also more. It updates classic liberalism to make it appropriate in an age of European integration and identity politics. At the same time it systematically holds apart the liberal pluralist principles from the liberal nationalist application of them. For Hume, nations are not present at the level of first principle, and come in only as the background understanding to the specific demands of level 2. This complex system of ideas cannot be understood simply by abstracting the pluralist, post-nationalist or nationalist premises used by Hume, nor evaluated by deciding whether he is 'really' post-nationalist or nationalist. It is rather a matter of identifying the system of ideas. This has many political virtues. Level 1 gives a language for political dialogue and a general legitimation of the specific demands. Level 2 places Hume firmly in the (liberal) nationalist tradition, (Cunningham, 1997; Longley, 1994) although willing to adapt that tradition in light of the more general principles. The lack of explicit articulation of nationalist premises gives political flexibility. In any situation Hume or the SDLP can emphasise or de-emphasise nationalist judgements: how far to emphasise the political salience of national identity and situation over regional and local, how far to emphasise the political relevance of the island of Ireland over other spatial units. The emphasis can shift in the light of dialogue with unionists or republicans, of changing attitudes in the population and of emerging political possibilities, without the need for any explicit revision of nationalist aims.

REPUBLICAN REVISIONS

Traditionally republicanism had combined classic nationalist axioms with an emphasis on the need for complete separation from Britain and for radical social change: in Adams's phrase, republicanism combined separatism, secularism, anti-sectarianism, nationalism and radicalism (Adams, 1986, pp. 132–3; see also Patterson, 1989). The republican emphasis on colonial conquest and conflict and on the need for a radical break from British cultural as well as political hegemony precluded any strategy which would accept partition or British rule even as an interim compromise. In the seminal republican writings there was an interrelation of nationalist aims and radical egalitarian democratic ideals (Pearse, 1966; Patterson, 1989, chapters 1–2; for anti-democratic tendencies, see Garvin, 1987, chapter 6). For the most part, however, republicans kept these radical ideals as resonances of separatist nationalist aims, as part of a republican culture which underlay and gave meaning to the nationalist goals which took the dominant role in the ideology.

In the recent phase of conflict in Northern Ireland (1969–94) Anthony McIntyre (1995) points out that British policies and unionist resistance meant that republican aims could only be pursued militantly. There were no real possibilities of a gradualist path to an Irish nation state: unionist resistance and British backing of unionism precluded it. McIntyre expresses the choice – as republicans saw it – starkly: the militant pursuit of anti-partitionism or the acceptance (like constitutional nationalists) of partition for the foreseeable future. Throughout the 1970s and much of the 1980s, republicans unambiguously chose the first option.

At the same time, republican strategy and ideology changed during this period (McIntyre, 1995; Clohessy, 1998; Patterson, 1989) and the changes did not leave the traditional goals untouched (Clohessy, 1998). The success of an electoral strategy after the hunger strikes of 1981, the increasing influence of the Irish government in Northern Ireland, the threatened marginalisation of republicans after the Anglo-Irish Agreement of 1985, and stalemate in the armed struggle, made for changes in both strategy and in ideology. With the peace process of the 1990s, these changes accelerated. The question is how to characterise the changes. For McIntyre, they represent a rejection of the core republican beliefs: like constitutional nationalists, leading republicans now accept the principle of majority/unionist consent to constitutional change and with it partition for the foreseeable future.

McIntyre's argument rests on taking one binary opposition (anti-partitionism vs partitionism) as the essential feature and organising core of republican ideology. Since anti-partitionism is equated with republicanism and militancy, and partitionism with constitutional nationalism and the principle of (unionist) consent to constitutional change, it follows that those who reject militant anti-partitionism have converted to constitutional nationalism. But what if, rather than republicans rejecting anti-partitionism for partitionism, they instead have rejected this organising ideological dichotomy. This would indeed be change, but to assess its extent would require analysis of the ideological system as a whole. Indeed when we consider 1990s republicanism as a complex ideological system, we see continuity with many elements of the tradition and a clear distinction from the ideological structure of Hume's constitutional nationalism. The system as a whole is presented by republicans as part of a continuous tradition: the changes are presented as better ways of achieving the aims and dealing with the problems which beset the tradition in the past (cf. MacIntyre, 1988, p. 7). The latter claim may be false, but to assess it requires an analysis of the system as a whole.

With the peace process, the republican leadership moved swiftly, but ambivalently, to embrace some aspects of Hume's dual-levelled ideology. The Hume–Adams statements of April and September 1993 reaffirmed the principle of national self-determination while accepting that its exercise is a matter for agreement among the people of Ireland, and stated that any viable agreement must earn 'the allegiance and agreement' of the different traditions on the island (Hume–Adams, 1993). From this point, a distinction was made clear between consensualist first principles aiming at agreement between the traditions, and the goal (Irish unity) of one of those traditions. Increasingly, leading republicans spoke in terms of universalisable first principles – democracy, justice, equality and the overcoming of oppression (McLaughlin, 1998), peace based on equality, justice and freedom (McGuinness, 1999), peace, justice and freedom (Adams, 1999a). The status of the traditional goal of Irish unity became more ambiguous (cf. Clohessy, 1998). Sometimes Irish unity was presented as the overriding aim: 'The objective remains the same: a united independent Ireland' (Doherty, 1999; IRA, 1999). At other times it was subsumed in vaguer references to constitutional and institutional change (Adams 1999a) or understood as an application of first principles (McLaughlin, 1998).

At the same time, republican ideology had a sharper critical edge than Hume's. Rather than Hume's emphasis on European models of gradualist change, there were analogies with South Africa (e.g. Sinn Féin, 1995, p. 39), and the clear assumption that the colonial structures of the society would have to be dismantled before a legitimate settlement was possible. The negative and problematic features of the British role in Northern Ireland were emphasised (Sinn Féin, 1995, pp. 35–6). There was a continuing emphasis on struggle, change and processual transformation (McLaughlin, 1998; Adams 1999a). The principle of legitimacy founded on agreement and allegiance was qualified by the assumption that radical change – an undoing of the causes of conflict – would be necessary to create the conditions for an agreed settlement (Adams, 1999b; McGuinness, 1999). The commitment to peaceful methods, dialogue and democratic procedures was combined with a commitment to removing the causes of violence and demilitarising the society (McGuinness, 1999). Radical principles of equality (including cultural and national equality, parity of esteem, institutional recognition of the political rights of republicans and of the legitimacy of republican aims) were core elements of the ideological system. Rather than Hume's emphasis on inclusive identities, unionist identity was characterised as oppositional and supremacist, and it was assumed that change in unionist identity and allegiance was both possible and necessary (e.g. IRA, 1999; McLaughlin, 1998, pp. 78–80; Adams, 1999a). In all these respects, a legitimate settlement would require radical change. But where that change would lead was no longer seen as predetermined: Irish unity was still the desired end but no longer the predetermined one (cf. McLaughlin, 1998).

Throughout most of the 1990s, these radical egalitarian democratic transformist principles were understood within a decolonising historical model. Into this fitted the classic nationalist premises. Colonisation and its effects were located in Ireland, and upheld by Britain (cf. McLaughlin, 1998; Sinn Féin, 1995). Decolonisation would involve the reaffirmation of an Irish national identity, the exercise of national self-determination (free of British interference), and the achievement of a united independent Ireland (the coincidence of Irish nation and state). After the Good Friday Agreement, however, colonial analogies all but disappeared from the discourse of leading republicans. At the same time, a re-evaluation of the European context began: the inequalities generated by European integration were criticised but now there was a commitment to work within the framework to increase equality (McLaughlin, 1999). The British state continued to be criticised, but it was also recognised as a possible facilitator of change.

Nationalist premises remained, not least the goal of a united Ireland, but their status within the ideological system was now less clear. Republicans recognised that a united Ireland might not be immediately possible and were open to constitutional compromise, but only if that compromise opened a path to Irish unity (Adams 1998a; 1998b). Whether such a compromise was to be justified in terms of liberal nationalist principles, in terms of egalitarian norms, or as a step on the way to Irish unity, was not clear. Equally, how the right of self-determination was to be exercised was not settled within republicanism. In 1995, in rejecting the principle of consent in the majority report of the Forum for Peace and Reconciliation, Sinn Féin continued to work with a majoritarian notion of self-determination. By the May 1998 referendum, the implicit message of republican support for the Agreement seemed to be that self-determination could be by each part of the island separately. But republicans themselves gave contrary indications (IRA 1998; Adams 1998b); they continued to describe Northern Ireland as an illegitimate political entity, even after the Agreement and referendums (Adams, 1999b).

In principle, the new republicanism had sharpened Hume's criteria of legitimacy and added to them classic nationalist principles. In practice, the strengthened normative criteria and their processual character and their combination with a now processually understood nationalism meant that any compromise settlement could not fully meet all the republican criteria of legitimacy. But one of the political purposes of the new republicanism was to open the way to interim political compromises. The conditions for legitimate compromise, (which did not, or did not yet, fully meet any or all of the republican criteria of legitimacy) remained unclear. The ambiguity was exacerbated because the ideology was still in flux, responding to new events and opportunities, jettisoning old themes and ideas, while attempting to keep continuity with the past. In this context of very rapid change, republican arguments wavered between three quite distinct structures of ideology.

In some republican discussions (see McLaughlin, 1998), there was a two-levelled ideological structure reminiscent of Hume. The emphasis was on first principles of democracy and equality. Irish unity and independence seemed to be demoted to second-level applications of first principles, and even then made into long term aims. Indeed in the year after the Good Friday Agreement, unity and independence all but disappeared from the discourse of leading republicans (Adams, 1999b; McGuinness, 1999; Kelly, 1999). Rather, more specific second-level aims were emphasised: a strong equality agenda incorporating radical reform of the police, total demilitarisation, and strong North/South linkages which would open the possibility of an eventual united Irish nation state. National self determination was affirmed, but its character (majoritarian or not) and its result (a united Ireland or another form of agreed Ireland) were left ambiguous. There were inherent problems in this approach.

Irish unity meant something different when relegated to a level 2 contingent long-term demand rather than a level 1 principle (cf. Clohessy, 1998). While the peace process had a strong momentum, some of the radical resonances which had cohered around the goal of unity could be transferred to the peace process itself, emphasising its dynamic and potentially emancipatory character in building a new (and implicitly united) Ireland. But what some saw as an ideological continuity in a new phase of struggle, others saw as a conversion to constitutional nationalism and a rejection of the old aims (McIntyre, 1995).

At the same time, the ideological changes were presented to supporters or militants as simply strategic changes: a new gradualist path to Irish unity through increasing republican and nationalist strength within Northern Ireland and a decrease in British and unionist power (Adams, 1998a; Adams 1998b). The objective of a united Ireland was reaffirmed (IRA, 1999; Doherty, 1999), sometimes within a timescale of 15 years. The attempt to present the changes as purely strategic was also problematic (cf. Clohessy, 1998). For the strategy to be effective, the new principles of agreement and allegiance, peace and justice had to be consistently and wholeheartedly affirmed, the aim of Irish unity had to drop from public view at least in the statements of republican leaders. In these circumstances it was reasonable to suppose that the leaders would be swayed by their own rhetoric; the strategy thus came to appear the more contingent

There is a third possibility, and one which perhaps best characterises the new republicanism (for a good example, see Sinn Féin, 1995). That involves an ideological symbiosis between the universalisable principles and the traditional goals. On the one hand there are the radical egalitarian transformist principles emphasising the need for fundamental change to achieve agreement on a legitimate political system. On the other hand – and equally important – there is a specific goal (Irish unity). The goal is presented as the best manifestation of the principles and the principles interpreted so as to lead to the goal. National self-determination is affirmed in two senses simultaneously. As a democratic principle of self-determination on the island free from British interference, it belongs with the first principles (and does not require a majoritarian interpretation). At the same time, in a majoritarian sense, it is the path to and the justification of Irish unity. But now Irish unity can be achieved incrementally. Thus the second-level aims – cultural equality including for the Irish language, radical reform of the police, total demilitarisation of British army presence and posts, and of the legally as well as illegally held weapons in the North, and strong North/South linkages which would open the possibility of an eventual united Irish nation state – are at once applications of the first principles and stages necessary to move towards the goal.

These second-level aims are, moreover, beneficial in themselves. Even if, once implemented, they do not lead to the desired goal of Irish unity, they are a gain for republicans and their constituency. For the new republicans, this approach offers the benefits of a strong, principled, egalitarian and democratic stance, a continuity in traditional aims, and achievable short-term goals: the moral high ground can be attained with an adaptation of means rather than a transformation of ends, and in the process bring immediate benefits (see Adams, 1998b). Moreover if the means, the second-level aims, do not lead to Irish unity, they can be adapted or changed without major disruption to the ideological system. The element of contingency in the second-level aims allows an openness to future developments, an ability to adapt to new circumstances without jettisoning the whole ideological tradition.

There are plenty of precedents for such an ideological symbiosis within democratic politics, not least in classic nationalism itself. The best analogy, however, is with strong advocates of European integration. Here universalisable first principles of peace, cooperation and prosperity are combined with a strong goal of European unity which is seen as the sole way to ensure the principles while the principles are interpreted in the light of the goal. Second-level aims – monetary union or a common defence force – are at once justified in light of the principles and seen as stages towards the goal. Just as Europeanists fight hard for their particular goals in the name of widely shared aims, so too can the new republicans. Just as Europeanists can emphasise the principles or the goal, as the situation demands, so too can republicans. Just as the viability of Europeanist ideology depends on the assumption that the second-level aims will in fact pave the way towards the goal, so too does the viability of the new republicanism. And just as Europeanists can change their second-level aims – from single market to single currency – so too can republicans.

If this third option gives an ideal type of the new republicanism, it was never fully fixed in republican discourse. The status of the goal of Irish unity remained unclear, and different statements of position veered to one side or another. The principle of national self-determination was sometimes interpreted in a majoritarian and sometimes in a non-majoritarian way. The result was a deep tension in the ideological structure of the new republicanism: the distinction between universal-isable first principles and the traditional goal of Irish unity was there, but the priorities were not made clear. What was change and what was continuity were hard to grasp in a context where the substantive aim of a united Ireland had remained constant, and strategies had been changing for decades. There was a sense of fluidity and experimentation in the discourse, expressing perhaps conflicting imperatives within the organisation, and possibly also within individuals themselves. As political pressures mounted during and after the Good Friday Agreement, it was to become even more difficult to assess the direction and assumptions of the new republicanism.

THE GOOD FRIDAY AGREEMENT: WHAT IT OFFERS TO NATIONALISTS AND REPUBLICANS

Even after the changes in nationalism and republicanism, the room for compromise with unionism remained slight. Unionists, if they recognised changes in republican ideology at all, were resolutely opposed to the new republicanism's transformism: their quest was for political stability within the constitutional status quo. Indeed unionism kept a clear distance from even the non-nationalist premises of constitutional nationalism. Unionists did not accept Hume's pluralist and communitarian premise that all identities require institutional recognition and respect (Aughey, 1989). They continued to emphasise the principle that they (as the majority in Northern Ireland) had the right to consent or withhold their consent to constitutional change. They remained committed to the union and to continued British sovereignty. One reason they rejected Hume's language was because it made fuzzy and ambiguous the question of sovereignty. Despite this, many unionists came to accept one of his core principles, that dialogue and agreement were necessary to create a settlement that was, and was seen to be, legitimate.

This might have been enough to get negotiations going but it certainly did not guarantee any agreement on substantive issues. Yet agreement there was. The compromise represented by the Good Friday Agreement was made possible because the Agreement at once incorporated distinctions made in the new nationalist and republican ideologies at the same time as it satisfied core unionist principles. As read by new nationalists and republicans, the Agreement promises to meet many of their substantive interests while balancing them against the constitutional guarantee to unionists. But at each point the interpretation is contestable and the balance delicate, and each may be overturned in the implementation of the Agreement.

On the constitutional level, the Good Friday Agreement recognises the existence of British sovereignty in Northern Ireland and its legitimacy while it is the majority wish. It enshrines the principle of majority consent to constitutional change in the Irish constitution. Republicans, in assenting to the Agreement, have implicitly accepted the principle of consent. This is rightly seen as a major achievement by pro-Agreement unionists. The achievement is, however, qualified by the increasingly formal character of sovereignty. From a nationalist and republican perspective, the institutional provisions of the Good Friday Agreement function more fully to integrate the Irish nation (in the sense of providing common institutions, norms and linkages) and to bring that part of it in Northern Ireland into closer relation with the Irish state, while simultaneously decreasing the British state's role in Northern Ireland. It is worth analysing these provisions in some detail.

(i) The equality agenda promises an end to structural inequality in the political and cultural as well as the economic spheres: it promises an equal relation of both communities to public institutions and to the public sphere in Northern Ireland, in terms of access, opportunity and, implicitly at least, in terms of culture (see Agreement, 1998, section on Rights, Safeguards and Equality of Opportunity, subsection on Human Rights, paragraphs 3 and 4).

(ii) The Irish cultural element in public institutions is to be increased, while Irish language activities and schools are to be supported (see Agreement, 1998, section on Rights, Safeguards and Equality of Opportunity, subsection on economic, social and cultural issues, paragraphs 3 and 4).

(iii) The role of the Irish state formally in the intergovernmental conference is as strong as in the Anglo-Irish Agreement (AIA) (see Agreement, 1998, Strand Three, section on British–Irish Intergovernmental Conference). Informally its involvement in the process of implementing the Agreement continues to increase.

(iv) The standards of human rights are to be equivalent in both parts of Ireland, and there is an implication that equality legislation will also begin to converge (Agreement, 1998, section on Rights, Safeguards and Equality of Opportunity, paragraph 9).

(v) Formal institutional linkages between North and South, which may be further expanded, are instituted in the North–South Council and implementation bodies (Agreement, 1998, Strand Two).

(vi) Informal linkages and political networks between North and South increased during the peace process, intensified during the multi-party negotiations, and are being sustained at present. There is pressure to intensify them further: for example republicans have asked that those elected MPs in Northern Ireland be permitted to attend the Dáil (rather than Westminster).

(vii) Economic linkages have been sustained by EU programmes and will be underpinned by the new North–South implementation bodies.

(viii) The changes also promise to dismantle the security apparatuses of the British state in Northern Ireland to a level appropriate to a normal peaceful society and to reconstruct the police in a way that will win widespread support (Agreement, section on Security, paragraphs 1 and 2, section on Policing and Justice, annex A).

None of these changes removes British power from Northern Ireland. It will remain in funding and finance, and in bearing ultimate responsibility for human rights and security decisions; the Irish government's input through the intergovernmental conference remains less than executive. Sovereignty still matters. But, as the Agreement is implemented, nationalists and republicans expect it to matter less than before. As the proposed changes are implemented, the value of cultural capital in Northern Ireland should change; Irish cultural values and mores should be as much institutionalised, embodied in public interactions and valued as British. As this takes place, the ease (and one might suppose also the frequency) of interaction, formal and informal, between North and South will increase. At the same time, those areas where the British state presently impinges on life in Northern Ireland should decrease: if the peace holds, the British security presence and security installations will be dismantled. The obviously British character of public institutions will be muted. Nationalists should no longer encounter a 'chill factor' in interaction with public authorities.

Nationalists can plausibly argue that these changes – if indeed they come about – will accomplish, through institutions and without impact on formal sovereignty, some of what classic nationalists wished to achieve by formal sovereignty. They will create institutions which integrate the Irish nation and interconnect with (although are not directly subject to the jurisdiction of) the Irish state. They will change the cultural substance of the public institutions in Northern Ireland so as in practice to equalise the relations of each community in Northern Ireland to these institutions: each can equally feel a sense of belonging in the public sphere. British power will remain substantively as well as in formal terms, and will be crucial on macroeconomic, international and military affairs. But, if the peace holds, in terms of the quality and ethos of daily life and interaction with public authorities, formal sovereignty may come – as Hume predicted – to matter relatively little. In these ways, the institutional changes at once remain strictly separate from formal sovereignty, and can begin to balance it in a compromise settlement.

Of course whether or not in practice these institutional changes 'balance' the constitutional guarantees to unionists, the 'fairness' of the compromise from a nationalist and republican standpoint, depends upon the degree of institutional change. On the nationalist and republican interpretation, the degree of change promised in the Agreement is quite extensive. This interpretation may not be borne out. The formation of an executive and North–South bodies has been blocked by the unionist refusal to enter an executive with Sinn Féin prior to decommissioning. Once the executive is formed, crucial issues (for example, the accountability of ministers in the North–South Council to the Assembly and the powers of committees in the Assembly to block North–South initiatives) remain to be worked out in practice and may in effect give a unionist veto on the North–South integration achieved by the Council and implementation bodies. And some contentious issues (most particularly reform of the police and timing of decommissioning and demilitarisation) were not agreed; their potential to generate conflict remains very great (see Ruane and Todd, this volume, p. 25 ff.).

At the same time, the potential dynamism which nationalists and republicans understand to be built into the institutions is central to their concept of a balanced settlement. The institutional changes discussed above do not necessitate any movement towards Irish unity and independence, but they can ease such movement by providing the infrastructural and institutional integration necessary for a viable transition to a united Ireland. The equality and security agendas have major symbolic aspects which may be expected to affect identities and allegiances. If the union can no longer be a means to maximise unionist power resources and if a united Ireland can no longer be a means of increasing Catholic/nationalist power, the conflicting nationalisms may start to lose their communal bases and become more genuinely civic and inclusivist. Demilitarisation, decommissioning, reform of the police, release of prisoners, all provide a clear symbolic break with the past which may allow further ideological movement in both unionist and nationalist/republican senses of allegiance and legitimacy. If these effects do not follow from the Good Friday Agreement, republicans in particular may come to revise their judgement that the agreement was a balanced one.

THE IDEOLOGICAL EFFECTS OF
THE GOOD FRIDAY AGREEMENT

The implementation of the Agreement is already affecting ideological development. For the SDLP, the Agreement and the new institutions it proposes confirm both their liberal pluralist principles and their liberal nationalist aims. The Agreement gives a broadly acceptable institutional framework which offers equality in Northern Ireland, closer North–South relations, and agreed East–West relations. It balances the affirmation of the constitutional status quo with institutional changes in Irish national integration which may have long-term effects on the constitutional status of Northern Ireland. It is an institutional arrangement which affirms an open future, to be decided by dialogue and agreement. The changes in North–South relations will be as quick or as gradual as the parties desire, thus approximating to the natural 'healing process' advocated by Hume. At the same time, the flexibility of Hume's ideology remains a practical virtue in post-Agreement circumstances: depending on the sorts of changes in nationalist sentiment and aspiration that follow from the implementation of the Agreement, the ideology can be more or less nationalist, more or less dialogic, more or less accepting of the status quo.

For republicans, the Good Friday Agreement brings sharply to the fore the unresolved question of the conditions of a legitimate compromise settlement. Is Northern Ireland after the Good Friday Agreement a legitimate entity, since the electorate in both parts of Ireland have ratified the Agreement? If not, will it become so as the Agreement is implemented? At what point in its implementation? And what if it turns out that the Agreement does not, as anticipated, open the way to a united Ireland? Unionists, by foregrounding the question of decommissioning (which at time of writing remains a core issue in dispute preventing the formation of the executive and the implementation of the agreement) have brought precisely these questions of legitimacy to the fore. For, unionists argue, if Northern Ireland is now a fully legitimate entity, there is no need for republicans to keep arms: and if republicans believe that it is not legitimate, have they not thereby reneged on the Good Friday Agreement? Commentators – and perhaps also political leaders – in the South have echoed the unionist questions, increasing the inherent tensions between Southern nationalism (which now accepts the legitimacy of Northern Ireland) and republicanism (which does not).

The republican response to the increasing pressure has been defensive. The Agreement is an 'accommodation', not a 'settlement', the two referenda do not constitute an act of self-determination and do not render Northern Ireland legitimate (IRA, 1998; Adams, 1998b; Adams, 1999b; Kelly, 1999). Yet the aims are stated minimally: the Agreement is 'an accommodation which, if implemented, has the inherent facility to enable us to live together with as much dignity as possible, to promote and develop tolerance, to agree to disagree, to pursue our political preferences in that context and through all of that to effect a real reconciliation, at all levels: local, communal, national and between Ireland and Britain' (Kelly, 1999). It is clear that republican strategy requires that they keep powerful (Irish government) allies and that they encourage the desired direction of government policies: at the same time, the governments and international mediators will have insisted that republicans encourage unionist reformism and avoid inciting unionist anger. It is perhaps this pressure that has led leading republicans to highlight first principles rather than ultimate aims. But such discourse is likely to lead to tensions, confusion and unease at the republican grass roots (cf. *Irish News*, 26 April 1999, p. 2).

The new republican ideology presupposes political movement. It mediates tensions between its nationalist goals and its egalitarian and dialogic principles by positing processes whereby interim goals, justified on egalitarian principles, will also further nationalist aims. A full implementation of the Agreement might bear out this republican interpretation. In this case, the new ideological trends would be confirmed as principles and goals begin to converge: the real possibility of a united Ireland would increase (through increased linkages and institutional networks) while changes in the views of all parties would open new possibilities of dialogue and agreement. In such circumstances, one may imagine a strengthened and stable yet politically flexible new republicanism, where universalisable first principles are combined with a flexibletimescale goal of Irish unity, and where the symbiosis is a source of strength for both sets of aims. The increasing all-island linkages, the decreasing import of British sovereignty, and the implementation of the equality and security agendas would of themselves serve to justify the ideological move, and allow an republican affirmation of the legitimacy of the political process in Northern Ireland (while the question of the legitimacy of the political entity of Northern Ireland would become practically irrelevant).

To date, however, the fraught political situation has instead revealed tensions in republican ideology between dialogic principles and nationalist goals. Over a year after the referendums endorsing the Agreement, even some of the interim republican aims – demilitarisation, participation in power, radical reform of the police, changes in the cultural ethos in Northern Ireland – have yet to occur (cf. McGuinness, 1999). The choice unionists have posed – democratic dialogue or a united Ireland – isolates the principle of democratic agreement from the context (egalitarianism and transformative change) in which republicans had understood it, and counterposes it against the classic nationalist goals. When forced to answer if Northern Ireland is now legitimate – after the Agreement but before its implementation – they say clearly no (Adams, 1999b).

Further political pressure on republicans to choose is likely to be counterproductive. To insist that republicans opt for the principles of democracy and dialogue abstracted from the wider transformative context in which republicans themselves had situated their democratic strategy, is to destroy the possibility of ideological change in republicanism. It is to force republicans to make a choice between, on the one hand, non-nationalist principles without clear transformative potential, and, on the other classic (and militant) nationalism. The new republicanism attempted to give an alternative to precisely this dichotomy. Logically, it cannot make a choice between what it has defined as a false dichotomy. Its ideological fragility in this situation must be recognised: the ideological changes can be sustained only if the institutional context gives an opening for republicans to pursue a 'third way' between classic nationalism and non-nationalist reformism.

Here the conflict with unionists – pro- as well as anti-Agreement – becomes evident. At base, it is the opposition between a settlement which will stabilise Northern Ireland and one which will transform it: between a political system which gives power to those who wish to transform the system, and one which marginalises them. The pro-Agreement unionists are not just attempting to win support from anti-Agreement unionists. They are also attempting to create a stable settlement in Northern Ireland. It is tempting, in the context of the battle between pro- and anti-Agreement unionists, for the unionist supporters of the Agreement to minimise the extent of ideological change which it implies and to press for maximum benefits within the Agreement (at whatever cost to republicans). This strategy, however, may well be counterproductive, confirming older ideological premises (minimise change and concession) which preclude a lasting agreement. But do pro-Agreement unionists have an alternative? Can they accommodate nationalists' and republicans' interpretations of the Good Friday Agreement? Alternatively – to rephrase the question in a way that can be answered within the confines of this chapter – can the revised nationalist/republican ideologies and understandings of the Good Friday Agreement accommodate unionists' interest in maintaining the union?

Despite the clear tensions and oppositions, a narrow possibility of compromise may still exist. For nationalists in the SDLP, the transformative potential of the institutions can be de-emphasised in order to maximise agreement. For them, the healing of divisions within Northern Ireland is as much a priority as the expansion of North–South linkages. Within the terms of the Agreement, the SDLP has room to compromise, to wait, to strengthen pro-Agreement unionism. For republicans, the issue is more difficult because of the transformist character of their perspective. But for them too, there is some ideological capacity to accommodate unionist interests within the terms of the Agreement. Republican transformism now incorporates an open, not a predetermined, future and leaves to dialogue and discussion the future development of the agreed institutions. The union might be viable within such an understanding.

This indeed would require a unionism which is willing to live with change and to affirm the Agreement as a process, rather than as a final settlement. But unionists may note that politics in Europe and Britain is also a politics of change, that change may also be slow and evolutionary, and that institutions to guide ordered, structured and agreed change in North–South and East–West relations have already been agreed. In short, an accommodation between unionism and republicanism within the framework of the Agreement is not in principle impossible, although it would most certainly involve continuing tension and conflict on the nature, extent and speed of change within each of the institutions of the Agreement. Whether unionism is willing to affirm its values within such a processual under-standing of the institutions, whether republicanism can accept a slow pace of change within the Agreement, and whether it is politically possible to continue to mediate tensions at once within unionism, within republicanism, and between unionism and republicanism, is much less clear.

CONCLUSION

This chapter has sketched quite radical changes in nationalist and republican ideologies. In Hume's nationalism, the first premises of classic nationalism – the right to self-determination and the need for nation and state to coincide – have been rejected. Now the first premises are non-nationalist ones, self-determination is redefined in terms of agreement, and much moderated nationalist aims (of increasing nation/state inte-gration, short of nation/state coincidence) are brought in as second-level interpretations of the first principles. In the new republicanism, new first principles are added to the traditional goal of Irish unity; whether this goal is justified in classic nationalist terms, as an application of the other first principles (à la Hume) or as a separate, symbiotic goal, is as yet unclear. The Good Friday Agreement, if fully implemented, may well sediment these ideological changes and produce further ideological development. In the short term, however, conflicts over its implementation have highlighted tensions in republicanism and have the potential for reversing the new ideological directions.

Theoretically, the analysis in this chapter has focused on ideologies as systems of ideas and principles. Within these systems, nationalist premises have been much adapted and revised. Even more important, their relation to other axioms has varied quite dramatically. Nationalist axioms can be held as overriding goals or they can be subordinated to other principles; they can be held co-equal with and informed by such other principles, or can be conjoined symbiotically with them. Each of these options opens different possibilities of compromise.

Identifying the systemic character of ideologies is a prerequisite to a judgement of the degree of change or continuity with ideologies of the past. It is not enough simply to abstract the 'nationalist' premises from the system as a whole and to compare them with the nationalist premises of previous decades. In both nationalism and republicanism, as we have seen, a level of ambiguity exists as to the exact status of these premises. In some respects they are left under-specified, to be articulated to meet the demands of particular situations. But it is the ideological system as a whole that contextualises the premises, and gives limits to the possibilities of change in them. And it is only by identifying the system as a whole that one can judge the complex mixture of change and continuity with the past, and the potential for the ideology to change the nationalist or republican tradition from within.

Finally, the chapter has suggested a clear relationship between institutional and ideological change. Institutional change has been crucial in revealing tensions within ideologies, in providing incentives for ideological reconstruction, and in providing new modes of activity which can cement and confirm ideological changes within a wider population. For example, when events revealed tensions in classic nationalism, sections of the political elite (in particular John Hume) developed a radically revised neo-nationalist ideology which in turn informed political and institutional developments (the Anglo-Irish Agreement) and facilitated wider ideological changes (in unionism and republicanism) which in turn allowed new institutional developments (the Good Friday Agreement) which may yet sediment the ideological changes. At the same time, the fragility of ideological change and its dependence on particular directions of institutional development are clear from the discussion of republicanism. The problem is that the conditions for compromise (in terms of the conflicting interests of the parties) remain extremely narrow. The Agreement defines such a compromise, but the balance it achieves is itself a developing and dynamic one in constant danger of collapse.

4

'QUIET DIPLOMACY AND PERSONAL CONVERSATION': TRACK TWO DIPLOMACY AND THE SEARCH FOR A SETTLEMENT IN NORTHERN IRELAND

Paul Arthur[1]

INTRODUCTION

'Quiet diplomacy and personal conversation' is a phrase borrowed from an address to the United Nations General Assembly by Jack Lynch, the Irish Taoiseach, in 1971. Though he referred to official methods of interstate conflict resolution (or Track One diplomacy) in the context of traditional Anglo-Irish relations, Mr Lynch's phrase is remarkably redolent of the type of activity which occurs in unofficial (or Track Two) diplomacy. For one who has been intimately associated with Track Two exercises, the similarity with Track One diplomacy is not much of a surprise. The most important theme of this chapter is that the incremental and cumulative nature of Track Two exercises may influence, sometimes quite profoundly, developments within official diplomatic activity during interstate conflicts. In the words of the Carnegie Commission on Preventing Deadly Conflict: 'So called Track Two diplomacy, long an informal staple in international negotiations and used by leaders who wanted to take informal soundings of adversaries' intentions, is increasingly the diplomacy of choice for problems beyond the reach of official efforts' (Carnegie Commission, 1997).

In this chapter we deal with two examples of Track Two diplomacy: the activities that led President Clinton to grant Gerry Adams a 48 hour visa early in 1994, and the informal workshops which brought together members of different political parties in Northern Ireland during the 1990s. We begin, however, with some observations on the nature of Track Two diplomacy and on the changing understanding of the conflict in Northern Ireland.

TRACK TWO DIPLOMACY

The most succinct definition of Track Two diplomacy describes it as:

> unofficial, informal interaction between representatives of adversary groups or nations which aims to develop strategies and create an environment which could contribute to the resolution of their conflict. It must be understood that track two diplomacy is in no way a substitute for official, 'track one' government-to-government or leader-to-leader contact. Rather, track two activity is designed to assist official leaders by compensating for the constraints imposed upon them by the psychologically understandable need for leaders to be, or at least *be seen* to be, strong, wary and indomitable in the face of the enemy. . . . Track Two diplomacy, then, is conceived of as several levels of process designed to assist official leadership in the task of resolving, or in the first instance, managing, conflict by exploring possible solutions, out of public view and without the requirement to formally negotiate or bargain for advantage. Track Two diplomacy on its more focused level seeks political formulae or scenarios which might satisfy the basic security and esteem needs of all parties to a dispute. On its more general level, it seeks to promote an environment in a political community, through the education of public opinion, that would make it safer for public opinion to take risks for peace (Montville, 1986, p. 1).

At the outset we need to be precise about the terms we shall be adopting. The literature on mediation serves as a good starting point. Mediation has been defined as:

> a process by which the participants together with the assistance of a neutral person or persons, systematically isolate disputed issues in order to develop options, consider alternatives, and reach a consensual settlement that will accommodate their needs. Mediation is a process that emphasises the participants' own responsibility for making decisions that affect their lives. It is therefore a self-empowering process (Folberg and Taylor, 1986, pp. 7–8).

In that respect it is an alternative which differs from the process of counselling, negotiation and arbitration. It is 'goal-directed, problem-solving intervention' which is different from the adjudicatory process where the emphasis is on 'establishing the rights and wrongs of a particular situation. It is a win/win process in which participants can formulate their own agreement and make an emotional investment in it' (Folberg and Taylor, 1986, pp. 8–10).

Of course mediation is only one device in a range of options open to those engaged in conflict transformation. It is not solution-directed but can assist in the process that leads towards a solution by allowing for the enlargement of a common ground based on establishing a common vocabulary, language and understanding. In the first instance, it is about analysis. Negotiation and implementation are much further down the line. As a process it can produce several results by sending substantive messages between parties, establishing informal networks and understandings, and ultimately changing hardened ideas. It is about what Pierre Wack (Montfleur, 1996, p. 6) has called the 'gentle art of reperceiving'. In broader terms, we are dealing with what Hal Saunders (1996, pp. 420–1) terms 'prenegotiation' and 'circum-negotiation'.

By its very nature, diplomacy is not a precise science (Sofer, 1997). We have to allow for what Machiavelli calls *fortuna*, for the role of unpredictability, of serendipity, of randomness and, above all, of confusion. Having no cognitive framework about a conflict is perhaps better than having a wrong cognitive framework, 'which is what happens if you prematurely close in on an understanding. There are no correct understandings but there are very bad ones' (Kurtzman, 1998). Much of Anglo-Irish diplomacy since the 1970s falls into this category of confusion, and a great deal of time was spent on trying to make sense of what was going on. Those who intervene need to be conscious of time frames and of process. We are also concerned with disequilibrium and with asymmetries. Essentially, this essay examines the *process* of conflict resolution, rather than the substance of the dispute.

A second consideration is ethical in nature. Unofficial diplomacy relies on confidentiality and discretion. Much of the activity described in the following pages could not have worked if participants were uncomfortable in any way with the process or with those leading the unofficial exercises. Bad practice undermines the efficacy of the approach, and this has a particular bearing where the work is ongoing. Thus when I describe my own contribution I can talk only in general terms; I will be concerned with examining trends and making comparative points rather than going into specifics. The subjective factor can interfere with objectivity: Track Two is part of the wider phenomenon of 'participant observation' – the 'empathic and analytic immersion into a social world' in which 'the "personal equation" suggests that the perceptions and interpretations of the research will be contingent on the values of the researcher' (Burton, 1987, pp. 165, 167).

THE CHANGING UNDERSTANDING OF THE CONFLICT: ANGLO-IRISH DIPLOMACY IN CONTEXT

Throughout the 1980s, it was fashionable to examine the three intractable conflicts of Northern Ireland, South Africa, and Israel, to study commonalities and to forecast likely outcomes. In 1989, for example, the Frederick Naumann Foundation and the Institute for a Democratic Alternative in South Africa (IDASA) held a conference in Bonn to make comparisons between these three case studies which produced a book, *The Elusive Search for Peace: South Africa, Israel, Northern Ireland* (Giliomee and Gagiano, 1990). One of the contributors, Bernard Crick (1990, p. 265), argued that the three problems were insoluble for two formal reasons: (i) that no internal solution likely to guarantee peace can possibly satisfy the announced principles of the main disputants; and (ii) that any external-imposed solution is likely to strengthen the desperation and self-righteousness of the threatened group. Moreover, there was a distinct feeling that Northern Ireland was the most intractable because there appeared to be no real desire to search for a solution – 'There has been no resolution [to the Northern Ireland conflict] because the violence has not been intolerable. By whatever calculus communities compute their interests, the price of compromise is still thought to be greater than the cost of violence' (Darby, 1986, p. vii). In the meantime, apartheid has been dismantled, and South Africa's pariah status has been removed; the Camp David Agreement of September 1978, and more latterly the Oslo Accord (with all its concomitant difficulties) produced a serious opening for peace in the Middle East; and finally Northern Ireland's peace agreement was signed in April 1998. Of course, none of these developments are immutable, but their relative success raises questions about 'intractability'.

Objectively, the Northern Ireland conflict should have been the 'least difficult' to solve. For the most part it was containable. The resolution to the conflict in South Africa, however, was part of a much more complex regional question with geopolitical overtones in which the United States began a diplomatic initiative for 'constructive engagement' in southern Africa in the early 1980s. It entailed linking apartheid to the issue of Namibian independence and the removal of 50,000 Cuban troops from Angola (Crocker, 1992). Similarly, the Palestinian question was bound up with the politics of the Cold War in an area in which three of the world's major religions were in dispute. In both the Middle East and South Africa, the role of unofficial diplomacy was crucial in supplementing official efforts.

In contrast the Northern Ireland problem was much less complex geopolitically. Traditionally Ireland was considered to be within the British sphere of responsibility in terms of the management of the international system, a factor underlined by the Anglo-American special relationship. Indeed as early as August 1969 the British and Northern Ireland prime ministers issued a statement in which they asserted that Northern Ireland was purely a matter of domestic jurisdiction with no role for the international community. Following serious rioting in Belfast which led to eight deaths and widespread destruction in Catholic areas in the summer of 1969, the Irish government tried to raise its concerns at the United Nations Security Council but it was politely rebuffed. The Irish government's move, however, was merely an act of catharsis, another example of the UN's significance as 'sacred drama'.

The conflict could not, however, be contained within the boundaries of Northern Ireland, or even the archipelago. An FBI report of 1973 commented on the 'embarrassment' to the administration that the US was being used as a source of IRA funding to secure weapons (Holland, 1987, p. 39). One of the themes of Ronald Reagan's presidency was the need to contain the 'network of international terrorism'. On 8 July 1985 he stated that Iran, North Korea, Cuba, Nicaragua, and Libya were 'members of a confederation of terrorist states' responsible for 'outright acts of war' against the US. When he launched an aerial attack on Tripoli on 14 April 1986, he was hitting one of the IRA's chief arms suppliers. Several IRA operations on the European mainland against British troops stationed there added another dimension to the conflict. At the same time, while IRA propaganda identified with the 'freedom struggles' of the ANC and PLO, none of these efforts were sustained enough to suggest that the conflict belonged to the wider concerns of the Cold War.

That is not to say that there were not those in British politics who attempted to place it in that context. Chief among those was the distinguished Conservative backbench Member of Parliament, J. Enoch Powell, who might be thought of as a high priest in paranoia. The psychologist, Ken Heskin (1989, p. 100), has described Northern Ireland between 1921–72 as a 'paranocracy' in which the basis of power 'was the successful appeal to paranoid fears in the Protestant electorate about the political, social, philosophical and military potential of their Catholic neighbours'. Powell took this outlook to new heights after the Northern Ireland parliament and government had been suspended in 1972, thereby shifting the problem from the 'narrow ground' of Northern Ireland to the broader canvas of Anglo-Irish relations. He argued that a consistent view in Irish nationalism was that the Republic could not annex Northern Ireland by force; and the ending of partition could come about only by the creation of an autonomous Ulster with 'guarantees' within a federal Irish state possibly in some loose relationship with Great Britain. This could be brought about only by British pressure when the United Kingdom decided that Irish unity was strategically necessary to her: 'Britain, like the USA, has been – perhaps this is now changing at last – convinced that the island of Ireland is vital to the defence of the west'. The task then was to get Northern Ireland into a direct relationship with the Republic 'sweetened by a British Isles totality or a Commonwealth or an EEC or a NATO dimension . . .' (Powell, 1983, p. 20). While this opinion was not widespread within the political community, it had a certain staying power inside the unionist hierarchy and impacted later on official diplomacy and on the role of the US as a prestigious third party.

The view of the Brussels-based international research and information centre, Pro Mundi Vita, was more realistic. It saw the conflict as a bitter communal strife defined by religion and national identity: 'One has to go back to the 17th century to find [a war] in which both sides find their focus of cohesion and of antagonism in a version of the Christian faith'. In that respect, the conflict was out of kilter with contemporaneous ethnic conflicts around the world and was an embarrassment within the European Community. The auditors of violence calculated its impact in a European setting thus: Northern Ireland has 'generated the most intense violence of any part of the contemporary UK, the highest levels of *internal* political violence of any member-state of the European Community, and the highest levels of internal political violence in any of the continuously liberal democratic states of the post-1948 world' (O'Leary and McGarry, 1993, p. 9). They concluded that '"being second to Lebanon" is an unenviable classification' (O'Leary and McGarry, 1993, p. 16).

The emergence of an adequate understanding of the conflict was, however, a slow process. The temptation to see it simply as being about 'terrorism' or 'repression' and, hence, to ignore the complex political issues, was all too prevalent. In the Anglo-Irish framework, one of the more revealing documents came when British and Irish officials on 30 January 1981 established a Joint Steering Group whose terms of reference included an analysis of 'the reasons for misconceptions in each country over attitudes and government policies in the other' and a consideration of 'measures which the two Governments might take, jointly or separately, to remove such misperceptions and improve mutual understanding' – this after a decade of communal blood letting and several centuries of (involuntary) propinquity. Not surprisingly, one observer of the peaks and troughs of Anglo-Irish relations in the 1970s was reminded of a 'fever chart' (Arthur, 1983).

The significance of such a Steering Group in achieving a more holistic view of the problem should not be underestimated:

> Communication entails recognition of the other, and 'the awareness of being separate and different from and strange to one another' opens up potentials of creative search for dialogue and for understanding of each other. This is also the essence of negotiations. Reaching common ground is not necessarily a product of similar opinions' (Sofer, 1997, p. 181).

The latter point is borne out very strongly if one examines the paradox of Anglo-Irish diplomatic relations in the 1980s: close and seemingly harmonious institutional co-operation culminating in the signing of the

Anglo-Irish Agreement on 15 November 1985, even as intense national suspicions continued. These suspicions can be personified through the memoirs of the two signatories of the Agreement, Garret FitzGerald and Margaret Thatcher (FitzGerald, 1991; Thatcher, 1993, esp. p. 415); or more brutally in the words of one right-wing commentator: 'Hillsborough is as pregnant with danger for Britain as Munich once was' (Alexander, 1986).

Despite such scepticism, one should not underemphasise the utility of communication in achieving understanding: where it does not seem to bear fruit immediately on Track One, it may play a meaningful role on the second track. This leads us to a consideration of proper time frames and of the concept of the 'hurting stalemate' (see below, pp. 78–80). One of the more insightful commentaries on the Agreement was provided by a former US Ambassador to Ireland, Bill Shannon. He concluded a fascinating article full of insider knowledge with some prescient remarks: 'The two governments have set in motion a process of change. The way ahead for this kind of intergovernmental cooperation is uncharted. It may be the end of the century before it finally becomes clear how far Northern Ireland has drifted from its old habits of conflict' (Shannon, 1986, p. 870). This forecast has a particular resonance in light of the signing of the (Belfast) Agreement on 10 April 1998; and it is unlikely that that Agreement would have been signed had there not been carefully placed landmarks along the way. These included the Brooke and Mayhew talks (convened by successive Secretaries of State between 1990 and 1993), the Downing Street Declaration signed by the Taoiseach and Prime Minister on 15 December 1993, and the Framework Document of 22 February 1995.

There is no need to rehearse the minutiae of these declarations, documents and events but simply to highlight their significance. For some years both governments had been attempting to move politics in Northern Ireland from zero-sum to win/win and to stress that political dialogue was not solely concerned with final status issues. In addition the declarations made the negotiations as inclusive as possible. The 'end result of the (1985) Agreement', for example, 'was to create the context for a real attempt at direct dialogue'; and the motivation of the Brooke talks (1990–92) had been a desire to bring the unionist parties and Sinn Féin out of their respective cul-de-sacs (Bloomfield, 1998, p. 179). Above all they were about defining the parameters of the problem – that the 'Northern Ireland problem' could not be contained within the narrow ground of the province. An ultimate solution entailed dealing with the relationships within Northern Ireland: relationships between the peoples of Ireland, north and south; and relationships between the islands of

Ireland and Britain (importantly, this archipelagian approach was influenced by developments within the European Union).

There were two hugely significant potential outcomes from this broader approach. First, it challenged narrow definitions of nationalisms (British and Irish) and opened the possibility of embracing polycentric nationalism:

> Inherent in nationalism is a recognition of the existence of others. It is the way in which the national group treats these others that distinguishes polycentric nationalism, which respects the other and sees each nation as enriching a common civilisation, from ethnocentric nationalism, which sees one's own nation as superior to all others and seeks domination (Tamir, 1995, p. 430).

Secondly, the European dimension could complement polycentric nationalism by stressing multiple identities through what Cathal McCall refers to as 'intimations of postmodernity' (McCall, 1999). All of this recognised the changes in the management of the international system in which the Anglo-Irish conflict had shifted from being solely within the British sphere of responsibility to being part of a 'functional regime' which 'unbundles' the package of rights inherent in territorial sovereignty. 'Functional regimes, it was hoped, would not only downgrade the importance of national boundaries but could, through the expansion of transboundary co-operative networks, lead to "peace in parts"' (Kratochwil, 1986, pp. 48–9).

These represented enormous shifts in official and political attitudes and were in sharp contrast to the sterility and frigidity of earlier Anglo-Irish diplomatic activity. They also challenged the communal calculus of being able to live with violence rather than accept compromise. Ready explanations for this shift can be furnished through an examination of the environment, external and internal, and through a consideration of the 'hurting stalemate'.

THE HURTING STALEMATE AND THE POTENTIAL FOR MEDIATION AND NEGOTIATION

When is the optimum moment to engage conflicting parties in mediation and negotiation? Obviously government has no choice but to be engaged at all times if only to regulate the conflict. More important is when a government judges that it can have a positive role to play in turning the conflict around and that the time is ripe for Track Two and/or prestigious third-party intervention. There is a school of thought which asserts that there may be a 'ripe moment' for intervention in conflicts which Schulze (1997) (citing Zartman) maintains is 'composed of a structural element, a party element, and a potential alternative outcome – that is, a mutually hurting stalemate, the presence of valid spokespersons, and a formula for a way out'. Schulze (1997, p. 104), places this in terms of the dynamics of the conflict when she considers the 'ripe moment' as a process rather than a specific point in time: 'While the "ripe moment" deals with the shift, theories on possible settlement are dealing with the end product. This leaves the highly important interim phase inadequately studied'. Northern Ireland may well be at that interim stage; and it may be prudent to recognise that a 'peace agreement' may only be the beginning of a process:

> One thing that is imperative is to establish realistic expectations about how much and how quickly a weak and tentative peace agreement can alter the basic nature of a long and profoundly bitter conflict. It is also important for the leaders on both sides to recognise that the game has changed, that the behaviour necessary to get to a provisional agreement is not always the behaviour appropriate for the post-agreement period: needs and priorities change, interests must be redefined or revisioned, and a joint learning process must be institutionalised and accelerated (Rothstein, 1996, p. 7).

Track Two exercises can be especially relevant in this context in terms of the joint learning process and in inducing behavioural transformation.

We should pause to consider some of the factors which might suggest that a hurting stalemate had imposed a ripe moment in Northern Ireland. One might be called the domino effect, as when incipient peace in the Middle East and South Africa spurs transformation within the Northern Ireland conflict. If one examines Irish republican propaganda and rhetoric, its symbolic capital and mythologies (Arthur, 1997a), one is struck by its identification with the PLO and the ANC and its positing of a global anti-colonial struggle for the dispossessed and the marginal. By implication, the Oslo accords, the dismantling of apartheid, the collapse of communism, the end of the Cold War, the reshaping of the European Union all had a profound effect on republican thinking and the realisation that there was a need for a new form of political discourse. All one has to do is to compare and contrast two of their key discussion papers: 'Towards a Strategy for Peace' (1988) and 'Towards a Lasting Peace in Ireland' (1992). The dates are important. The former precedes the collapse of the Berlin Wall and belongs to Cold War rhetoric. The 1992 document recognised that traditional sovereignties were eroding, jurisdictions in flux and boundaries altering. It rediscovered an Irish republicanism 'which has its root in the crucible of Europe during the great French Revolution'; and saw the political and economic transformation of the new Europe as providing 'a golden opportunity to finally resolve its British problem'.

Equally there were very powerful endogenous factors. The IRA's military campaign had been diminished by the security implications of the

Anglo-Irish Agreement. Its dual strategy of 'the armalite and the ballot box' was perceived as contradictory the more that Sinn Féin involved itself in the political process. The 'Long War' as a war of attrition was becoming too long, and war weariness was manifesting itself within republican support groups. From the late 1980s onwards, the IRA had admitted to a series of 'mistakes' whereby they had hit the wrong targets, and their own supporters and families were becoming the victims of a more focused loyalist murder campaign.

On the positive side, supporters of constitutional nationalism were engaged in serious dialogue with republicans. The British had stated that they had no selfish strategic or economic interest in remaining in Northern Ireland, and an emissary of the British government had been engaging in secret discussions with Sinn Féin's Martin McGuinness between 1990 and 1993. Also, Irish America was reinventing itself and beginning to act in unison for the first time this century with the support of a proactive Clinton administration. The importance of these Track Two activities was to become evident in the decision by the President to grant a 48 hour visa to Gerry Adams early in 1994.

TRACK TWO DIPLOMACY: THE ADAMS VISA

Instant journalism produced several explanations for the US visa grant to Gerry Adams. Some asserted that a unique set of circumstances in the Irish peace process coincided 'with a once-in-a-century placement of the right people at the right time in positions of authority and influence in the United States' (O'Clery, 1997, p. 245); others emphasised the fall and rise of the US–British 'special relationship' (Blumenthal, 1997) although there are sharply contrasting views on the nature of that relationship (Arthur, 1997b); still others saw the president's Irish policy 'as part of a broader strategy to enhance his image as an international statesman and thus win higher approval ratings from the entire American electorate' (Wilson, 1997).

No single explanation gives due weight to the complexity of the issue. It ignores what Enoch Powell calls 'the pre-play', that period of gestation when an issue is being shaped. In this context, changes in the international system had a role to play and have been well documented. Less noted has been the shift in Irish–American attitudes in more recent years. Historically, Irish–Americans have been among the most divided ethnic groups in the United States. In addition they suffered from the myth that the US could fulfil the role of a 'second front' in the effort towards Irish unity. That was to be rudely shattered throughout the 1970s and was reinforced by Irish–American disharmony.

The situation was reversed only by a very gradual convergence of Irish–American opinion. There had been a disparity between, on the one hand, the 'tree-tops' led by senior Democratic Party politicians like Senators Kennedy and Moynihan, and, on the other hand, the 'grass-roots' represented by Northern Aid (or Noraid, an Irish republican support group), the Congressional Ad Hoc committee and the Irish National Caucus, all of which were perceived as being more sympathetic to the Irish republican cause. With the election of Ronald Reagan and the twelve-year incumbency of the Republican Party in the US, the 'tree-tops' became more inclusive in that they formed themselves into a bipartisan group, the Friends of Ireland. Nonetheless the gap between the two groups remained and centred on conflicting attitudes towards Irish republican *means* rather than *ends*. Convergence centred on

> the effectiveness with which Irish–Americans have used the language of American public life to state their case – equal opportunities, civil rights, freedom of expression, pluralism – and mobilised multiethnic coalitions to advance their programme. Unionists have been much less effective. The contrast is not simply one of political capacity; the Catholic case lends itself more easily to articulation in those terms (Ruane and Todd, 1996, pp. 278–9).

But even at this level there was room for disagreement (Arthur, 1991).

Irish–America displayed an unusual capacity for coalition-building over the question of immigration, which stood out as one unifying issue among Irish–Americans. One of those most closely involved with these changes asserted, in a private interview with me, that 'in some sense it was a question of accident with a somnambulant Irish–American group being confronted by young Irish immigrants – the Irish Immigrant Reform Movement – pushing on an issue which we thought had no chance. What we were about was to try to transcend all sides'. The passing of an immigration Bill embracing Hispanics, Asians, Irish, etc., had a galvanising effect on this group: 'It was the first time in a generation that Irish America had flexed its muscles and won in a way that was different'.

The 'accident' of the immigration issue illustrated that a new generation of leaders had emerged and many of them came from the corporate sector. Their emergence had been tracked (and encouraged) in the pages of a glossy magazine, *Irish America*, founded in 1986. It produced an annual 'Top 100 Irish Americans'. The 1998 list opened with the words: 'As we enter the last years of the 20th century, the Irish in the US have reached a level of success unimagined even fifty years ago'. It was from among these numbers that several of the key players in the Adams visa process appeared. Some were to play a crucial role in Bill Clinton's candidacy for the Presidency in 1992 through the formation of Americans for a New Irish Agenda (O'Clery, 1997).

They were helped by the fact that a convergence was happening in Ireland as well in a very intense dialogue between John Hume and Gerry Adams assisted by the Irish government. The dialogue was prompted by a desire to end the 'Long War' and to move republicanism solely into the political camp. This called for a new nationalist consensus in which Irish–America would have a prominent role. Ever since 1984, Democratic nominees for President supported a policy of appointing a 'peace envoy' to Ireland. Bill Clinton endorsed this policy and went one stage further when he promised publicly to consider giving Gerry Adams a US visa. When an attempt was made to secure him one in the summer of 1993, the administration demurred. The time was not right. There was strong resistance within the National Security Council (NSC). In a confidential interview, one of those who was pressing most strongly on the visa issue said that National Security Adviser Anthony Lake was very dismissive and considered Ireland to be a second rate subject matter – 'This was *not* the Middle East'. He also said that Lake's assistant, Nancy Soderberg, came with what he called 'her Kennedy baggage' (that is, before joining the NSC she had worked for Senator Edward Kennedy who was perceived to be very anti-IRA).

Yet less than six months later – and against the strong advice of the US Departments of State and Justice, the FBI, CIA, and especially the British government – Gerry Adams was given a visa to enter the US for a 48 hour period at the end of January 1994. Since the summer a number of things had happened. A prominent Irish–American delegation had visited Ireland for one week in September during which time the IRA maintained a ceasefire. The delegation's purpose was twofold: to argue that a solution lay in a synergy of the economic and the political; and to urge the creation of an envoy through which the President could play a catalytic role. Following the Joint Declaration signed by the Taoiseach and Prime Minister on 15 December 1993, Bill Flynn, President and CEO of Mutual of America, inserted a one-page advertisement in the *New York Times* seeking a visa for Adams. It was an intuitive decision taken without any advice but the response was very positive and it was probably the first occasion in which the Irish–American corporate sector raised its head above the parapet in an overtly political manner. Less than six weeks later the Sinn Féin President got his visa; and on 1 December 1994, President Clinton appointed former Senate majority leader George Mitchell to be special economic adviser on Ireland.

It is difficult to exaggerate the importance of the visa issue. It is inconceivable that a peace process could have been established separate from it. That was to be the catalyst. Everything else flowed from that, including the unique role played by George Mitchell. Following the first

Adams visa, the United States' diplomatic effort accelerated even after the IRA renewed hostilities in February 1996. The groundwork lay in the Track Two exercises which had been conducted since 1987. Trust and convergence were the elements that drove the process forward. Irish republicans trusted their American interlocutors, some of whom had continued to maintain contact throughout the 1980s when republicans were being marginalised. The Administration, especially the President himself, trusted the interlocutors because they were committed to a process which eschewed violence in any shape or form. And the President would not have granted a visa had he not been supported by the 'treetops' (Senators Kennedy and Dodd and Ambassador Jean Kennedy Smith). In turn, they had taken advice from John Hume and the Irish government. That support would not have been forthcoming had there not been some form of strategic convergence within Ireland. Here was a classic example of Track Two feeding into Track One in a spectacular fashion.

TRACK TWO INITIATIVES: INFORMAL POLITICAL WORKSHOPS

We look now at a second arena of Track Two diplomacy: a series of informal political workshops which brought leading representatives of the Northern Ireland political parties together at a number of different venues during the 1990s, and which served to build trust in a political culture which can be characterised as factionalised, underdeveloped, intimidatory, and demotic (Arthur, 1990).

South Africa illustrates the advantage of such workshops in building a strong civil society. Between 1990 and 1994, many 'forums' were set up in South Africa creating temporary structures that gathered together the broadest possible range of stakeholders. The dates are significant in that these meetings took place between the release of Nelson Mandela from prison along with the unbanning of the ANC and other organisations, and the holding of democratic elections in April 1994. The breadth and depth of these forums was an indication of how '[s]trikingly few conflict-torn societies possess anything approaching the wealth of civil society institutions, mediation and negotiation skills and leadership depth found in the South Africa of the 1980s and 1990s' (Crocker, 1996 , p. 193). The (unhappy) contrast with Northern Ireland goes without saying.

There are few successful examples of reconciliation exercises within Northern Ireland: a deviant political culture does not respond well to exercises in reconciliation. The problem was compounded by clumsy official initiatives in the early 1970s when the Northern Ireland government established a Ministry of Community Relations serviced by a

Community Relations Commission. Its very first Minister, for example, was a political appointee who on his appointment resigned from the Orange Order, an exclusively Protestant body which was perceived as being rabidly anti-Catholic. The first Chairman of the Commission was a prominent Catholic civil servant, Maurice Hayes, who was seconded to the position initially for only one day and a half each week.

The chairmanship became a full-time post eventually but it was not the most suitable device for sensitive community relations work. In his evaluation many years later, Hayes observed that:

> it is probably not unfair to say that the government did not see community relations as having much to do with civil and human rights; rather it was all to do with socialising and getting to know you. Any idea that the government itself, or the system, was in any way responsible was far from government ministers' minds. . . . Neither at ministerial nor official level was there any real attempt to conceptualise what it is they were about, there was no attempt to analyse the problems, or to develop a strategy to deal with them (Hayes, 1995, 84).

He went on to detect one of the classic dilemmas of community development in a divided society: 'to balance the desire for self-sufficiency, self-confidence and a secure identity with the need to relate in the wider society to other communities holding utterly different sets of values'. Hence he found a social as well as religious (even theological) factor: 'Protestantism as a system of belief puts more emphasis on individual responsibility, Catholicism puts a higher value on community'. These competing mind-sets were a real challenge to Track Two.

The community development strategy may have failed to attract Protestant support 'because politics had atrophied in Protestant areas through a belief (mistaken as it appeared) that the Unionist Party in power would look after its own' (Hayes, 1995, pp. 94-5). That experiment in inducing attitudinal change failed perhaps because it had been imposed by a government which had demonstrated over the previous half century that it did not believe in the policies it was attempting to implement. Whatever the reasons for failure, Hayes resigned in the aftermath of 'Bloody Sunday' when British paratroopers shot dead 14 unarmed civilians in Londonderry in January 1972, and the Commission itself was suspended early in 1974.

There had been unsuccessful workshops. One of these was the 'Belfast Workshop' which took place at the University of Stirling in Scotland, 19–28 August 1972. It was described by its creators William Doob and William Foltz (a psychologist and political scientist from Yale University) thus:

> Through an intervention design which combined Tavistock and National Training Laboratory group dynamics, a team of American social scientists

attempted to assist the 56 [Catholic and Protestant citizens of Belfast] to learn about their behaviour in organised groups and better to understand their political opponents' situation. The workshop sought further to provide a protected setting wherein groups might explore modes of intercommunal cooperation that could later be implemented back in Belfast (Doob and Foltz, 1973, p. 489).

They described it as a 'high-risk, high-gain project'. All the evidence suggests that the former was true but that there was little sign of the latter. The workshop led to bitter recriminations in the press and in academic journals. Two who had been recruited as 'deputies' – they preferred the term 'administrators' – withdrew from the project 'in profound disagreement with its methods and objective'. They summarised their objections as follows:

> It is our feeling that the goals of the exercise were confused and unsubstantiated either theoretically or practically and that this confusion allowed for serious errors of judgement regarding the political and ethical propriety of the exercise. All of this is somewhat disguised by the haphazard nature of the research methodology which made evaluation more a matter of guesswork than anything else (Boehringer et al., 1974, pp. 274–5).

Further, they complained that it 'could not have taken place without the prevalence of the 'mandarin' attitude among many conflict researchers . . . the greatest mistake an applied social scientist can make is to regard people as data' (Boehringer et al., 1974). Under these circumstances people became very wary of participating in any such future activities.

Stirling also had a serious effect on applied conflict research. There was a great uneasiness about researchers being parachuted in with neither the requisite knowledge nor sensitivity to the cultural and psychological underpinnings of the problem.

Another Track Two initiative in 1988 caused problems for the participants. On 14–15 October, a workshop was convened by a lawyer and Lutheran ecumenist, Dr Eberhard Spreicher, in Duisburg (Germany). Dr Spreicher had organised similar meetings with churchmen, politicians and paramilitaries from Northern Ireland. At Duisburg he had proposed a four-point agenda. But that was soon abandoned and discussion centred on a way around the fixed positions each party had adopted ever since the signing of the Anglo-Irish Agreement of 1985. There was a leak that the meeting had taken place – the main BBC News broadcast led with the item on 1 February 1989 and suggested that it was potentially the most significant breakthrough since partition. The politicians who had been present were embarrassed by the leak and were accused of negotiating without the imprimatur of their party leaders. It emerged later that someone who was perceived as a proxy for Sinn Féin, Father Alex Reid, had also been present (Coogan, 1995, p. 335). Though the four party representatives probably had no idea that such a person was to attend, the essential prerequisite of trust had been shattered.

More recent workshops have had a more fruitful outcome. Given their discreet nature, it is difficult to know exactly how many there have been. With various colleagues I have organised seven in all. In addition workshops have been sponsored by the National Democratic Institute (NDI) with the Northern Ireland parties in which the emphasis has been on training and technique rather than peer learning. More recently, a session was organised in South Africa (28 May–2 June 1997) to enable those parties elected to the Northern Ireland Forum on 30 June 1996 to learn from South Africa's apparently successful transition from apartheid to a democracy undergoing the rigours of reconstruction and develop-ment. Given the discreet nature of Track Two exercises, it is possible that others have taken place without my knowledge.

What follows describes the seven workshops in which I was involved. These took place in Virginia, USA (January 1990), Grenoble, France (August 1990), Des Moines, Iowa (December 1991), Strasbourg, France (December 1993), South Africa (April 1994), Belfast (June 1995) and Harvard University (July 1996). These workshops were not conceived ini-tially as part of a package but were rather initiated in response to offers from external third parties to assist the political process. The sum total of these meetings, however, had a positive incremental effect on the formal political negotiations. However not all the workshops were equally useful, and the discussion will focus on the most useful exercises.

Two of the workshops were sequential and complemented each other. The workshop at the Airlie House Conference Centre in Virginia (28 January to 2 February 1990) and the workshop at the Centre for Defence and International Studies at the University of Social Sciences, Grenoble, France (27–30 August 1990) were each organised by the same teams from the Centre for the Study of Conflict, University of Ulster and the Centre for Conflict Analysis and Resolution, George Mason University. Both involved the same set of politicians (although they added to their numbers for the Grenoble workshop). Together they resulted in a single product – a proposal for the establishment of a Northern Ireland Centre in Europe (NICE) – which made a significant impact on the political process in Northern Ireland. Two were freestanding – Des Moines and Strasbourg – but complemented each other insofar as they were concerned with a Bill of Rights and a human rights culture. Two – South Africa and Harvard – were more reflective in that the participants learned from experts and activists about conflict resolution elsewhere. Belfast was the only workshop which was totally public and which involved large numbers of people.

With the exception of the Belfast workshop all were held outside Northern Ireland. This allowed for valuable distance from media distortion and peer group pressure. It gave a safe, neutral and supportive environment where each delegation started from the same equal footing and with the capacity to use an extensive support network. The fact that the workshops took place in a scholarly setting was advantageous because journalists were inclined to dismiss them as being merely 'academic'. The politicians were invited in their individual capacities rather than as representatives of their respective parties. Each party delegation decided whether or not to issue press communiqués before or after each event. Some issued deliberately bland statements to satisfy their absent party colleagues.

The key aim of the workshops was to build up a culture of trust among politicians who, for the most part, occupied second tier positions within their parties. They addressed transitional issues, rather than questions of final status. Virginia and Grenoble had as their theme 'Northern Ireland in Europe: 1992'. Des Moines was billed as a seminar on the feasibility of a Bill of Rights for Northern Ireland; Strasbourg as a seminar on 'Constitutional Protection of Human Rights: Comparative Experiences'; and South Africa was an opportunity to listen to those from every point of the South African political spectrum who were participating in the transition. The Kennedy School of Government at Harvard billed their case study method as 'Managing Change in a Diverse Society'.

In each case, location and format were significant. Participants were housed in comfortable surroundings all under the same roof and all on the same corridor. (Harvard was an exception to this arrangement, but even there, accommodation consisted of executive-style apartments with adjacent space to hold informal meetings.) A common meeting place was established, and it was the practice to eat together. This was not compulsory; a high degree of leisure time was built into most exercises. The South African trip included an overnight stay at a game park; at Harvard, participants attended a baseball game, a reception in a Boston art gallery, and visited Martha's Vineyard. In all these ways, informal interaction was encouraged. The opportunity to meet at the margins of the formal workshops proved to be a vital component in the success of the workshops.

The workshops took place against a backdrop of continuous tension where politicians had often adopted adversarial positions. The absence of the media – a policy which the participants had fully endorsed – meant that there was no need to strike poses. A parallel can be drawn with the Oslo process, where the secret negotiations in Norway produced results which would have been inconceivable from the official and public negotiations (Egeland, 1994). Of course the parallel is not precise. Oslo was about negotiation; the Northern Ireland workshops were not. But the absence of the media and the opportunity to build on a collegial spirit had an effect which should not be underestimated. The workshop settings tended to be formal and formidable. They enabled the participants to hone their political skills. Leisure time allowed for building personal relationships and trust. For example, I have a vivid recollection of a conversation between a nationalist and a unionist in a Strasbourg restaurant in December 1993 when the latter explained his concept of an 'agreed Ireland' and gave a graphic description of the physical and emotional damage visited on him and on his family by supporters of the IRA. The sheer emotion of the occasion impacted on both men and on those who had the privilege of listening in on this dialogue. At a less dramatic level, the opportunity for private conversations over a meal or in hotel bedrooms increased the sense of collegiality and assisted the formal workshop sessions occurring in civilised fashion.

The Harvard workshop provides a contrast. It was the first occasion in which Sinn Féin participated alongside the Ulster Unionist Party (UUP). The other unionist parties with parliamentary representation, the Democratic Unionist Party and the United Kingdom Unionist Party, did not participate. That put some pressure on the UUP representation since they could not afford to consort with Sinn Féin. They were in the same workshop as Sinn Féin but they refused to socialise outside. They would not share the same dining tables nor would they sit together for the group photograph. One can understand the constraints, electoral and otherwise, that they worked under, but the consequence was that they appeared foolish.

The quality of the workshop teams and the role of third parties were central to the success of the workshops. Ideally, the teams needed to be tolerant, respected and representative. All of this is relative. Tolerance simply means a willingness to listen to and work with others. Since the politicians were willing to participate, *ipso facto* they were tolerant. Because some workshops reflected rising tension on the ground in Northern Ireland, dialogue could be robust, but generally it was pursued in a civilised and inquiring manner. In a divided society a respected politician who has the capacity to transcend that division is a very rare bird: in this context 'respected' means within one's own community. They need not necessarily hold official positions – indeed it may be an advantage to target emerging talent where the conflict is complex and tortuous. Two criteria were adopted in the workshops under discussion: the politicians were all either potentially part of their respective negotiating teams or they were perceived as emerging leaders. The result was that the workshops were dominated by the secondary leaderships.

The representativeness of the participants is more difficult to assess. The participants chosen were – to an extent at least – determined by the third parties who organised the workshops. My standing with individual politicians was crucial. Initially, I approached politicians with whom I had some previous relationship either through interviewing them for academic projects or some other involvement. These were people with whom I had established a degree of mutual trust and respect. In every instance, the same cadre of politicians was called upon, and if their leading members were not available they would nominate like-minded individuals. In this sense, the selection of politicians tended to be self-fulfilling and over a period of six years a small group of politicians became versed in the process of shared learning.[2]

At the start, there was a certain arbitrariness to the selection of participants. I judged that two of the party leaders would have considered the type of exercise in which we were involved to be foreign to their way of doing business. But I made a conscious effort to identify those who might make a political impact in the longer term and who represented a newer generation. Total consistency was impossible because so much depended on the vagaries of timing. Each workshop had its own pre-play and could take a few years to plan. Once a date had been set, we came up against parliamentary and personal time tables. More important, however, than the selection of participants was the fact that parties had accepted that this type of exercise complemented Track One efforts.

In some respects the participants were not statistically representative. There was no female representation before the Strasbourg workshop in December 1993. Indeed the issue of gender did not properly surface until the formation of the Northern Ireland Women's Coalition in June 1996. In more recent workshops an attempt has been made to establish a more equitable balance. More generally, however, the participants will never be fully representative in that they will not contain those who spurn 'the gentle art of reperceiving'. In place of an ideal statistical form of representation, my colleagues and I sought instead to concentrate on those who had leadership qualities and the ability to move some of their own intransigent colleagues.

The workshops in Virginia and Grenoble were among the most successful. They had a beginning, a middle and an end; they were designed to complement each other; and they yielded an outcome. The theme of 'Northern Ireland in Europe' after 1992 had been chosen for a number of reasons. The introduction of the Single European Act was going to change the nature of the political game with the reduction in boundaries across Europe. It had the potential to have positive or negative impact on regions such as Northern Ireland. So the topic had a practical content: how does Northern Ireland prepare itself for the Single European Act? It was believed that, while some thought had been devoted to the economic implications of the Act, there had been little anticipatory thinking on the likely political and social consequences of 'a Europe without boundaries'. It was hoped that the workshop might allow some shared agreement to develop about the opportunities and problems the new Europe was likely to present to the people of Northern Ireland.

The theme also had a symbolic content in that it was concerned with questions of sovereignty and subsidiarity. Traditionally, the unionist parties were seen as antithetical to the European vision, whereas the Social Democratic and Labour Party was very pro-European. Despite this symbolic input, the topic was perceived as being sufficiently non-contentious to enable the politicians to use the workshops to cover any issue they desired.

Discussion at the workshops focused on the implications of the Single European Act, and specifically on how this might affect the relationships among the various Northern Ireland parties and other interested parties elsewhere. One theme which emerged was a strong feeling that Northern Ireland's interests were not well represented in the European Community in spite of the efforts of its Members of European Parliament (MEPs). Hence it was suggested that a Northern Ireland input in Brussels could take the form of a Northern Ireland Centre in Europe (NICE), and a tentative draft proposal for exploring the possibilities of establishing such a centre was drawn up. Following the Airlie House workshop, the three Northern Ireland MEPs were apprised of the deliberations and agreed in principle to support the establishment of NICE. On 16 March 1990, the Northern Ireland participants met at a neutral and secluded venue in Belfast and requested a study of the feasibility of NICE.

With a grant I had received from the Ireland Funds, I commissioned a retired civil servant to conduct a feasibility study. His study was considered by the Northern Ireland participants in Belfast on 6 July 1990 and was judged to form a firm basis for progress. It was decided to hold a second workshop to expedite the business of establishing NICE. In the meantime, I had learned that sections of the business community were proceeding with a similar model that was to be launched by the Secretary of State in September. I conveyed this information at the outset of the second workshop in Grenoble. The information angered some of the participants. They were aware that their standing in the community was low because it was perceived that they did not cooperate across the sectarian divide. Here was an example of practical cooperation in which they were engaged, which now looked as if it was not going to be recognised. They conveyed their anger to the Northern Ireland Office and had the proposed launch postponed. This was a rare example of Track One clashing with Track Two.

The participants used their visit to Grenoble to study at first hand how other European regions were preparing for the impact of the Single European Market. A visit to the Rhone-Alps Regional Office in Lyon enabled them to question local officials concerned about their region's relationship with the wider world and, especially, the axis of development it had cultivated with Baden-Württemberg (Germany), Catalonia (Spain), and Lombardy (Italy). As a result of the workshop the feasibility study was amended and it was agreed that it would be published to engender public debate about 'Northern Ireland in Europe: 1992'. That debate led eventually to the establishment of NICE in a partnership between the political parties and the business community. The feasibility report acted as the catalyst for NICE. Funding was to be derived from a combination of public and private sources, and it was recognised that the project could succeed only if it had a broad base of support from political, economic and institutional interests in Northern Ireland.

The NICE project was a successful proactive exercise. It also served as a useful reminder of how third parties can be facilitators. And it gave the political participants the space to explore the more pressing demands arising from the conflict. The project was serviced throughout by academics from both sides of the Atlantic, some of whom had considerable experience in this type of exercise. It might be said that the Northern Ireland academics provided the linkage to, and a sense of the integrity of, the conflict, whereas others provided most of the technical expertise. The combination produced a level playing field in which both sides to the conflict knew that they could call on the existing support system. The very first workshop in Virginia, for example, was opened with a mildly provocative philosophical paper from a distinguished practitioner in conflict resolution who had some experience of Northern Ireland at the early stages of the conflict. He was *au fait* with the nature of the problem, sufficiently distanced from the action, and sufficiently skilful in drawing the politicians into dialogue. That was particularly important for the unionist politicians worried about the burgeoning relationship between the governments in London and Dublin. In addition, the participants were able to call on academic expertise ranging from knowledge of the evolution of the European Union to workshop experience concerning the conflicts in Cyprus and the south Atlantic.[3]

The workshops also produced what one participant described as 'shared learning'. Not only were the participants able to take advantage of the technical expertise available, they acquired a better understanding of their political adversaries.[4] Discussions went well beyond the European question. Even on that level, many of the myths about the EU were exposed, and the notion that 1992 would 'open up the possibility of manipulative politics' (according to one unionist participant), whereby the Single European Act would be utilised to force Northern Ireland into a closer relationship with the Republic of Ireland, was fully rehearsed.

The participants were concerned that their constituents back home might not recognise the distance between analysis and negotiation (shades of Duisburg!), and they wished to ensure that that distance was maintained. They used the cover of Virginia and Grenoble to tease out a formula which would allow them to re-enter political dialogue without an apparent loss of face. The phraseology they produced was remarkably close to the formulation devised by the two governments at a later stage to keep the peace process in existence. Similarly the SDLP participants used these exercises to talk down some of the unionist fears about the Irish dimension and the Anglo-Irish Agreement of 1985. These shared understandings enabled bilateral and multilateral Track One exercises to proceed more smoothly than might have been expected, a fact confirmed by the interviewees.

The visit to South Africa in 1994 was not so much a single workshop as a series of consultations with parties inside South Africa to enable Northern Ireland participants to gain first hand experience of the South African negotiation process. The consultations were sponsored by the Institute for Democracy in South Africa (IDASA) and designed to provide key players with an opportunity to reflect on their own process in the light of the South African experience: 'In IDASA we have seen the value of such exposure programmes for our own process and a similar value might be expected for the participants'. On the question of participation, IDASA accepted that it might have to 'exclude some sections of opinion who will have to be drawn into the process at a later stage. South Africa has lessons for how the various groups were negotiated into the settlement at various times as well' (communication from IDASA, 16 September 1994). That last comment was shorthand for the inclusion of Sinn Féin because, as the link person to Northern Ireland, I was pressured (slightly) by South Africans to have Sinn Féin included. Since this was prior to the IRA cease-fire and since I knew that unionists would not participate in those circumstances, nothing came of the suggestion.

The 1994 South Africa exercise should be examined in conjunction with the subsequent 1997 South African visit (with which I was not involved). The latter was the first fully inclusive process in that it contained high-powered delegations on all points of the political spectrum including

Sinn Féin and the fringe loyalist parties (it also was graced with a visit from President Mandela). It indicated too how useful peer learning could be when the participants were learning from another conflict. South Africa had moved beyond its pariah status in the international community and had illustrated that 'intractable' problems need not necessarily be intractable. It was a shining example of what could be achieved if the will was there.

Together, the trips produced a palpable product. Sinn Féin representatives involved in the multi-party talks later referred frequently to their South African experience. At the formal opening of substantive talks in Belfast on 7 October 1997 the Alliance leader, Lord Alderdice, said that the 'message Northern Ireland politicians learned from the recent examination of the South African experience was that if deadlines were not met "you never achieve the outcome you want to achieve"' (*The Irish Times*, 8 October 1997). An Alliance participant made the point in interview that workshops such as Des Moines were about looking at particular pieces of content whereas South Africa was mostly looking at process – how to get from Point A to Point B. He believed that South Africa pointed out design faults in the Northern Ireland process.

Specifically, the South African participants took away three messages: how to make use of technical committees to further the process; the value of the notion of 'sufficient consensus' (it became part of the political furniture in the multi-party talks); and the need for parties not to allow themselves to be left behind by the process. Individuals took away other ideas on specific matters such as policing. Most important of all, the South African visit helped to make relationships more manageable and allowed the multi-party talks negotiators to use the same language and have a clearer idea of what was possible. Some used the South African experience in talks with government and in discussions within the Democratic Unionist Party. One participant asserted that if Des Moines was 'nearest to Track Two then South Africa was more like Track One and a half'.

CONCLUSION

By the 1990s, the Anglo-Irish conflict had reached the stage of a 'hurting stalemate'. It was clear to the parties to the conflict that something needed to be done, and they were ready at the very least to explore each other's options. In this context, Track Two initiatives became important, both in increasing the incentives for exploration and negotiation and in providing the best opportunities for initial exploration. These factors illustrate Crocker's observation that the way in which 'third parties can intervene most effectively depends upon (1) their own capabilities, leverage, and linkage to the conflict; (2) the conflict's status, form, and ripeness; and (3) the character of the parties to the conflict, their accessibility, and their decision-making systems' (Crocker, 1996, p. 187).

The granting of the Adams visa had a major effect on Track One diplomacy; it is a near perfect example of the symmetry of intervention and leverage. Informal contacts where trust was built, involving at once third parties, key political actors in Northern Ireland, and the US 'treetops', came together in this crucial Track Two initiative to confirm trust and create incentive for Track One progress.

The workshops had more indirect but still important incremental effects. They did not directly complement the official mediation, though the participants certainly used their unofficial experience to rehearse positions taken up at the formal level. They assisted a key cadre of politicians to gain from the process at a technical level and to learn to trust each other. At the very least, these politicians were already familiar with each other when entering the official bilateral and multilateral meetings convened by government. It is true that each party entered the workshops with their separate agendas and extracted their own lessons. This suggests that they participated with no very high general expectations. Yet in some instances there were palpable products – emotional, intellectual, and institutional. Common themes emerged, and there was a commonality on how to use the process.

The process was credible in that the participants became advocates for the process and, while using it to present their own positions, also demonstrated a capacity to grow and learn. It was reflective in that the participants absorbed considerable new information, technical and otherwise. They were prepared to assert their opinions but also to listen carefully to those of others. Many of them matured as a result of the process. With the passage of time, the process became more inclusive of diverse voices from Northern Ireland. Indeed, a group dynamic had established itself as early as 1990. On the last day of the Grenoble meeting one of the politicians made the point that 'contacts are now established and we don't need academics to keep them up'. Nevertheless academics were called upon on quite a few other occasions in the years that followed.

It is difficult to be precise about the extent to which ideas emanating from the workshops reached a wider audience. Most of my interviewees maintained that they discussed the outcome of the different workshops with a small coterie of political friends, although one said that he passed on much of his experience to the party through speeches and articles. The role of wider political opinion is also difficult to assess. One workshop participant considered that the most important measure of success is the extent to which party leaders have become engaged in the whole process because they are the only ones who can deliver. However the Belfast Agreement might call this into question. Here was an Agreement which was driven by the two governments because they perceived that in a demotic culture there was a real desire for change. This was contrary to the strongly held opinions of some political leaders.

The Belfast Agreement serves as an indication of how far we have moved towards process and inclusivity. As implementation proceeds, it shows whether we have gone beyond the need for analysis and are beginning to look at decision making and implementation, and whether we have moved beyond confusion and are working through more realistic – and shared – cognitive frameworks. It should tell us, too, whether Track Two in Northern Ireland needs to move into a new phase in which leaders and third parties recognise that the rules of the game have changed. As the institutions of the Agreement begin to function, the new sets of rules, problems and opportunities for intervention will become clear. But always we should keep in mind that *fortuna* lurks in the political undergrowth.

NOTES

[1] This paper was prepared while the author was a Jennings Randolph Senior Fellow at the United States Institute of Peace, Washington DC, 1997–8.
[2] It is vital to note that the participants were there in an individual capacity and not as official representatives of their respective parties.
[3] A similar support system existed in Grenoble where a different set of experts shared their knowledge on human rights issues.
[4] We see this in the context of the workships (in Virginia and Grenoble) which produced the schema for a Northern Ireland Centre in Europe.

5

EQUALITY AND THE GOOD FRIDAY AGREEMENT

Christopher McCrudden[1]

INTRODUCTION

In Northern Ireland talk of equality and human rights has often been ignored or marginalised. It has been perceived by too many in positions of power as divisive, as ignoring 'the real problems', even as subversive. During 1998 something remarkable happened. Discussions about equality and human rights moved from the margins into the mainstream. The Good Friday Agreement, drawing on the best international and European practice, identified equality and human rights as a central element in a new constitutional settlement. The purpose of this chapter is to discuss this sea change. Following the Agreement, there was a real danger that equality would be pushed back to the margins. However, as we will see, a coalition of the disadvantaged and politicians ensured that this did not happen. The Northern Ireland Act 1998 taken together with the Human Rights Act 1998 now accurately reflects the Agreement's human rights and equality requirements.

The chapter focuses on three aspects: first, the emergence and development of the equality agenda in Northern Ireland from the initial anti-discrimination legislation to the development of 'mainstreaming' as a political and legal approach to equality; second, the convergence of the political and equality agendas in the negotiations leading up to the Agreement; third, the strengthening of the equality agenda in the Agreement and its subsequent incorporation into the Northern Ireland Act 1998, the legal basis for the new constitutional settlement in Northern Ireland. But first, what does mainstreaming equality mean?

In essence 'mainstreaming' is the principle that equality be seen as an integral part of all public policy making and implementation, rather than something separated off in a policy or institutional ghetto. The concept has emerged from several sources, of which the most important are debates about how best to advance women's equality. One early, 1980s, source was the attempt to integrate gender issues into policy making in the area of development assistance, such as lending by the World Bank or decision making in the United Nations Development Programme (Razavi and Miller, 1995). Since then, the concept has been adopted in ever expanding areas. Mainstreaming was adopted as a policy goal at the Fourth United Nations World Conference on Women in 1995 (UN, 1995). More recently, the European Commission has become involved in developing such approaches in Europe (European Commission, 1997, pp. 15–20). The Council of Europe convened a group of specialists on mainstreaming in February 1996; their report in March 1998 presented a conceptual framework, a methodology for conducting mainstreaming, and a discussion of 'good practice' in the area (Council of Europe, 1998). At the national level also there are examples of mainstreaming policies, some already in existence, some in embryo, in the Netherlands, Sweden, Denmark, Flanders, Portugal, Finland, Ireland, Canada, Australia, and New Zealand (see McCrudden, 1999a).

We shall see below that the concept is not free of ambiguities and problems, some of which are brought into greater clarity by the experience of constitutionalising mainstreaming in Northern Ireland. The Northern Ireland model is unusual, if not unique, in two respects. First, the mainstreaming undertaken goes beyond gender. In particular, it focuses attention on equality between the two religio-political communities in Northern Ireland. Second, it is underpinned by a firm legal foundation. How did this come about? To understand fully the development of mainstreaming in Northern Ireland, we need to begin the story much earlier, with the civil rights movement of the late 1960s.

DEVELOPING AN ANTI-DISCRIMINATION AGENDA IN NORTHERN IRELAND

The Northern Ireland civil rights campaign of the 1960s focused on the need to eradicate discrimination between Catholics and Protestants (Cameron, 1969). This movement led to some action by the then Northern Ireland Government, but anti-discrimination legislation as such began after the Northern Ireland Government was suspended in 1972 and 'direct rule' was introduced. The Northern Ireland Constitution Act 1973 made it unlawful for a public authority carrying out functions relating to Northern Ireland to discriminate, or to aid or incite another person to discriminate, against a person or class of person on the ground of religious belief or political opinion. Two features of the Act's approach are important. First, it protected from discrimination only in the religio-political context. Second, it protected only from direct discrimination, that is (to put it somewhat over-simplistically) discrimination which arises from an intentional act. There was, as a consequence, little litigation under these provisions.

The second major development in anti-discrimination legislation was in the area of employment. A government committee (the van Straubenzee committee) considered the question of discrimination in the private sector of employment in 1973 and produced a penetrating report (Working Party, 1973). The Fair Employment Act 1976 partially implemented this report, and addressed also employment in the public sector. A Fair Employment Agency was established to enforce the legislation in 1977. However, the legislation had little effect on employers' practices. Research carried out by the Policy Studies Institute in 1987 showed that the vast majority of employers believed that the Act had made little, if any, impact on their behaviour (Smith and Chambers, 1991). The research also confirmed the extent of the economic inequality between the two communities in Northern Ireland. According to the PSI study, for example, Catholic male unemployment, then at 35 per cent, was two and a half times that of Protestant male unemployment, and continued at this level despite there being over 100,000 job changes a year.

From the mid-1980s, inequality of opportunity between Catholics and Protestants again became a key political issue, largely due to pressure from outside Northern Ireland. A campaign was begun in the United States to bring pressure to bear on American corporations, state legislatures and municipal governments with investments in Northern Ireland to adopt a tougher set of anti-discrimination principles (called the 'MacBride Principles') and sought to encourage employers to engage in affirmative action (McCrudden, 1999b). The MacBride campaign met with opposition from the British government, but proved popular with American state and city legislators. A number of states enacted legislation requiring US companies in which they invested to ensure fair employment practices in their Northern Ireland subsidiaries. This US campaign began to fill, however partially and inadequately, the vacuum caused by the failure of institutions in Northern Ireland to address the issue adequately.

Partly in response, in 1986 the Northern Ireland Department of Economic Development proposed new legislation that offered hope of a more robust approach, but the proposals, emphasising voluntary compliance, fell short of what was likely to be effective (Department of Economic Development, 1986). In October 1987 the Standing Advisory Commission on Human Rights (SACHR) published a major report providing a comprehensive and authoritative analysis of the problem and a detailed set of proposals for legislation and other government initiatives (SACHR, 1987). Crucially the report shifted the terms of the debate from the eradication of prejudiced discrimination to the reduction of unjustified structural inequality in the employment market, whether caused by discrimination or not. In December 1988 the Government responded by publishing new legislation. After significant amendments this was passed in July 1989 (McCrudden, 1991). The new Fair Employment Act 1989 marked a departure from existing approaches, emphasising compulsory rather than voluntary compliance, giving broader powers to the enforcement agency (the Fair Employment Commission), and requiring limited affirmative action and compulsory monitoring.

'POLICY APPRAISAL AND FAIR TREATMENT' (PAFT)

Anti-discrimination law was, however, gradually perceived as insufficient to achieve the substantial change that the 1987 SACHR Report had defined as necessary. In its Second Report (1990) SACHR argued that the government should establish machinery which would monitor the impacts of legislation, policy and administration on equality of opportunity and on relations between the two sections of the community.

Another development at this time involved the reform of 'community relations' policy making within the Northern Ireland Office. In September 1987 Tom King, then Secretary of State for Northern Ireland, announced the establishment of a Central Community Relations Unit within the Central Secretariat of the Northern Ireland Office. The purpose of this reorganisation, according to the announcement, was to ensure that in 'every decision we take, whether it is in the fields of housing, education, planning or employment, or any other fields of government, . . . we have taken into account any community relations aspects there may be' (Northern Ireland Information Service, 1987). The new unit would coordinate all Northern Ireland policy making. In discussions with the Northern Ireland Office before the new initiative was announced, SACHR was informed that it was intended that a senior officer in each department would be made responsible for examining policies and proposals in relation to their community impact. If, in the view of that officer, any such policy or proposal might have a disparate community impact, the matter could be taken to the Permanent Secretary and ultimately to the Secretary of State for decision.

More generally, British administrative policy in the rest of the United Kingdom was becoming more favourably disposed to attempts to engage systematically in 'policy appraisal', and to 'mainstream' other policies in government (see McCrudden, 1999a for more detail). Since the 1980s regulatory impact assessments had often been required, as had occasional cost/benefit analyses of proposed projects. In addition, 'proofing' government policy proposals to ensure compliance with certain obligations was becoming more common.

All these elements contributed to the announcement by government in 1990 that a non-statutory policy of 'equality proofing' would be introduced in Northern Ireland. A circular was issued giving advice to all Northern Ireland departments about the need to consider discrimination in relation to religious affiliation, political opinion and gender (Central Secretariat Circular, January 1990). This was coordinated with an initiative launched in the UK by the ministerial group on women's issues that encouraged all Government Departments to develop basic guidance on equality proofing throughout the United Kingdom.

There were several years of controversy over the content of the guidelines in Northern Ireland, including the failure to cover areas such as race, disability and age. Revised and more inclusive guidelines, renamed the Policy Appraisal and Fair Treatment guidelines (PAFT), came into effect in January 1994. The groups coming within the scope of its guidelines went beyond the two religious communities, and included people of different gender, age, ethnic origin, marital and family status and sexual orientation, and the disabled. PAFT was an attempt to establish a procedure within Government decision making by which the principles of equity and equality could be made effective. 'Equality and equity', it said, 'are central issues which must condition and influence policy making in all spheres and at all levels of Government activity' (Central Secretariat Circular, May 1993). We can see here the crucial shift from an anti-discrimination to a mainstreaming approach. But little detailed guidance was given to departments or other public bodies as to how to accomplish this task, although a commitment was subsequently given that the Annual Report on PAFT implementation by the Central Community Relations Unit (CCRU) would be published, providing a degree of transparency to the process.

There were, moreover, a number of unresolved ambiguities. First, it was unclear how far the government was willing to go beyond action of an anti-discrimination kind. Second, it was unclear whether the initiative was much more than 'window dressing' in response to political pressure, particularly from the United States. Third, many aspects of the guidelines – the stress on the UK context, their inclusiveness, the use of international human rights language and concepts – seem to have been designed to make more acceptable to civil servants and public opinion an initiative whose primary rationale was the need to tackle Catholic disadvantage.

The inclusive, broad and radical-sounding nature of the initiative raised expectations that proved difficult to satisfy in practice. Unlike the equivalent guidelines in the rest of the United Kingdom, the PAFT guidelines were available from government on request and were widely circulated by NGOs among the relevant groups. Perhaps naively, they took the PAFT guidelines at face value, expected fairness, and behaved accordingly. When the promise was not delivered, not surprisingly, they mobilised. The guidelines were soon embroiled in public controversy. Unison, the public sector trade union, took judicial review proceedings against one of the public bodies that intended to privatise its services on the grounds that to do so discriminated against women. The judicial review was ultimately unsuccessful, but two things emerged. First, the PAFT guidelines had not formally been issued to the public body concerned, which was a considerable embarrassment for the government. Second, the court held that, had the guidelines been issued properly, the public body would have been legally required to take them into account. This appeared to give the guidelines a legal status, something that had hitherto not been clear.

It became clear later, however, that while departments had to take the guidelines into account, once they did so, it would be difficult to contest their decision legally, whatever the result of that consideration – in short that PAFT was legally enforceable procedurally but not substantively. However, the effect of all this was to raise the political status of the guidelines in the eyes of both the public bodies and departments to which they applied and the campaigning groups. In a sustained attempt to encourage groups to use the guidelines, the Committee on the Administration of Justice (CAJ), a Northern Ireland human rights NGO, organised briefing sessions on the guidelines for a range of interested voluntary and community organisations. The NGOs responded with enthusiasm. A loose coalition was born that was dedicated to putting PAFT into effect.

Meanwhile, another factor played an important role in making PAFT a major focus of political interest. During the passage of the Fair Employment Act 1989, the government committed itself to conducting a formal review of the operation of the legislation and other government policy in this area within five years of its commencement. Originally, this task was given to the Central Community Relations Unit within the Northern Ireland Office, the government department responsible for Northern Ireland, but responsibility was later transferred to SACHR. SACHR commissioned research into several areas of government policy as part of its enquiry. Particularly important among this research was a short but highly critical piece on the operation of PAFT, which showed that PAFT appeared to be largely ignored by substantial sections of the policy-making apparatus of government (Osborne et al., 1996). Increasingly, the focus of political attention shifted from concern about the operation of the Fair Employment Act narrowly conceived, to the ineffectiveness of the policy that had been seen as a necessary complement to the legislation – PAFT.

EMERGENCE OF ALTERNATIVE
MODELS OF MAINSTREAMING

The potential for a mainstreaming approach to impact significantly on inequality, combined with evidence of the lack of such impact in practice, contributed to pressure for reform. Unison, the union involved in the initial judicial review, commissioned the author to prepare a study on reform of PAFT. A discussion paper – 'Mainstreaming Fairness' – was produced which set out various options and raised questions for further consideration (McCrudden, 1996). A possible model for a statutorily-based PAFT was tentatively suggested to stimulate debate. The proposals included provision for a statutory duty to be imposed on the Secretary of State and on public bodies to ensure that material inequalities between certain groups should be progressively reduced.

In November 1996 the Committee on the Administration of Justice (CAJ), an influential human rights NGO in Northern Ireland, circulated the paper extensively among opinion formers, trade unions, voluntary groups, lawyers, politicians, and civil servants in Northern Ireland, and requested comments. Significantly, one of the earliest responses to the paper was in the form of an extensive discussion by one of the researchers within SACHR (Hutson, 1996). This developed the 'Mainstreaming Fairness' proposal further, suggesting the establishment of an Equality Commission to oversee public sector application of equality proofing mechanisms.

In early 1997 the Government responded to both papers with a detailed critique (Commentary, 1997). Prominent civil servants had earlier expressed concern at the growing pressure to give legislative force to PAFT (Watkins, 1997). Now, a sustained attack was mounted against the idea. It was argued that the proposals would 'effectively constitutionalize [sic]' the equality aspiration in a manner which 'would seek to dictate the socio-economic policies of future Governments, irrespective of electoral mandates or budgetary constraints' (Watkins, 1997), and that the emphasis on consultation and external participation could undermine representative democracy. Other concerns were also raised, including the bureaucratic burden and extra costs in implementing PAFT.

Despite these objections, the 'Mainstreaming Fairness' proposal was substantially taken up by SACHR and became one of its central recommendations for reform. SACHR reported in June 1997, criticising the existing implementation of PAFT and making detailed recommendations for a revised scheme (SACHR, 1997). The report recommended, as a minimum, that a number of measures should be incorporated into the PAFT system. These included, 'effective political control over, and responsibility for, the policy on both direct and indirect effects on equality generally and community differentials in particular', 'adequate monitoring of both the direct and indirect impacts of policy on community differentials, and other equality measures', 'full consideration of alternative policies which might give effect to government objectives but reduce or avoid unwelcome effects on equality generally and community differentials in particular', 'greater transparency in the manner in which government policy is assessed' and 'greater accountability in the manner in which the civil service and public bodies fulfil their remit to promote equality'. More far-reaching still, the SACHR report recommended that the policy on PAFT be given legislative form, with enforcement based on an internal NIO unit, such as a strengthened CCRU.

THE GOOD FRIDAY AGREEMENT AND EQUALITY

The Good Friday Agreement had a crucial impact on the development of these issues. Up to then the debate had only indirect relevance for, or input into, the search for a constitutional settlement to the conflict. By 1997, however, a new politics was emerging in Northern Ireland that meant that previous approaches to resolving the problem were to be supplemented with a new concentration on equality. The debate on equality issues, including PAFT, previously separate from the political negotiations, now became entangled with them. In particular, both the revision of the 'Mainstreaming Fairness' proposal, and the British Government's response to the SACHR report, have to be seen in the context of the peace negotiations which culminated in the Good Friday Agreement.

Several developments affected the ultimate outcome. First, in May 1997, a new Labour Government was elected, committed to breathing new life into the constitutional talks, unencumbered by a unionist veto and backed by a substantial majority in the House of Commons. Soon after, the IRA resumed its ceasefire. Suddenly it seemed as if a peace settlement might actually emerge. The two issues – equality and the search for a settlement – now became intertwined. For the two Governments, equality issues were perceived as an important part of 'confidence building' in the Catholic/nationalist community and, from then on, policy proposals on equality were affected significantly by the talks process.

Second, while earlier attempts at establishing peace in Northern Ireland had addressed questions of discrimination and human rights, this time the talks involved parties which had not participated previously, and which viewed equality and human rights issues as particularly salient, including

Sinn Féin and the various fringe Loyalist parties. For these parties, failure to address successfully equality and human rights issues important to their communities would make it much more difficult for them to 'sell' any agreement. Once human rights were identified as an area that was important, particularly to Sinn Féin, it then became important for those who wanted to keep Sinn Féin 'on board' to include it. The SDLP, Sinn Féin and the PUP all embraced a reform of PAFT as a part of its strategy on equality. So too did the Women's Coalition, which played an important role in keeping the issues to the fore in the negotiations. For the Ulster Unionist Party, equality was either an issue that it considered it could not oppose, or did not consider sufficiently important to make a priority.

Third, there developed outside the formal talks process what the journalist, Mary Holland, called a 'parallel peace process', involving an informal coalition of such bodies as the Committee on the Administration of Justice, Unison, the Women's Support Network, and many other community and NGO groups in Northern Ireland (Holland, 1998). This loose network had contacts within the talks process, in particular through the Women's Coalition, and succeeded in setting at least part of the human rights and equality agenda in the negotiations both before and during the final frenzied days.

Fourth, the new Labour Government was more comfortable with a strong 'rights' approach than the earlier Conservative government had been. The new Secretary of State, Mo Mowlam, whilst in Opposition, had supported draft legislation on equality, and was much closer to the 'parallel peace process' than any of her predecessors had been. Before the election she publicly announced that she intended 'to make it a statutory duty for government bodies to take equality of opportunity into account through more rigorous enforcement of the Policy Appraisal and Fair Treatment guidelines' (Mowlam, 1997).

Negotiations on the equality agenda in the talks took place largely in the months of December 1997 to April 1998. In January 1998 the British and Irish governments published a joint statement – the so-called 'Heads of Agreement' paper – setting out their best guess on the bare bones of a settlement. The statement included a paragraph on human rights and equality that envisaged provisions to safeguard the rights of both communities in Northern Ireland 'to achieve full respect for the principles of equity of treatment and freedom from discrimination, and the cultural identity and ethos of both communities'. The use of the term 'equity', rather than the stronger term 'equality', met with a hostile response from both nationalist commentators and human rights advocates. This appears to have concentrated Irish government minds further on the equality issue (O'Dowd, 1998; McCrudden, 1998a; Ahern 1998a; 1998b).

In February 1998 the Committee on the Administration of Justice published a revised proposal by the present author – 'Benchmarks for Change' (McCrudden, 1998b). It proposed replacing PAFT with a statutory obligation to promote equality of opportunity and establishing a strong mechanism within the Northern Ireland civil service to monitor and enforce this obligation. It also envisaged a high degree of involvement by those outside government in the assessment and development of equality issues, including those affected by policy proposals and the statutory equality agencies. The proposal received extensive support across the range of groups most affected. Several of the political parties picked up aspects of it, as did the Irish government.

The Government's proposals were set out in the White Paper, 'Partnership for Equality', published in March 1998. From the perspective of what subsequently occurred, two proposals were particularly important. First, the Government proposed a new statutory framework to supersede the PAFT's administrative guidelines. There would be a statutory obligation on Northern Ireland 'public sector bodies' (including District Councils and United Kingdom Departments operating in Northern Ireland, as well as the Northern Ireland Departments) to ensure that 'consistent with their other responsibilities', their various functions 'are carried out with due regard to the need to promote equality of opportunity in those areas covered by the current PAFT guidelines'. Each public body would be required to adopt a statutory scheme setting out 'how it proposed to take regard of its new statutory obligations in its day-to-day work'.

Second, the Government proposed, subject to public consultation, to create a new unified statutory authority bringing together the existing Northern Ireland equality agencies: the Fair Employment Commission, the Equal Opportunities Commission, the Commission for Racial Equality and the Northern Ireland Disability Council. The intention was to provide an institutional mechanism to monitor and enforce the new statutory duty. The new body, external to the civil service, would provide the various public bodies with the assistance necessary to enable them to implement the duty effectively. The proposed amalgamation of the existing bodies was to prove the most controversial element of the White Paper, giving rise to considerable unease amongst the equality bodies themselves (with the exception of the Fair Employment Commission) and many of the NGO groups.

One of the key issues urged on the parties to the negotiations was the centrality of the human rights and equality issues to the success of the peace process. Moreover a consensus emerged that discussion should go beyond a classical, narrow definition of rights centred on political and civil rights, to include social, cultural and economic rights, and that equality issues should be mainstreamed. In the months of negotiation, it also emerged that there was significant support across the political spectrum for the CAJ and SACHR approach to the replacement for PAFT. It was feared that the British Government would seize the opportunity of the negotiations to bolster its White Paper proposals with the authority of a peace agreement. Arguments were put to several of the parties to the negotiations to try to prevent this, and to have stronger proposals inserted in the final text.

All this activity was reflected in the 'Mitchell Document' that was presented by the Chairmen of the talks at the beginning of April 1998 as a draft paper for discussion. The bones, and much of the flesh of the ultimate Agreement, were in the Mitchell Document, including the sections on equality and human rights. However, some significant changes regarding equality were made to these aspects of the document in the run-up to final agreement on 10 April. Also, the Agreement departed from the White Paper proposals in some important respects.

Two equality agendas were addressed in the Agreement, one national, the other social. The national equality agenda – equal respect for the two different allegiances, Irish and British – was reflected in the institutional provisions designed to ensure fair representation in the Assembly and Executive, and in the establishment of North–South institutions. Beyond these arrangements, however, the parties affirmed a list of important rights: the right of free political thought; the right to freedom and expression of religion; the right to pursue democratically national and political aspirations; and the right to seek constitutional change by peaceful and legitimate means. A new Bill of Rights, supplementing the European Convention on Human Rights, was envisaged to reflect the principles of 'mutual respect for the identity and ethos of both communities and parity of esteem'. In addition, there were new obligations on government to encourage the use of the Irish language.

The Agreement was equally forthright and inclusive on social equality. The parties affirmed 'the right to equal opportunity in all social and economic activity, regardless of class, creed, disability, gender or ethnicity; . . . and the right of women to full and equal political participation'. (The references to disability, ethnicity and participation by women were inserted by the negotiators during the final days.)

Provisions governing Ministers in the new Executive Authority, in particular the Pledge of Office, required Ministers 'to serve all the people of Northern Ireland equally, and to act in accordance with the general obligations on government to promote equality and prevent discrimination'. (This was also inserted in the last few days of the negotiations.) Under the Code of Conduct for Ministers, Ministers were required to 'operate in a way conducive to promoting good community relations and equality of treatment'. Moreover, an individual 'may be removed from office following a decision of the Assembly taken on a cross-community basis, . . . for failure to meet his or her responsibilities including, inter alia, those set out in the Pledge of Office' which included the duty of equality and impartiality.

Pending the devolution of powers to a new Northern Ireland Assembly, the British Government committed itself to pursuing policies for sustained economic growth and stability in Northern Ireland and for promoting social inclusion, including in particular community development and the advancement of women in public life. Subject to public consultation, the British Government would also develop a new regional development strategy for Northern Ireland, for consideration in due course by the Assembly. This would aim to tackle the problems of a divided society and social cohesion in urban, rural and border areas. The government also planned to introduce a range of measures aimed at combating unemployment and progressively eliminating the differential in unemployment rates between the two communities by targeting objective need.

A new Northern Ireland Human Rights Commission would be established, with membership 'reflecting the community balance'. This would be established by Westminster legislation, independent of Government, with an extended and enhanced role beyond that exercised by the Standing Advisory Commission on Human Rights. Its duties would include keeping under review the adequacy and effectiveness of laws and practices, making recommendations to Government, providing information and promoting awareness of human rights, considering draft legislation referred to it by the new Assembly and 'in appropriate cases' bringing court proceedings or providing assistance to individuals doing so. It would consult and advise on 'the scope for defining, in Westminster legislation, rights supplementary to those in the European Convention on Human Rights, to reflect the particular circumstances of Northern Ireland, drawing as appropriate on international instruments and experience'. It would also give consideration to offering 'a clear formulation of the rights not to be discriminated against and to equality of opportunity in both the public and private sectors'. In this respect, the Agreement kept open the possibility that a Northern Ireland Bill of Rights would include the concept of 'indirect discrimination' in any new anti-discrimination duty applying to the actions of public bodies in Northern Ireland, an idea which was rejected in the earlier White Paper.

The Agreement noted that '[s]ubject to the outcome of public consultation underway, the British Government intends, as a particular priority, to create a statutory obligation on public authorities in Northern Ireland to carry out all their functions with due regard to the need to promote equality of opportunity in relation to religion and political opinion; gender; race; disability; age; marital status; dependants; and sexual orientation'. Under the Agreement, '[p]ublic bodies [would] be required to draw up statutory schemes showing how they would implement this obligation'. As part of the equality duty, they would be required to include 'arrangements for policy appraisal, including an assessment of impact on relevant categories'. The references to impact assessment and information were added at a late stage of the negotiations. In these respects the Agreement went further than the White Paper.

The Agreement additionally proposed 'arrangements to provide that key decisions and legislation are proofed to ensure that they do not infringe the ECHR and any Bill of Rights for Northern Ireland'. The Assembly 'may appoint a special Committee to examine and report on whether a measure or proposal for legislation is in conformity with equality requirements, including the ECHR/Bill of Rights'. This was not included in the White Paper. The Assembly 'shall then consider the report of the Committee and can determine the matter in accordance with the cross-community consent procedure'. It would be 'open to the new Northern Assembly to consider bringing together its responsibilities for these matters into a dedicated Department of Equality'. These elements were added at a late stage.

The Agreement noted that the British Government proposed to create a new statutory Equality Commission to replace the Fair Employment Commission, the Equal Opportunities Commission (NI), the Commission for Racial Equality (NI) and the Disability Council. Such a unified Commission would 'advise on, validate and monitor the statutory equality obligation and will investigate complaints of default'. However this proposal, which did not have the support of the negotiating parties or the Irish Government, was 'subject to the outcome of public consultation currently underway', a condition which had not been included in the original Mitchell document.

The new British–Irish Intergovernmental Conference was also given significant human rights responsibilities. Strand Three provided that '[i]n recognition of the Irish Government's special interest in Northern Ireland and of the extent to which issues of mutual concern arise in relation to Northern Ireland, there will be regular and frequent meetings of the Conference concerned with non-devolved Northern Ireland matters, on which the Irish Government may put forward views and proposals. These meetings, to be co-chaired by the Minister for Foreign Affairs and the Secretary of State for Northern Ireland, would also deal with all-island and cross-border cooperation on non-devolved issues. The Conference . . . will address . . . the areas of rights . . . in Northern Ireland (unless and until responsibility is devolved to a Northern Ireland administration)'.

IMPLEMENTING THE EQUALITY
ASPECTS OF THE AGREEMENT

The Agreement thus contained strong provisions on equality. The question was whether these would be adequately reflected in the implementing legislation. For campaigners, the issue became how to translate what appeared to be a breakthrough at the political level into legislative text. This was to prove a difficult task. The period between the conclusion of the Agreement in April, and the publication of the Bill implementing that Agreement in July, saw 123 submissions on the government's White Paper of March, 'Partnership for Equality'. All but two of these were received after the Agreement was concluded and many took account of the Agreement in their submission. Most endorsed the principle that equality of opportunity should be placed on a statutory basis, though a substantial proportion questioned whether the government proposals would achieve their stated objective. Many also opposed the creation of a unified Equality Commission.

In May, an alternative proposal to that adopted in the White Paper was submitted to the Secretary of State suggesting that, in the light of the Agreement, several features of the White Paper's proposals should be revised (McCrudden, 1998c). It argued that the enforcement and monitoring of the equality of opportunity duty on the public sector should be carried out by establishing an effective internal monitoring and enforcement mechanism within the Northern Ireland Civil Service/ Executive. This should be complemented by mechanisms for increased public participation and a role for the existing equality commissions. The powers that the White Paper recommended for the Secretary of State to intervene, where there was a breach of the equality duty by a public body, should be strengthened and clarified. Further research was necessary to assess the effect of the amalgamation of existing equality bodies into one equality body (or into a new Human Rights Commission) before a decision on amalgamation should take place.

The Secretary of State announced her decisions on the equality aspects of the Bill on 10 July. Her announcement made it clear that the campaign to modify the Government's proposals on amalgamating the equality Commissions into a new Equality Commission had been unsuccessful. The Equality Commission envisaged by the White Paper would be set up. At the same time she was concerned to reassure critics that the White Paper proposals 'seemed to pass responsibility for the promotion and oversight of the equality of opportunity obligation to an external body' and stressed that 'internal arrangements for coordinating, promoting and monitoring the activities of Government Departments and public bodies must also be rigorous and effective.' (Northern Ireland Information

Service, 1998). To meet the criticism that issues of religious equality would dominate the working of the new body, she indicated that the legislation would require the Equality Commission to devote appropriate resources to gender, race and disability issues. It would also allow the Commission to establish consultative councils on these issues.

The Secretary of State also responded to public consultations on the White Paper on the matter of the form and content of the equality duty on public authorities. She indicated that several criticisms of the proposals contained in the White Paper 'were based on misapprehensions'. It was not the intention 'to leave substantial areas of discretion to those in the public sector'. 'To remove any ambiguity, the requirements on the public sector to carry out appraisals of policies, including equality impact assessments, to consult with representatives of interests which might be affected, and to publish information on appraisals, will all be clarified in the Bill'.

The Government introduced the Northern Ireland Bill into the House of Commons on 15 July. It received its second reading on 20 July. Clause-by-clause consideration of the contents of the Bill took place (first in Committee, then at Report stage) between then and 31 July when the Bill was given its Third Reading. During the summer, further intensive consultations took place between the Government and interested groups (including the Northern Ireland political parties). The Bill was then given its second reading in the House of Lords on 5 October (again the debate focused on the principles underlying the Bill). This was followed by detailed clause-by-clause consideration of the Bill at the Committee and Report stages on 26 October and 10–11 November respectively. The Lords Third Reading debate took place on 17 November. The next day the Commons considered the Lords amendments, and agreed them. The Bill received the Royal Assent on 19 November 1998 and became law.

The politics of the Bill's passage is important for an understanding of what transpired during the Parliamentary phase. The Government commanded a sizeable majority in the House of Commons and there was never any doubt that it could push the legislation through in any form that it wished. Nor was there any serious prospect that the Conservative majority in the House of Lords would chose the legislation implementing the Agreement as a basis for attacking the Government. Indeed, neither in the Lords nor in the Commons did the Conservative opposition appear to have played much of a role in the negotiations surrounding the Bill's passage. The Government ministers involved were Paul Murphy, MP, in the Commons, and Lord Williams and Lord Dubs in the Lords. Behind Mr Murphy stood the Central Community Relations Unit of the Northern Ireland Office (based in Belfast) and the Northern Ireland Office civil servants in London. The other principal actors on the Parliamentary stage, as regards the equality aspects of the Bill, were the Northern Ireland MPs in the Commons, and a few Labour backbenchers. In particular Kevin McNamara, MP, in the Commons and Lord Archer of Sandhill in the Lords both played key roles. Finally, Lord Lester of Herne Hill was the Liberal Democrat front-bench spokesperson on the equality aspects of the Bill in the Lords.

Outside the Houses of Parliament, the main actors were the Northern Ireland political parties, the Irish Government, the statutory equality agencies, and the loose coalition (including such bodies as the Northern Ireland Council on Ethnic Minorities, Unison and Disability Action) that took its cue largely from the briefings of the CAJ. Behind the scenes (only when the Bill was in its final stages was there any attempt to 'go public' on these issues), the CAJ and members of the coalition briefed influential figures in the United States Administration and Congress, British parliamentarians, the Irish Government and other NGOs, whilst also being consulted directly by Paul Murphy. Particular attention was paid by the CAJ and the statutory agencies to constructing a sufficient consensus across the Northern Ireland parties to make it difficult for others to argue that the Government should not 'take sides' between the parties on these issues. This resulted in several amendments being jointly supported by Ulster Unionists, the SDLP, and Liberal Democrats.

In the Commons Second Reading debate, considerable attention was given to the issue of amalgamation of the existing equality commissions, rather than the issues surrounding the equality duty on public authorities. Both the Secretary of State and Mr Murphy made a strong commitment to engage in further consultations during the summer months after the Bill had left the Commons and to amend the equality aspects of the Bill before consideration in the Lords. During the summer, Paul Murphy consulted extensively on the equality and human rights aspects of the Bill with the political parties represented in the Assembly, the chairs of the existing equality commissions, the CAJ, members of the coalition, and others. As a result of these meetings, it became clear that the Government was prepared to introduce extensive amendments on the equality aspects of the Bill.

On 14 October, a few days before the Committee stage was to begin, Mr Murphy announced the Government's response to the summer consultations on the equality issues in the Bill, and the type of amendments that it would support in the Lords. First, during the summer, confusion had arisen as to the allocation of responsibility for equality issues once powers were devolved to the new Assembly and Executive. The Murphy announcement proposed that the provisions of the Bill on equality (basically the Equality Commission and the equality duty) would be reserved matters. That meant that the Secretary of State would continue to have responsibility for them, although the Assembly would be able to legislate on these issues with the permission of the Secretary of State. However, the existing bodies of law on fair employment, gender equality, race relations and disability discrimination in Northern Ireland would become transferred matters, on which the Assembly would have legislative responsibility. The Bill would be amended, in addition, to ensure that the Assembly would be kept more closely informed on the enforcement of the new statutory equality duty.

Second, there was further clarification of the equality duty. The obligation would apply to UK government departments operating in Northern Ireland (including the Northern Ireland Office) as well as to Northern Ireland Departments and public bodies. Public bodies would be required to produce equality schemes, without being requested by the Equality Commission to do so, as had been the proposal until then. Greater detail would be included on what would be required to assess the impact of various policies on equality of opportunity. Assessments would include, for instance, consideration of alternatives that would better promote equality of opportunity. Public bodies would also be required to review their equality schemes on a five-yearly basis.

Some of the amendments introduced by the government at Committee stage reflected this announcement in a straightforward manner. However, others did not. First, although the amended legislation now imposed a duty on most public authorities to produce schemes, it included the awkward provision that the Equality Commission would have to ask new public authorities to produce a scheme. Second, the amendments meant that the Equality Commission would be able to specify that only some functions of a public authority would be affected by the requirement to produce a scheme. Third, there were no amendments requiring several other important aspects of impact analysis, including specification of the aims and purposes of the policy under assessment, specification of alternatives, specification of consultation procedures prior to decision making and specification of the reasons for the policy eventually adopted by the authority. Nor did the amendments include requirement of a five-yearly review by public authorities of the measures taken to comply with the equality duty. Taken together, the Government's amendments seemed to reflect neither the summer consultations nor the Murphy announcement.

Several other issues had arisen during the summer that needed clarification. First, the consultations indicated that an amendment would be forthcoming which permitted an 'affirmative action' exception to the 'equality of opportunity' duty on public authorities. There was a concern that, without this, the equality of opportunity duty could be used to argue against measures that aimed at the reduction of disadvantage. There was some evidence that the PAFT guidelines had been mistakenly interpreted by some government departments to undermine just such provisions (Department of Health and Social Services, 1997, annex 8). There was also a precedent for such an amendment. The Fair Employment Act 1976, which included an equality of opportunity provision, was amended in 1989 to include protection for affirmative action measures. Yet no such amendment appeared. Second, the schedule that included the details of the enforcement procedures on the equality duty was potentially ambiguous as to whether the impact of all policies would have to be assessed, or just those policies specifically concerned with equality of opportunity.

The Lords Committee stage debate saw a detailed consideration of all the outstanding equality issues. The main challenge to the Government was led by Lord Archer and Lord Lester, both briefed extensively by the Committee on the Administration of Justice, the coalition, the statutory agencies and others. The outcome was that between the Committee stage and Report stage in the House of Lords, the Government came up with many amendments or statements of clarification which met the concerns of those arguing for a more explicit approach, particularly on the equality duty on public authorities. Moreover, where Government felt an amendment was unnecessary, interpretative statements by Ministers often indicated why that was so.

THE NORTHERN IRELAND ACT 1998 AND EQUALITY

What, then, was the result of all these amendments and commitments? What does the Act, as finally passed, require? The Act establishes a new Equality Commission for Northern Ireland, to consist of not less than 14 nor more than 20 Commissioners appointed by the Secretary of State. The Secretary of State is to appoint one Commissioner as Chief Commissioner, and at least one Commissioner as Deputy Chief Commissioner. In making appointments, the Secretary of State is required, as far as practicable, to secure that the Commissioners, as a group, are representative of the community in Northern Ireland.

The Commission takes over the functions of the Fair Employment Commission for Northern Ireland, the Equal Opportunities Commission for Northern Ireland, the Commission for Racial Equality for Northern Ireland, and the Northern Ireland Disability Council, which are abolished. In exercising its functions the Equality Commission is required to aim to

secure an appropriate division of resources between the functions previously exercisable by each of these bodies, and to have regard to advice
offered by a 'consultative council'. This will be a group of people selected
by the Commission to advise in relation to the functions in question.

The provisions of the Bill on equality – basically the Equality
Commission and the equality duty – are to be reserved matters for which
the Secretary of State will have responsibility. The Assembly will be able
to legislate on these matters with the permission of the Secretary of State.
The existing bodies of law on fair employment, gender equality, race
relations and disability discrimination in Northern Ireland will become
transferred matters, on which the Assembly will have legislative responsibility. The Bill was amended to reflect this demarcation of responsibility.
In addition, further amendments were introduced to ensure that the
Assembly will be kept closely informed on the enforcement of the new
statutory equality duty.

Important safeguards are included in the Act. Potentially, any legislation
in the equality area can be made subject to the condition of cross-
community support. Also, the Assembly cannot legislate in a way that is
incompatible with rights under the European Convention on Human
Rights or European Community law (which is particularly relevant to
gender discrimination issues). Nor may the Assembly legislate in a way
that discriminates directly on grounds of religious belief or political
opinion. In addition, if the Assembly legislates in a way incompatible
with the UK's international obligations, the Secretary of State may decide
not to submit such a Bill for Royal Assent.

Section 75 provides that each 'public authority' is required, in carrying
out its functions relating to Northern Ireland, to have due regard to the
need to promote equality of opportunity between certain different
individuals and groups. The relevant categories here are persons of
different religious belief, political opinion, racial group, age, marital
status or sexual orientation; between men and women generally; persons
with a disability and persons without; and persons with dependants and
persons without. Without prejudice to these obligations, a public authority
in Northern Ireland is also, in carrying out its functions, to have regard to
the desirability of promoting good relations between persons of different
religious belief, political opinion or racial group. Schedule 9 makes
detailed provisions for the enforcement of these duties.

All public authorities included within the definition of public authority
are required to submit an equality scheme to the Equality Commission.
Only where a public authority has been notified in writing by the
Commission that it does not need to, is it exempted from producing
such a scheme. In Parliament, concern was expressed at the apparently

open-ended power of exemption granted to the Equality Commission. In response, the Government made it clear that it was only in very limited circumstances that the Government envisaged such exemptions being granted by the Commission either to a body entirely, or with regard to particular functions of a body (Murphy, 1998).

An equality scheme shall show how the public authority proposes to fulfil the duties imposed by section 75 in relation to the relevant functions, and specify a timetable for measures proposed in the scheme. The Act sets out in some detail (without being exhaustive) what an equality scheme must contain in order to be in compliance with the legislation. The list includes the authority's arrangements for assessing compliance with the duties under section 75, for consulting on matters to which a duty under that section is likely to be relevant (including details of the persons to be consulted), for assessing and consulting on the likely impact of policies adopted or proposed to be adopted by the authority on the promotion of equality of opportunity, for monitoring any adverse impact of policies adopted by the authority on the promotion of equality of opportunity, for publishing the results of such assessments and such monitoring, for training staff, and for ensuring, and assessing, public access to information and to services provided by the authority. In addition, an equality scheme shall conform to any guidelines as to form or content which are issued by the Equality Commission. These guidelines are subject to the approval of the Secretary of State.

The legislation also details what is required in an authority's publishing of its assessments. It must state the aims of the policy to which the assessment relates, details of any consideration given by the authority to measures which might mitigate any adverse impact of that policy on the promotion of equality of opportunity, and alternative policies which might better achieve the promotion of equality of opportunity. Also, in making any decision with respect to a policy adopted or proposed to be adopted by it, the authority is required to take into account any such assessment and consultation carried out in relation to the policy. The government also made it clear that it expected consultation 'to embrace those directly affected by a policy as well as non-governmental organisations and relevant statutory bodies' (Dubs, 1998).

What happens after a scheme is submitted for approval to the Equality Commission depends on what type of public body is involved. A distinction is made between Northern Ireland departments and public bodies, and United Kingdom-wide public bodies. A 'public authority' is defined to include any department, corporation or body listed in Schedule 2 to the Parliamentary Commissioner Act 1967 and designated for the purposes of this section by order made by the Secretary of State. The inclusion of these latter bodies, being mainly United Kingdom-wide government departments, has resulted in special arrangements being devised relating to the procedures with which they must comply regarding equality schemes.

We describe first what happens in the former case. On receipt of a scheme the Commission shall approve it, or refer it to the Secretary of State. Where the Commission refers a scheme to the Secretary of State, the Commission is required to notify the Northern Ireland Assembly in writing that it has done so and send the Assembly a copy of the scheme. Where a scheme is referred to the Secretary of State, he or she has three options: to approve it, to request the public authority to make a revised scheme, or to make a scheme for the public authority. Where the Secretary of State requests a revised scheme, or makes a scheme himself or herself, he or she shall notify the Assembly in writing. Where the Secretary of State has made a scheme for the public authority, he or she is required also to send the Assembly a copy of the scheme.

Certain of these provisions do not apply in the case of United Kingdom-wide departments. On receipt of a scheme submitted by a UK government department the Commission shall approve it, or itself request the department to make a revised scheme. Where such a request is made, the government department shall, if it does not submit a revised scheme to the Commission in the time provided, send to the Commission a written statement of the reasons for not doing so. The provisions relating to notification of the Assembly do not apply. Nor do the provisions empowering the Secretary of State to make schemes for the public body directly. These provisions are intended to 'avoid a situation where the Secretary of State must reach a decision or issue a direction in a case involving her Department or that of a Cabinet colleague' (Murphy, 1998).

If the Commission receives a complaint, made in accordance with certain formalities, of failure by a public authority to comply with an equality scheme approved by the Commission or made by the Secretary of State, it is required to investigate the complaint, or give the complainant reasons for not investigating. The formalities with which complaints must comply are that the complaint must be made in writing by a person who claims to have been directly affected by the failure. A complaint must also be sent to the Commission during the period of 12 months starting with the day on which the complainant first knew of the matters alleged. Before making a complaint the complainant must bring the complaint to the notice of the public authority, and give the public authority a reasonable opportunity to respond.

In addition to investigating on the basis of a complaint, however, it appears that the Equality Commission itself has power to carry out an investigation into the compliance by a public authority with an equality scheme without having received a valid complaint. Although there is room for doubt, the power to carry out such an investigation appears to be derived from the Equality Commission's general duty to keep under review the effectiveness of the duties imposed by section 75. Paragraph 11 of the Schedule, in addition, provides explicitly for the same conditions to be applied to investigations which arise from complaints as investigations which are 'carried out by the Commission where it believes that a public authority may have failed to comply with a scheme'.

What happens to the results of these investigations depends on the type of public authority involved. Again, a distinction is drawn between Northern Ireland and United Kingdom-wide public bodies. In the case of the former, the Commission is required to send a report of both types of investigation to the public authority concerned, the Secretary of State, the Assembly, and the complainant. If a report recommends action by the public authority concerned and the Commission considers that the action is not taken within a reasonable time, the Commission may refer the matter to the Secretary of State. Where a matter is referred to the Secretary of State, the Secretary of State may give directions to the public authority in respect of any matter referred to him. Where the Commission refers a matter to the Secretary of State it shall also notify the Assembly in writing that it has done so. Where the Secretary of State gives directions to a public authority, he or she shall notify the Assembly in writing that he or she has done so.

Somewhat different provisions apply in the case of United Kingdom-wide bodies. Certain of these provisions do not apply, particularly those empowering the Secretary of State to give directions to the public authority in respect of its failure to present a scheme. Instead, the Commission may lay before Parliament and the Assembly a report of any investigation regarding compliance with an equality scheme by such a department.

DELIVERING ON THE EQUALITY PROVISIONS OF THE AGREEMENT

The equality provisions of the Agreement represent a major development in efforts to create a more equal society in Northern Ireland – a shift from an anti-discrimination to a mainstreaming approach. Before looking at the problems that may arise in implementing this, it is important to stress their innovative nature both in Northern Ireland and in international terms.

Governments in North America, Western Europe, and the Commonwealth have sought to address the disadvantaged position of ethnic groups, women and others by developing anti-discrimination law in specific areas such as employment or housing, particularly in the private sector. In all countries of Western Europe, and much of the Common-wealth, such legislation is now in place. The Northern Ireland experience suggests, however, that while such legislation is necessary, it is insufficient by itself. The legislation is essentially negative, aiming to prevent discrimination, rather than positively to promote equality. There is, moreover, growing concern in many countries about the extent to which anti-discrimination norms are practically effective (Blumrosen, 1993). Attempts have been made to develop mechanisms to ensure greater compliance, for instance by creating specialised bodies tasked with enforcement, but these often have little effect on key government deci-sions. There have also been attempts to develop policies that bring the weight of government to bear more directly, for example, by making government contracts and grants to the private sector conditional on implementing equality policies. However, their influence touches only a limited sphere of activity.

In this chapter we have been examining an attempt to go several steps further to require government and public bodies to weave policies of equality and non-discrimination into the fabric of decision making across all spheres of government – in short, to 'mainstream' fairness issues in public policy. This attempt is particularly important if the problem is defined, as it increasingly is, as involving not only the problem of 'discrimination,' but the larger issue of unacceptable inequalities affecting women and particular minority groups, whether caused by discrimination or not.

How does mainstreaming differ from traditional anti-discrimination approaches? The most important difference is that it concentrates on achieving equality rather than simply eliminating discrimination. Mainstreaming involves government proactively taking equality into account. It is intended to be anticipatory rather than retrospective, to be extensively participatory rather than limited to small groups of the knowledgeable, and to be integrated into the activities of those involved in policy making. The motivation for mainstreaming lies in the realisation that unless special attention is paid to equality in policy making, it becomes too easily sidelined and submerged in the day-to-day concerns of policy makers who do not view equality as central to their concerns. Mainstreaming, by definition, attempts to address this problem by requiring all government departments to engage directly with equality issues.

Mainstreaming will have other, more indirect, consequences. One of these is to encourage greater transparency in decision making since it necessitates defining the likely impact of policies at an earlier stage of policy making, more systematically and to a greater extent than is usually contemplated. It will also encourage greater participation in policy making. Unlike more traditional mechanisms of consultation, mainstreaming as now to be practised in Northern Ireland requires impact assessments of a degree of specificity that establishes a clear agenda for discussion between policy makers and those most affected. In combination, impact assessment and participation will develop links between government and 'civil society', encouraging greater participation in decision making by marginal groups and lessening the democratic deficit.

There are dangers and limitations to mainstreaming. In particular, it may result in the over-fragmentation of equality policy, especially if it becomes an alternative to traditional anti-discrimination and other equality mechanisms. If all public bodies have responsibility for equality, there is the danger that none will regard it as an important part of their function. There is need, therefore, for some centralised responsibility within government to ensure that mainstreaming is consistently applied, according to common standards. Nor should one overlook the fact that building such a requirement into civil service decision making will require considerable cultural change. Apart from practical issues, there are problems of departmental exclusiveness and collective responsibility. Mainstreaming may well cut across the working practices, and potentially the ethos, of civil service bureaucracy. The dismal experience in Northern Ireland of the non-statutory PAFT approach to mainstreaming before the reforms introduced by the Northern Ireland Act 1998 is eloquent testimony to this.

The implication is that a strong political commitment to mainstreaming is absolutely crucial and must drive the new approach being taken by departments and other public bodies. But it means more than that. It means also that the legal status of mainstreaming needs to be considered. It is noticeable that many of the jurisdictions that have introduced mainstreaming have done so without according it any clear legal status. Mostly, mainstreaming has been introduced administratively by circular, without any formal legal underpinnings. At best, the status of mainstreaming in many countries is that of 'soft law'. The Northern Ireland experience points to the inadequacy of a 'soft law' approach. Whether a 'hard law' approach will be any more successful in Northern Ireland remains to be seen. It is to that issue that we now turn.

What are the prospects of the legal mainstreaming approach adopted in Northern Ireland being effective? The provisions of the Act are promises, not reality. They are a necessary part of the process of achieving substantive equality, fairness, and justice. But neither the provisions of the Agreement nor the Act itself delivers such change directly. This delivery will require political will at all levels. The provisions of the Act, in other words, represent the potential for change. The provisions will reframe the debate. But we must ensure that change actually occurs, particularly in the areas of greatest disadvantage.

The provisions will need to be put into effective operation. In this context there is a real difficulty. Ultimately, those who will have to operate this system day-to-day are the civil service and other public servants. The response of parts, and I stress parts, of the public service to these initiatives has been problematic in the past. Often it has been ungenerous and lacking in imagination. Sometimes, it seems that it has been actively opposed to necessary change. If the Agreement is to mark a new beginning for Northern Ireland, as is the wish of the vast majority of the population, all institutions have the obligation to change and adapt. The public service cannot be an exception to this, however difficult it must be for some to give up the almost unrestrained power they were able to exercise for a generation. For its own sake, as well as that of Northern Ireland as a whole, the civil service must not be seen as obstructive to this aspect of the Agreement. The Equality Commission can no doubt play a role in assisting the public service to adapt, but ultimately the responsibility will lie with the public service itself, the members of the Executive, and, of course, the Assembly, if it is established. (It is important to note, in passing, that the equality provisions of the Agreement incorporated in the Northern Ireland Act, including the equality duty, do not depend on the implementation of the other parts of the Agreement, for example those relating to the establishment of the Executive and the transfer of functions to the Assembly.)

The Assembly can provide an important forum in which the successes and problems of the equality provisions of the Agreement are monitored. It will be vital to build up a cooperative relationship between the Assembly and the major statutory body in the area, the Equality Commission, as well as with the various constituencies directly. The relationship between the Assembly and the Commission will be of considerable importance in the future. At several points there will be significant contact: the funding for the Equality Commission will come from Northern Ireland Departmental budgets overseen by the Executive and the Assembly. The Equality Commission will be reviewing the schemes which public bodies, including those overseen by the Executive and the Assembly, produce.

The relationship between the Assembly and the Equality Commission has considerable potential for problems. Two possibilities suggest themselves. A confrontational attitude could develop in which the Assembly sees the Commission as hostile and a threat, and engages in a war of attrition against it. Alternatively, the Assembly could regard the Commission as rather useful to it, forewarning it of problems that have not yet turned ugly, and enabling it to tackle them in a sensible way out of the glare of hostile publicity or international pressure. I suggest that the second, cooperative approach is the sensible way forward. For it to work, the Assembly's relevant committees need to develop a harmonious working relationship with the membership of the Commission, one based on a mutual respect and recognition of the different roles that each plays in the overall structure.

Much depends on the quality of people appointed to the new Equality Commission and on its effectiveness in managing the transition from four separate bodies into one. Initially, the operation of the new equality duty imposed on public authorities will depend on the Equality Commission's guidelines as to the criteria to be followed to comply with their statutory duty. Thereafter, it will be important to ensure that the guidelines are adhered to by the public authorities in their day-to-day practice. There will be substantial opportunity for the groups most affected to insert themselves into the policy-making process.

How far the promise of the Agreement's equality provisions is delivered will depend, therefore, on the commitment, determination and skill of all the parties in the Assembly, on a strong, well-financed, and independent Equality Commission, effective NGOs, and, crucially, on the political will to place equality at the heart of decision making. Using the new tools will be a challenge for politicians to ensure that human rights and equality remain central to political life, for the civil service and public authorities to incorporate a culture of human rights into administration, and for civil society to use these tools imaginatively and persistently. A lasting peace depends upon them all.

NOTES

[1] For further details and discussion of matters raised in this chapter, see McCrudden, 1999a.

6

A NEW BEGINNING? THE PROSPECTS FOR A POLITICS OF CIVILITY IN NORTHERN IRELAND

Arthur Aughey

INTRODUCTION

The Belfast Agreement of 10 April 1998 ideally established the possibility for a new beginning in relationships within Northern Ireland and between Northern Ireland and the Republic of Ireland. What this chapter suggests is that the possibility implicit in the Belfast Agreement is the ideal of political civility. The 'project' of the Agreement, therefore, might be termed the attempt to inscribe the *politics of civility* as the new political code for Northern Ireland and for the engagement between North and South. However, the Agreement has equally the potential to secure the old political code, that familiar code which inscribes sectarian rancour in the conduct of public life in Northern Ireland. If the old Stormont parliament used to be called 'a factory of grievances' then the new devolved administration, if it survives, could very well become 'an assembly of antagonisms'. This prospect would mean the survival of what might be called the *politics of incivility*. This chapter explores contemporary politics in Northern Ireland using the civility/incivility index as a way to measure the post-Agreement challenges to, as well as opportunities for, parties and their electorates. It also considers 'the limits of tolerance' within which democratic politics may be said to work effectively.

Recent commentary on Northern Ireland politics has emphasised the need for trust. Indeed, one phrase abstracted from the body of conflict resolution theory – 'confidence-building measures' – has become part of the small change of popular discourse in the aftermath of the Belfast Agreement. It may be suggested that what is broadly intimated in this particular expression is the need to make the transition from one style of politics – the politics of incivility – to another style of politics – the politics of civility. This chapter assesses the respective qualities of both these codes. It begins with an extended examination of the condition of civility. This is followed by a much briefer distillation of the condition of incivility, brief because of its local familiarity. The provisions of the Belfast Agreement are then assessed in the light of this discussion.

THE CONDITION OF CIVILITY

Political civility involves a style of politics which acknowledges difference and diversity but also acknowledges a common interest beyond difference and diversity. That common interest can be taken to mean subscription to a notion of the general good or it can be taken to mean acknowledgement of the mutual advantage of common institutions, which acknowledgement itself constitutes a moral (as distinct from an instrumental) practice. Political civility, then, is more than a mere style of interpersonal good will. It is also more than a mere style of government (though it can be also both of these things). Rather, the politics of civility assumes a specific sort of relationship between individuals and between communities. It assumes a relationship of obligation and recognition which governs the contest between the interests and parties in a political association. In the last decade, and corresponding with the fall of communism, there has been increased interest in the ideal of 'civil society' and the relationship between the 'civil condition' and contemporary liberal democratic politics. This has generated quite a large and stimulating literature (Keane, 1988; Seligman, 1992; Tester, 1992; Gellner, 1996; Hann and Dunn, 1996; Fine and Rai, 1997). However, consideration of what is distinctive about the condition of civility has a much longer history than this recent flurry of interest. Reference to two acute students of that condition may provide a guide to its attributes. The first of these writers, Edward Shils, may be taken to be a theorist of a politics of civility involving the idea of a common good. The second, Michael Oakeshott, may be taken to be a theorist of a more formal ideal of civility which does not rest on any purposeful or substantive common good.

In an extended study of the sociology of modernity, Edward Shils has argued that liberal democratic institutions cannot work without a minimum of civility (even though he could provide no exact calculus with which to determine precisely what that minimum might be). For Shils, civility may be defined as an attitude of attachment to the whole of society. It is 'simultaneously individualistic, parochial and "holistic"'. More fundamentally 'civility is the conduct of a person whose individual self-consciousness had been partly superseded by his collective self-consciousness, the society as a whole and the institution of civil society being the referents of his collective self-consciousness' (Shils and Grosby,

1997, p. 335). The practical political relevance of this definition becomes clearer in the following statement:

> Civility as a feature of civil society considers others as fellow citizens of equal dignity in their rights and obligations as members of civil society; it means regarding other persons, including one's adversaries, as members of the same inclusive collectivity, i.e., as members of the same society, even though they belong to different parties or to different religious communities or to different ethnic groups. Civility in the former sense is included in civility in the latter sense. But in the latter sense, it includes concern for the good of adversaries as well as for the good of allies (pp. 338–9).

It is in this way, argues Shils, that one can specify the distinction between civility 'understood as good manners or courtesy and civility as the virtue of civil society' (p. 339). And as Shils is at pains to make clear, civility so understood and civility so achieved in the everyday practice of liberal democratic politics liberates that politics from the threatening antagonisms of Carl Schmitt's friend/enemy dichotomy (see below, p. 133). What Shils recommends is something which Schmitt himself acknowledged as an achievement of civilisation. For instance, Schmitt was fond of quoting Arthur Balfour's introduction to Bagehot's *The English Constitution* to the effect that the 'whole political machinery presupposes a people so fundamentally at one that they can safely afford to bicker; and so sure of their own moderation that they are not dangerously disturbed by the never-ending din of political conflict' (Schmitt, 1985a, p. xxii). That satisfactory condition, one experienced by settled political associations, is characteristic of a tradition of civility. It has not been, however, the characteristic of political life in Northern Ireland.

Of course, the pluralism of a modern democratic society will not resolve all antagonisms. Indeed, it will actually bring forth new conflicts and differences. Like Isaiah Berlin, Shils assumes a pluralism which acknowledges that ideals and interests are incommensurate (Berlin, 1990). This does not weaken the practicality of the politics of civility. Rather, it gives added force to the value of civility for the 'rules of pluralist society not only permit these conflicts; they even arouse them to greater intensity. Civility diminishes the intensity of these conflicts' (p. 343). It does not rule them out. Shils, though, tends to contradict this open ended pluralism with the suggestion that the greatest value of civility is 'to permit government to work effectively towards the common good' (p. 347). Put in this fashion, it suggests a substantive purpose for government and implies a special wisdom as the criterion for public office. Shils is aware of this problem and defines the common good as civil society itself. Civility becomes the concern to maintain civil society *as a civil society*. 'Civility is therefore a concern to reconcile – not abolish –

divergent interests'(p. 346). Nevertheless, the tension between divergent interests on the one hand and a single common good as the end of government policy on the other remains unresolved in Shils's many essays on the subject.

A more rigorously philosophical approach is to be found in the work of Michael Oakeshott, particularly in his most comprehensive work *On Human Conduct* (1975). Oakeshott defines political civility in the following manner:

> Engagement in politics entails a disciplined imagination. It is to put by for another occasion the cloudy enchantments of Schlafraffenland, the earth flowing with milk and honey and the sea transmuted into ginger beer, it is to forswear the large consideration of human happiness and virtue, the mysteries of human destiny, the rift that lies between the aspiration of human beings and the conditions of human life, and even the consideration of the most profitable or least burdensome manner of satisfying current wants, and to focus attention upon civility; that is, upon a practice of just conduct and upon the conditions which should be required to be acknowledged and subscribed to under threat of civil penalty or sentence of civil disability (1975, p. 164).

It cannot be doubted that Oakeshott's characteristic conservatism is implicated in this appeal to a politics of modesty. It has about it the ring of Paul Kornfeld's appeal (Richie 1998, p. 333) to fellow Expressionists during the travails of the Weimar Republic: 'Let us hear no more about war, revolution and the salvation of the world. Let us be modest and turn our attention to smaller things'. If it was true that political debate in Weimar was devoid of a modest and practical consideration of political aims and means then it has been equally true of political debate in Northern Ireland. The Belfast Agreement may be read as an invitation to make do with smaller but achievable things. If so, then Oakeshott's appeal is of relevance.

By civility Oakeshott, like Shils, does not mean decency or politesse. It is not a mere aristocratic affectation of manners. The term 'civility' is a way of talking about the relationship between citizens or (as Oakeshott chooses to call them) *cives*. It involves the following engagement:

> a common concern that the pursuit of all purposes and the promotion of all interests, the satisfaction of all wants and the propagation of all beliefs shall be in subscription to conditions formulated in rules indifferent to the merits of any interest or the truth or error of any belief and consequently not itself a substantial interest or doctrine (p. 172).

The sometimes delphic formulation that Oakeshott employs may be taken to mean that the relationship of civility consists in relative strangers being just to one another, tolerating diversity and respecting the freedom of other citizens. Civility, as Oakeshott portrays it, is an order of moral and not instrumental considerations. Its authority is to be found within the practice itself and not in its conformity to some basic, extra-historical norm nor, certainly, in its attachment to some ultimate end of human struggle. It finds its expression in 'agents exploring their relations in terms of a language of understanding and intercourse which is native to and is continuously re-enacted by those who use it' (p. 124). The use of the expression 'native to' does not suggest primordiality. From the text of *On Human Conduct* it can only be taken to imply something which is historically achieved and contingently preserved. The traditional character it may attain is based on its continued authority. In turn that authority is based on its continued use.

According to Paul Franco, Oakeshott's evocation of the condition of civility reminds us of Hegel's notion of *Sittlichkeit*. This is important, argues Franco, when it comes to differentiating Oakeshott's notion of civility from that of the theorists of a formal *Rechtstaat* as well as those who would interpret his theory as being 'value-neutral' (Franco, 1990, pp. 182–3). For Oakeshott, the neutrality of civil prescriptions is only a half-truth, the formal side of a deeply human (and humane) disposition. This is because Oakeshott's understanding, despite its abstract language, is thoroughly historical. The principles of civility are an abridgement of the practice of civility, a practice achieved, in its variety, by liberal democratic polities. We only become confused if we give priority to the abstraction (rationalism) over the varied practice. Civility, then, is the articulating principle of a distinctive way of political life. It requires common subscription to 'rules; the language of civil intercourse is the language of rules; *civitas* is rule-articulated association' (Oakeshott, 1975, p. 124). But, it must be emphasised again, these rules together constitute a genuine morality and not an abstract shell. Nor is it a case of historical luck – you either inherit the practice of civility (good luck) or you never have it (bad luck). To argue this would be submit to another abstraction, that of historical determinism. Oakeshott does not evade the burden of responsibility which attends the activity of politics. In a criticism of the sort of discourse theory which attempts to reach demonstrable truth (and thus denies the choices which politicians have to make) Oakeshott noted (1991, p. 95):

> a craving for demonstrative political argument may corrupt us by suggesting that we have not got to make choices, sometimes on little more than the courage of our convictions, or by suggesting that we can pass off the responsibility for making these choices upon some axiom or 'law' for which, in turn, we have no justification.

It is possible for circumstances to change because politics can draw upon creative and imaginative resources. And that change, inscribed in the practice of a community, can become habitual and conventional. And at some future date a popular historian, forgetting its contingency, may come to describe it as the 'genius' of the people. In truth, argued Oakeshott, this relies on the continued performance by individuals of the '"historic" self-enacted reflective consciousness' (1975, p. 56).

This is a very subtle and elusive idea and it may be useful to use a sporting analogy to help bring out its meaning. Writing about the conventions of sport and their connections with the 'ethico-philosophic' character of the game, Simon Barnes identifies them with what might be called the 'the spirit of fair play'. He argues that the 'spirit of cricket exists, but like the spirit of football or the spirit of anything, it is elusive of definition. The attempt to define it with words assumes that the spirit can be separated from the body, that it exists, as it were, platonically' (Barnes, *The Times*, 1999). This is an impossibility for 'the spirit of any game only exists as a living thing, as part of the comings and goings of the game'. The significance of sporting conventions lies in this. They are 'courtesies that demonstrate that the encounter between the players is not a serious matter. Serious, I mean, as in life in death'. Just so for sport. In politics this can be true only up to a point. Political civility also resembles an encounter of this sort except that it is a serious matter. It *is* about life and death and so requires 'civil penalty' for those in breach of it. Or, as the Weimar jurist Hermann Heller once put it, the value of a culture of civility lies in the 'belief in the existence of a common ground for discussion and in *fair play* for the opponent, with whom one wants to reach agreement under conditions that exclude naked force' (Schmitt, 1985 b, p. xxxviii). (The open question of Northern Ireland politics – the Agreement notwithstanding – has been and remains whether such common ground exists, whether people are agreed on the meaning of fair play or, indeed, whether they want to reach agreement under any acceptable conditions.) These observations need further specification.

It is necessary, first of all, to state what the politics of civility does *not* mean. It does not mean that 'anything goes' and that there are no boundaries or limits to what is acceptable. This notion is inconsistent with the politics of civility. The simple view of celebrating diversity for its own sake is reminiscent of what the American novelist Kurt Vonnegut, in *The Sirens of Titan*, called a 'chrono-synclastic infundibulum'. A chrono-synclastic infundibulum is that place in the universe where all the different kinds of truths fit together as nicely as the parts of a watch. In a chrono-synclastic infundibulum we would not have to worry about making choices or deciding between acceptable and unacceptable behaviour for everything would be permitted. That might be magnificent but it is not politics.

Neither does it mean the absolute triumph of what George Santayana called dismissively 'vacant liberty'. Santayana's problem with the prescriptions of traditional liberalism is also the problem many have with some of the propositions of contemporary multi-culturalism. The problem is a simple one. It is the problem of abstract rationalism, a high-minded egalitarianism of respect, and of esteem, which is at logical odds with the very pluralism it seeks to promote. In the politically incorrect language of *Dominations and Powers* Santayana put the objection thus:

> Merely to relax order and to be more and more tolerant will not therefore secure peace, unless the liberal peace works as a magic sedative, and gently destroys the possibility of discontent. Such was perhaps the secret expectation of liberal statesmen. Open every door, let in the light and air, smile upon the Red Indian in his feathers and the Chinaman in his pigtail, and the diffused and placid twilight of goodwill would bathe the moral universe for ever. Everybody would be happy at home, like the Englishman having his solitary tea in his garden; and all wars would be at an end because, at heart, there would be nothing left to fight for. Good will and mutual acquaintance would gradually rub off those remaining differences (1951, p. 449).

For Santayana all that such unlimited toleration would achieve – theoretically, not practically, for it is impossible to achieve practically, even within liberalism's own terms of reference – is the 'euthanasia of differences'. As a consequence everybody 'would be free to be what he liked, and no one would care to be anything but what pleased everybody'. The substance of Santayana's point is clear. Liberal abstraction, found sometimes in the simple incantation of human rights, is disposed to defend difference in theory but cannot really come to terms with it in practice when it discovers that goodwill alone is not enough.

As a disposition in politics, as a disposition to avoid conflict at all costs, this is one familiar aspect of the ideology of peace in Northern Ireland. What frequently characterises these contributions is a hostility to party politics itself, a style of politics which is thought to be an obstacle to the moral universe of goodwill. Democratic Dialogue, for example, took to calling local politicians a 'partitocrazia' (the reference was obvious), who were blocking the reconstitution of politics in Northern Ireland. The premise was that those 'who would advocate a multi-ethnic, multi-cultural approach arguably comprise a political majority . . . yet are currently divided across a range of parties, as well as being heavily represented outside all of them' (1996, p. 64). What Democratic Dialogue envisaged was a 'rapid rush towards the political centre (in nationalist–unionist terms) and new political formations' (p. 65). Santayana's view about such hopes in *Domination and Powers* is perhaps quite instructive: 'Concession and tolerance and equality would thus have really led to peace, and to peace of the most radical kind, the peace of moral extinction. Between two nothings there is eternal peace; but between two somethings if they come within range of each other, there is always danger of war' (p. 449).

The tragedy here is the tragedy of those whose politics aspire to do as they wish (eternal peace) but who end up never getting what they want because of the impossibility of inclusivity without limit (danger of war). And in a nutshell, that is the frustrating danger and the ultimate illusion of a thoroughgoing philosophy of inclusiveness. It has a tendency to lead towards a politics of non-negotiable demands based either on felt need or on communal self-esteem. The way to avoid this consequence, Santayana believed, was through what he called chivalry. While quaint, the term does come close to the idea of civil politics. As Noel O'Sullivan interprets it, chivalry 'does not require any abandonment of one's own interests; it does not aim, as liberalism aims, at the elimination of power from the world; what it does is reject man's tendency to attach absolute significance to those interests' (O'Sullivan, 1992, p. 88). There are, of course, many problems with Santayana's critique of modern political illusions, so many indeed that it would be inappropriate to consider them in this chapter. Nevertheless, his earthy naturalism, his sense of the determinateness of human existence and therefore of politics and, in particular, his refusal to be diverted from the fact of power at the core of the political is a useful corrective to the idealisation of civil society and to the demonisation of party politics.

Nor is the politics of civility simply a way of stating in another form the 'ideal speech situation' of Jürgen Habermas. His vision of a decision-making process informed by the principle of discussion free from domination is certainly an attractive one. The distinction between purposive-rational action, governed by technical rules and concerned with choosing means to an end, and communicative action, governed by binding consensual norms which define reciprocal expectations and are ends in themselves, is an important one. It is not unique, however, and the philosophical lineage of it may be traced – with a very different emphasis – in the work of Oakeshott as well. The idea of communicative action, indeed, does capture much of the character of political civility. Moreover, the symmetrical relationship Habermas requires of communication identifies the importance of freedom and equality of citizenship which must be always at the heart of civil politics. The intimation, though, that somehow differences can be resolved because it is possible to achieve perfect clarity is fatal to a civil politics. It neglects the limits to communication and the requirement for decision. As Robert Berki brilliantly points out, Habermas's theory cannot avoid, by a redescription of the contrast, all the problems of the Marxist distinction between alienation and communist freedom. Berki continues that 'one might respond to his thesis by arguing that in the "ideal speech-situation" there would be nothing to talk about; if there were no domination and roles were really interchangeable, then the ideal notions of "truth", "freedom" and "justice" would entirely lose their meaning' (Berki, 1981, pp. 253–4). Or, as one hostile critic put it, 'Habermas's linguistic emancipation could be secured by commanding universal silence' (Scruton, 1985, p. 123). Like the vacant liberals criticised by Santayana, in this view Habermas either wants to abolish power by equating the political with the rational or to make the universality of the rational a power to command silence. A local example of this is worthy of comment.

Exploring the appropriateness of Habermasian discourse ethics to the Northern Ireland crisis Shane O'Neill (1994) also reveals the limitation of that approach. He asserts that since unionists 'have failed to provide Nationalists with a moral justification for the border, they have had to rely on coercion to uphold their unequal status. The Union with Britain has been defended not with reasons but with power' (p. 375). Reciprocally, of course, as far as the first part goes, it could be said that nationalists have never provided unionists with a moral justification for removing the border. The reason for this is that, until recently, nationalists have rarely bothered to address their arguments to unionists at all. They have been more concerned to have British governments do their arguing for them, i.e. that it is the task of the British government to coerce unionists into accepting the 'moral justification' of the nationalist case (i.e. to see reason). As far as the second part of O'Neill's statement is concerned it is simply untrue to argue that the Union has never been defended with 'reasons'. The truth is rather different. It is that the reasons proposed by unionists have been either dismissed by nationalists as self-serving sophistry or they have gone unnoticed because it is assumed that unionists, by definition, have no rational arguments to make (which appears to be O'Neill's view). Finally, of course power is a vital element of the political and not a contingent one. There is no political order in which this is not the case. O'Neill's recommendation in favour of 'the sharper normative bite that discourse ethics provides' resolves itself into the republican fantasy that the political talks about the future of Northern Ireland could ignore the fact of the Union and popular support for it. In other words, the rationalism of discourse ethics abstracts Northern Ireland from its historical, constitutional and normative situation. 'Nothing', argues O'Neill, 'is ruled out nor is anything guaranteed, least of all the boundaries, or indeed the existence, of the political entity of Northern Ireland' (p. 377). Silence is commanded on history and on the principle of consent. Unionists must be made to see reason. They need to be forced to be free.

So much for 'reason'. So much for 'power'. O'Neill, by the wonders of discourse ethics, has become in his own terms a 'Unionist' – someone whose argument relies not on 'reason' alone but also on 'power'. It must also be said that his argument then becomes politically intelligible if politically unpersuasive. It is unpersuasive not because it infringes the requirements of discourse ethics. It is unpersuasive because it has lost touch with the requirements of liberal democratic politics.

In sum, the ideal of civility is the acknowledgement and acceptance of diversity within a framework of formal rules. Identification with those rules and procedures creates a political association of a definite and distinctive kind. That association is defined not by a common purpose but by the acceptance of a mode of relationship to others within that association. The rules of political civility together constitute a grammar of conduct in which we disclose our wants and enact (honour/dishonour) the virtue or spirit of the association. The rules do not assume a rational consensus about the 'ends' of politics. If this is taken to be a simple conservative notion tied to a limited conception of the political then it is interesting to note that the most suggestive exploration of its character recently has been by the French radical feminist, Chantal Mouffe.

Mouffe's recent work, *The Return of the Political*, is a unique appropriation of ideas from an eclectic range of theorists bringing together as it does thinkers normally associated with the authoritarian right, like Schmitt, thinkers normally associated with liberal conservatism, like Oakeshott, and thinkers of the left, most notably MacPherson, Skinner and Gramsci. *The Return of the Political* is an attempt to restate the ideal of civil association in a manner capable of sustaining the achievements of a modern liberal democracy without surrendering those achievements to the market liberals' 'evasion of the political'. Mouffe takes issue with much of what informs thinking about democratic politics today. This contemporary thinking, argues Mouffe, 'can be characterised as rationalist, universalist and individualist'. As she explains it in her introduction:

> Once we accept the necessity of the political and the impossibility of a world without antagonism, what needs to be envisaged is how it is possible under those conditions to create or maintain a pluralistic democratic order. Such an order is based on a distinction between 'enemy' and 'adversary'. It requires that, within the context of the political community, the opponent should be considered not as an enemy to be destroyed, but as an adversary whose existence is legitimate and must be tolerated. We will fight against his ideas but we will not question his right to defend them. The category of the 'enemy' does not disappear but is displaced; it remains pertinent with respect to those who do not accept the democratic 'rules of the game' and who thereby exclude themselves from the political community (1993, p. 4).

Antagonistic forces will never disappear in political life. These antagonistic forces, however, can be accommodated by creative political thinking. But there remain those who cannot be included because their inclusion contradicts the very character of the association:

> Political life concerns collective, public action; it aims at constructing a 'we' in a context of diversity and conflict. But to construct a 'we' it must be distinguished from a 'them', and that means establishing a frontier, defining an 'enemy'. Therefore, while politics aims at constructing a political community and creating a unity, a fully inclusive political community and a final unity can never be realized [sic] since there will permanently be a 'constitutive outside', an exterior to the community that makes its existence possible (p. 69).

In other words, a political association survives on the basis of making hard decisions about what is acceptable and what is unacceptable behaviour. But lest Mouffe may seem to read like an unreconstructed authoritarian, the bond of the association is defined openly and liberally. What binds citizens together 'is their common recognition of a set of ethico-political values. In this case, citizenship is not just one identity among others, as in liberalism, or the dominant identity that overrides all others, as in civic republicanism. It is an articulating principle that affects the different subject positions of the social agent . . . while allowing for a plurality of specific allegiances and for respect of individual liberty' (p. 70). Mouffe, like Oakeshott, here acknowledges the *sittlich* quality of civility. It is not an abstract identity or political persona but a real flow of sympathy within the public realm. Her exploration of this sympathy in contemporary Europe is a *tour de force*. It is also relevant to politics in Northern Ireland. Let us now turn our attention briefly to the politics of incivility.

THE INEVITABILITY OF INCIVILITY?

Political incivility, at its most extreme, is the politics of violent confrontation, the persistence of civil conflict. Such violent confrontation has been taken, with good reason, to be typical of the political code in Northern Ireland. However, even in a situation where active paramilitarism is absent, political incivility can take the form of communal self-assertion and mutual provocation. And it is this pervasive sort of corrosive and purposefully destabilising incivility which has been a characteristic of traditional political life in Northern Ireland even when there has been an absence of violence. As a code it has appeared to embody the truth of Carl Schmitt's observation in his influential study, *The Concept of the Political*. If the appropriate distinctions in morality are good and evil, in aesthetics beautiful and ugly, in economics profitable and unprofitable, then for Schmitt the specific 'distinction to which political actions and motives can be reduced is that between friend and enemy' (Schmitt, 1976, p. 27).

The 'friend/enemy' distinction is a criterion denoting 'the utmost degree of intensity of a union or separation, of an association or dissociation'. Political life in Northern Ireland has been taken to reveal the condition and the consequences of such communal separation and dissociation. Politics, in this view, is about winning and losing, about victory and surrender, about mastery and humiliation. That, it is believed, is the true nature of the political. Real enemies have nothing to discuss. They can only manoeuvre. The enemy, as Schmitt made clear, need not be 'personal'. Individual relationships and encounters could very well be cordial. But at the collective level in Northern Ireland relationships could be nothing other than confrontational and potentially threatening. This relationship does not always and necessarily entail widespread and overt inter-communal violence. As Richard Rose once observed, what was distinctive about the old Stormont regime before 1969 was its stability (Rose, 1971).

The assumption that there does indeed exist the real possibility of such violence informs political attitudes in Northern Ireland. More to the point, that assumption helps to explain why disagreements *within* communities about the nature of the struggle *between* the communities frequently tend to be so bitter. For example, Sinn Féin until very recently was in the habit of calling the SDLP the 'Stoop Down Low Party'. The word 'Lundy' has never been far from the lips of members of the DUP in their description of Ulster Unionist Party leaders. Since the outbreak of the Troubles the view that communal antagonism is irremovable has been more than a countervailing force to political models of institutional accommodation or exhortations to respect the diversity of cultural traditions. The business of definitive compromise usually has been interpreted by political leaders and their communities as a threat to their own positions and interests without coming close to satisfying the ambitions of the enemy. Much of what has happened in the political life of Northern Ireland over the last 30 years may be gauged by that practical rule of thumb. Indeed, right up until the very moment when the Agreement was signed the expectation of most people was that it would not happen. The assumption was that the parties could never agree. (If that proved to be a negative myth then a subsequent positive myth has emerged, namely, that the parties to the peace process will always over-come their difficulties. This, it must be remembered, *is* a myth, albeit a useful one.) The relationship of political incivility, of course, has deep histo-rical roots. It is necessary only to take a few examples of insight into this.

For instance, Donald Akenson's exploration of the cultural and social characteristics of Ireland in the nineteenth century showed how, by their self-referential and self-enclosed views, ordinary Protestants and Catholics magnified their (small) cultural differences out of reasonable proportion, thereby encouraging the potential for political violence.

> So strong was each belief system that in local societies individual Catholics and Protestants could cooperate effectively on small matters without undercutting their respective sets of beliefs. There was room in each system for the honourable exception, the Protestant who turned Nationalist, the Catholic who voted Unionist, and for the everyday good neighbour. On divisive matters, Protestants and Catholics lived in different mental worlds and on occasions (as in 1920–2), these worlds collided disastrously (Akenson, 1991, p. 148).

Writing in 1961 and during a period of relative security and prosperity, the Quakers Barritt and Carter noted that there was no assurance that the sort of divisions of the past described by Akenson were becoming any softer. Though 'the two communities in Northern Ireland live side by side, generally at peace' and though the people are linked by 'many ties of personal friendship, and by occasional ventures in co-operation' the potential for violent confrontation still existed. They observed that a 'divided education and a divided social and political life tend to deepen and confirm the fundamental cleavage' (Barritt and Carter, 1962, pp. 1–2). And with all the realism that their historical and empirical research obliged them to believe, they concluded their study by remarking: 'even when the divisions in the Northern Ireland community have been freed of all the accretions of emotional unreason, they remain real and profound' (p. 152). Barritt and Carter, though, certainly did not imagine that within a decade of the publication of their subtle and seminal work that bitter sectarian violence and overt communal strife would be taken for granted as the basic norm of political life in Northern Ireland.

Two political generations later and even the normally optimistic Democratic Dialogue remained cautious about the possibilities of a shift to a new political code and the emergence of a less uncivil style of politics – at least if that shift was to depend on the parties to achieve it. In frustration at what seemed the unchanging constancy of traditional politics in Northern Ireland, Democratic Dialogue could look only to an idealised 'civil society' as the catalyst for change. Writing in October 1997, only six months before the signing of the Belfast Agreement, Democratic Dialogue (1997, p. 12) argued:

> While one *could* envisage the building of trust overtime, thereby rendering unionists less fevered about their Britishness and northern nationalists less fundamentalist about their Irishness, in today's atmosphere – more polarised

than in 1973 – a dangerously high degree of wishful thinking seems required to anticipate such a benign scenario. More plausible is that recently held out by one of Ireland's most respected businessmen: 20, 30 or 40 years of further constitutional protagonism – peaceful or otherwise.

Moreover, there have been and there remain those who argue that a policy which seeks a balanced accommodation in Northern Ireland has never understood the nature of the struggle. To take one example, Robert McCartney has proposed consistently that it is a logically impossible prospectus which claims that two mutually antagonistic positions can be satisfied. The Belfast Agreement would be yet another example of this impossibilism. It cannot possibly be true that at one and the same time unionists can argue that the Agreement means that Northern Ireland's place within the United Kingdom is not only safe but strengthened and that nationalists and republicans can argue that the Agreement means that the objective of working towards Irish unity has been substantially advanced. Furthermore, the political structures of the Agreement, when and if they became operative, will simply become the focus of intense destabilisation. This view is composed of a number of parts.

On the unionist side it is believed that the politics of revolutionary movements like Sinn Féin/IRA is all about manoeuvre and manipulation, the intention of which is to weaken communal opponents. The institutions of the Agreement, far from providing a forum in which intercommunal bargains can be translated into collective stability, will become yet another site of sectarian disorder. The advanced nationalism of Sinn Féin will drag the moderates of the SDLP reluctantly in its wake. On the nationalist side, it is often held that the hostility to change which defines unionism means that it is incapable of making the required adjustments to the demands of equality and political consensus. Thirdly, many – unionist and nationalist – assume that it will not be possible to form a coherent government, because the parties are actually antagonistic to one another. As a result, the political game will become one of shifting the blame. The parties will blame the Secretary of State for inadequate financial resources, and other parties for failing to agree to their own favourite schemes. Add to this the presence of one or more parties with a vested interest in destabilising the state, and the prospects for good government are poor. Even if there is no return to full-scale political violence, the politics of incivility will triumph. For some there is no escape from that fate and it is cruel for politicians and commentators to suggest otherwise. The faith placed in a transition to political civility is the politics of cloud-cuckoo land.

Some of these observations on the cultural depth of political antagonism in Northern Ireland and the historical continuity of communalism are well made. They stand as a warning and a reminder of the difficulties which attend the politics of civility. However realistic they may be about the character of sectarianism, taken absolutely they do have their limitations for a complete understanding of political activity. Straightforward communalism or communitarianism, especially of a fatalistic or historically inevitable character, cannot do full justice to the political and its relative autonomy. It takes too narrow a view of what constitutes 'community' and what constitutes 'tradition' and, therefore, what might be possible politically. Rather like Hegel's moral – that one cannot learn to swim without getting wet – sometimes taking the political plunge (the famous Disraelian 'leap in the dark') creates a new set of circumstances which can transform what is considered practicable. And this, of course, depends on leadership and good judgement and what Harold Macmillan was wont to call 'events' (cf. Oakeshott above).

A rather good example of the intellectual limitation of the communitarian approach is Norman Porter's otherwise valuable book, *Rethinking Unionism*. This is not to argue that this book advocates incivility. Indeed, it argues quite the reverse. It is merely to illustrate the weakness of its high moralism which, because of philosophical assumptions about politics, could never explain the real process of negotiating the Agreement. Thus Porter argued, on the one hand, that unionist politics has only a narrow communally defined vision of politics, confined to 'paltry forms of political conduct which betray a narrowness of mind and a miserliness of spirit'; and on the other hand, to propose that the objective of political activity should be to transform the condition of unionism into a civic one which would 'celebrate the centrality of dialogue in political affairs and the need to be open to horizons beyond one's own' (1996, p. 11). But if, as Porter has argued, this civic tradition falls outside unionism's 'visual range' and 'lies beyond the horizon' of individual unionists then this is a self-defeating and yet, at the same time, a self-fulfilling mission. On the one hand, if agreement did come about Porter could claim that his book had made unionists see the light. On the other hand, if there was no agreement then he could equally claim that it proved his thesis about unionist narrowness of mind. It was a philosopher's no-loss case. Indeed, Porter (1998) appears to claim both of these things at once in the revised edition of his book – the Agreement is a model of his view of politics and its difficulties are to be found in a unionist narrowness of mind. There is no intimation, however, in the first edition of Porter's book that unionists, intellectually limited as they are, could ever sign up to the arrangements of the Belfast Agreement without, in an essential way, *ceasing to be unionists* (ironically, the very same sort of accusation made against the Ulster Unionist Party by its critics who oppose the Belfast Agreement). And the reason for this is clear.

The situated (unionist) self assumed by Porter's communitarianism is a caricature of the multiple, contradictory and diverse influences which together constitute unionist politics in particular and the situation in which unionists find themselves in general. His unionist – of whatever variety – was an abstraction from a complex and contradictory reality. Porter also ignored the possibility that cultural mentalities do not limit absolutely the possibilities of political choice. Porter's classification did not exhaust what one might understand by the term 'tradition'. Indeed, the tradition in which unionist politics can situate itself may be as wide as liberal democracy itself. This provides it with large rhetorical room for manoeuvre given appropriate leadership and appropriate encouragement. In other words, as Michael Oakeshott once argued, tradition is not a fixed and inflexible manner of doing things. It is not a groove along which people are condemned to live out their existence. It is 'a flow of sympathy' with the past and is open to modification by chance and circumstance. The help we may get from a tradition 'shared by a number of societies' is 'conditional upon our being able to assimilate them to our own arrangements and our own manner of attending to our arrangements' (Oakeshott, 1991, p. 59).

Porter's hermeneutical communalism does not allow sufficient play for such assimilation, for the contingency of politics or for the integrity of the political. Nor, as David Trimble himself noted in a speech to his party conference in 1996, had Porter been attentive to the changes in commitments which had taken place in Ulster Unionist policy in the previous decade (Bew, 1999, p. 5). Many of the changes he demanded in order for unionists to become 'civic' had already been accepted by the Ulster Unionist Party in the Brooke/Mayhew talks of 1991–2. Porter's analysis left unionism (in this case) standing on the Irish equivalent of Dover Beach. This was certainly not as Porter would have desired it but it is where his logic led. His book exemplified the limitation of the 'cultural' approach identified by Ruane and Todd, that approach in which the solution to the problem is to be sought 'in education, exhortation and the reconciliation of traditions' (Ruane and Todd, 1991, p. 27). It had no place for David Trimble's calculations and judgement.

History bears down on the present and politicians shoulder its weight. It can fix them with its gravity in the positive sense in which people speak of roots. It can also encourage politicians to act only on the basis of what experience obliges them to believe. And this can sometimes lead to a perversely conservative judgement that nothing can ever be other than what it has been. The history of the last 30 years in Northern Ireland, the history of violence and confrontation, has made it difficult to envisage a world in which things could be otherwise. Which helps explain that culture of pessimism which has infected unionist thinking (and beyond) and takes as its measure the thought that nothing will ever change. In that reading of history there is no way out.

It is that reading of history within unionism which Trimble has challenged. He was able to do so by drawing upon the fragments of unionist tradition (for instance, the example of the Craig–Collins Pact) in order to justify a new adventure in the present. And these fragments of unionist tradition became attached to a wider democratic discourse. And in the process something new, if fragile and challenged, came into being, albeit something new which claimed for itself a distinguished unionist heritage. And it came to define itself more clearly as the challenges to it intensified after 10 April 1998. This definition was not just tactical.

What relevance do any of these considerations have for the prospects of a politics of civility in Northern Ireland under the terms of the Belfast Agreement? This has to be considered under two notional headings: the achievement of the Agreement and what is required to make that Agreement operative (if you like, these two things together constitute the body and spirit of the Agreement).

THE BELFAST AGREEMENT

It could be argued that supporters of the Agreement made a rational wager on the future. It could be argued further that this was an affair of reason and not of the heart. In other words, the sceptic might propose that the cold print of the Agreement reflects a form of rationalism in politics – itself a faith – disconnected from what Santayana would have called the 'generative' forces in Northern Ireland politics, its roots in communal hostility. This rationalist view could be said to involve three interlocking assumptions. First, that a distinction can be made between symbol and substance; secondly, that politicians are capable of recognising the distinction between symbol and substance; and thirdly, that it is possible to arrive at a deal on the basis of politicians accepting the value of substantial advantages even if they had to swallow a certain amount of distasteful symbolism. In short, unionists would have to swallow the symbolism of cross-border cooperation with the Republic of Ireland in order to secure the substance of Northern Ireland's place within the United Kingdom, albeit on a consensual, cross-community model of government; and nationalists would have to swallow the symbolism of Northern Ireland's place within the United Kingdom in order to secure the substance of parity of esteem for their own tradition. (That Sinn Féin entered the talks which led to the Agreement in the expectation that unionists could not accept equality and that the Ulster Unionist Party stayed in the talks because it believed that Sinn Féin could never accept a partitionist settlement does not invalidate the rationalism of the final formula.)

But reason, of course, can only take you so far. There are two extravagances, wrote Pascal: to exclude reason and to admit only reason. Some might see in this a caricature of Northern Ireland politics itself, politics which swing between absolute pessimism and absolute optimism. And as that wise diplomat Count Leinsdorf acknowledged in Robert Musil's *The Man Without Qualities*, government machinery alone is not enough. There has to be something else – 'thought, morality, the idea . . . !' That Habsburgian sensibility might perhaps be too baroque for an island people. Then again, perhaps not. What this chapter suggests is that the 'thought, morality, the idea' in the Belfast Agreement is the ideal of political civility, the ideal sketched out in the work of Shils and Oakeshott though, above all, in the work of Mouffe. It can be argued that the Agreement creates the conditions for a politics of civility in the following ways.

First, the Agreement can be said to provide an escape route from the violent and self-destructive code – political incivility – which has characterised politics in Northern Ireland for the last 30 years. In the light of what might now appear possible, political parties and paramilitary groups can acknowledge the self-defeating commitments formerly and dogmatically held. The Agreement provides a potential escape from the view that nothing can be otherwise, the pessimistic mantra of inevitability. The past can be conveniently revised and reinterpreted in the light of what might now appear possible. We were all, one might say, victims of a series of events. But that was then and this is now. It was with this sort of understanding in mind – and in the distinctive language of the politics of civility – that David Trimble could define his aspiration to a 'pluralist parliament for a pluralist people'. That this was a conscious historical reference and therefore contrast to Lord Craigavon's 'protestant parliament for a protestant people' did not go unnoticed. No politician, of course, can by an act of will or turn of phrase overturn history. But a politician can by an act of will or turn of phrase identify politics with a new, more fruitful paradigm – that is with the politics of civility. And this is what Trimble tried to do.

Secondly, the possibility provided for in the Agreement is the consolidation of what might be called 'middle Ulster', those of whatever class and whatever religion and whatever party who have an interest in peace, security and stability. In short, instead of bitter contention it is now possible to envisage connection between unionist and nationalist on the 'ethico-principles' of public life. This does not mean a substantive consensus or a collectively held world view. It means simply a consolidation of interests around what are the boundaries, the limits and the expectations of political behaviour. In the jargon of contemporary political theory this may be a 'thin' identity but it would be an identity nonetheless. Furthermore, this middle Ulster now has the opportunity to engage intelligently once again with 'middle Ireland' in the Republic. This connection potentially puts together an island-wide constituency having a common interest in stability. The politics of civility is not divorced from the politics of self-interest and could not survive if it were (this is the truth of Santayana's observation). It is about specifying the new context of self-interest and respecting the plurality of such interests. One might tentatively argue that it could address satisfactorily for the first time in recent Irish history what may be called the Sudeten syndrome. As Konrad Henlein explained it in 1938: 'We must always demand so much that we cannot be satisfied' (cited in Bullock, 1998, p. 622). To which one might also add the contra-Sudeten syndrome: 'We must always offer so little that they can never be satisfied'. The Agreement could just possibly ameliorate, by reformulating, the confrontational dynamic of that syndrome.

Thirdly, the Agreement provides for a new and potentially decisive condition. Post referendum, that condition may be taken to represent an act of self-determination within the terms of the Downing Street Declaration of December 1993, namely that 'it is for the people of the island of Ireland alone, by agreement between the two parts respectively, to exercise their right of self-determination on the basis of consent, freely and concurrently given, North and South'. It is that 'self-determined' condition which could ultimately provide the legitimate basis for post-Agreement politics.

It is a measure of the ambition of the Agreement that the major parties of unionism and nationalism are required, almost overnight, to transform their character from instruments of rhetoric, opposition and mutual frustration into instruments of policy and government. The politics of civility is essential to make this transformation possible. The parties need to have some common point of reference and a common sense of popular responsibility. Over the last 30 years it has sometimes appeared that the parties in Northern Ireland shared the same ambition which the English historian A.J.P. Taylor attributed to central European politicians under the Habsburg Monarchy, namely endless and futile opposition. The Agreement holds out the opportunity that this can now change and change for the better. The principles of the Agreement might become diffused in a new spirit of public association. This does not mean the unionists must come to love nationalists or vice versa. It does mean that if the expectations of the Agreement are to be fulfilled, either adequately or at all, then a new practical and workable political code needs to establish itself. The functional success of this code implies also a common identification with what Mouffe would call 'the ethico-values' of the Agreement. It assumes also with Oakeshott the common acceptance of the conditions which should be acknowledged and subscribed to under threat of civil penalty or sentence of civil disability. It assumes, in short, the transition from the politics of incivility to the politics of civility. What does this require of the parties?

First, it means that there is a contradiction between enjoying the rules of liberal democratic procedure while denying them in practice oneself. That contradiction is exemplified by a form of criminal behaviour which usually justifies itself politically by proclaiming that the end justifies the means. The means may be murder, intimidation, personation and extortion. In a civil politics of the sort implied in the Agreement, however, the end can never be greater than democratic procedure or the civil law. Accepting the Agreement means, in effect, surrendering the priority of the end to the priority of the values embodied in the provisions of the Agreement, what Mouffe would call its 'ethico-political principles'.

Secondly, there is equally a fundamental contradiction between subscribing to the particulars of a peaceful resolution of disputes and at the same time denying its essential, general condition – the complete renunciation of violence to achieve political ends. This apparent subscription to the conditions of lawful procedures while denying the ethical requirement of those procedures is what is otherwise called fraud. Fraud would equally apply to the behaviour of politicians who sought to avoid fulfilling their obligations under the Agreement – like participation in North–South cooperation – while benefiting from the advantages of public office. While the terms of the Agreement are explicit as regards the relevant procedures on the second of these points it is vague on the first of them. Nonetheless, the *ethico-political* requirement of civility is far from vague.

Thirdly, then, one can argue that the commitment to civil procedures specified in the Agreement must be willed rationally by those who would seek to work fully – without criminality or fraud – the democratic process. Such subscription is the condition for inclusion within the bounds of civil politics. Failure to subscribe to these procedures would put one, using Mouffe's formulation, beyond the bounds of civil politics. Or, to put that another way, the politics of civility intimated in the Agreement can be inclusive only of those who subscribe *equally* to liberal democratic procedure. All parties must *equally* esteem the value of exclusively peaceful methods. No party can reserve to itself the right to equivocate on peace or democracy for that would be tantamount to the politics of threat. No party can claim a mandate to do wrong. No party can profit from the advantages of democracy but refuse, at the same time, to accept its obligations. The politics of civility must have its own exclusions. It cannot be, to use Santayana's expression, 'vacant'. Furthermore, the politics of civility cannot be an empty formula. Nor is it a suicide pact for those virtuous enough to take the risks, given Northern Ireland's violent past, of making the transition from the code of incivility to that of civility. The politics of civility cannot be value-neutral. It does not involve an equal chance for every party irrespective of its commitments.

This, it would appear, was the conclusion arrived at by the Prime Minister of the Irish Republic, Bertie Ahern, in his comments to *The Sunday Times* published on 14 February 1999. Albeit in the blunt language of a practical politician what Mr Ahern was expressing was the essence of the politics of civility. His contribution helped to place the whole question of 'decommissioning' into the proper context, a context which goes beyond legalistic pedantry and which addresses the 'ethico-political' values without which such legalism is anyway an empty shell. Mr Ahern said that it was 'illogical, unfair and unreasonable' for Sinn Féin (or any other paramilitary grouping) to expect to take the general advantages of the Agreement without fulfilling its particular responsibilities. Intimating a new condition of civility and a common set of expectations North and South, he argued that: 'Being part of a government, or part of an executive, [is not possible] without at least a commencement of decommissioning, and that would apply in the North and in the South. That is what we need to achieve'. This position was fully in line with the logic of the points sketched out in this section of the chapter in both its positives and its negatives and it is an effective summary of its requirements. Its logic was incorporated by the British and Irish Governments into the Hillsborough Declaration of 1 April 1999 which tried to address the decommissioning issue by requiring a voluntary act on the part of paramilitaries to put some weapons beyond use before power was devolved to the Northern Ireland Assembly. The 'failure' of the Hillsborough Declaration does not remove that 'civil' logic.

CONCLUSION

Can the Belfast Agreement work? That is a large question which is impossible to answer in any concise manner for it involves too many variations on the word 'work'. Viewed in the light of the preceding discussion, the question might be restated thus: does it seem likely that Northern Ireland can make the transition from the politics of incivility to the politics of civility? In this case it is worth making the following concluding observations, observations which are specifically addressed to the subject of this chapter, the politics of civility.

In his recent book, *The Ghosts of Berlin,* Brian Ladd tells of a vast lot at the junction of the districts of Pankow and Wedding where the huge slabs of concrete used in building the wall are now being ground up for usable gravel. The wall, he writes, had been Berlin's premier tourist attraction. He continues: 'If a monument can be decommissioned, that is apparently what has happened to the Berlin Wall' (1997, p. 7). The concrete has lost its aura. It has, so to speak, lost its power to kill. It no longer has its murderous properties. What happened on 9 November 1989 did not remove the Wall immediately. 'What had disappeared, rather, was the symbolic Wall – which meant that the concrete and the symbol were no longer the same' (p. 8).

Yet before the Wall could be forgotten, before the city could regain its completeness, the Wall had to be physically removed. Unfortunately in Northern Ireland, both the symbolism and the concrete reality of illegal weaponry remains. So too does the intense incivility of sectarian contention as witnessed at Drumcree. And so long as illegal weapons are held by paramilitary groups then there can be no real sense that the war is over. And so long as sectarian confrontation continues in the manner of Drumcree it will be difficult for the politics of civility to take root. Together these things constitute the politics of threat. Possibly the greatest obstacle to the politics of civility today is the persistence of the politics of threat. The politics of threat is at odds with the spirit of the Agreement. It is the politics of threat which still makes people feel vulnerable and exposed. It is the politics of threat which means that many – especially unionists – remain unpersuaded of the advantages of the Agreement. The incivility of the 'enemy' who refuses to become exclusively a civil political 'adversary' constantly taunts both sides.

Freudian analysts would call this condition 'castration anxiety'. Castration anxiety is that point at which a threat takes precedence over actuality and produces real effects. In the unionist case the threat of IRA arms is as good a reason for resistance as the actual use of IRA arms. Power, they might argue, can be exercised by threat. By keeping its force in reserve, republican strategy could be more effective than the actual use of violence. It is the threat of IRA weaponry, the threat of a return to war, which, so it is feared, will be used to skew democratic procedure and influence policy. The republican rejection of the Hillsborough Declaration, of its voluntary requirement to put some arms beyond use before the establishment of the Executive, does not inspire unionist confidence (to say the least) in Sinn Féin's willingness to move to a politics of civility. Unionists believe that this episode is an example of the politics of threat.

All that can be said at the time of writing (April 1999) is that the transition to civility can take place only when people are confident that the politics of threat has been removed. That point has not yet been reached. What the President of the Republic of Ireland (McAleese, 1999) called establishing 'a culture of consensus out of the ruins of a culture of conflict' remains still an aspiration.

7

THE END OF (IRISH) HISTORY? THREE READINGS OF THE CURRENT CONJUNCTURE

Joseph Ruane

In the summer of 1989, just as the collapse of communism in eastern Europe was beginning, Francis Fukuyama published an article whose title – 'The end of history' – still powerfully evokes the extraordinary events of that period (Fukuyama, 1989). The title was both misleading and misunderstood: many of its readers understood it to be an argument about history as 'the occurrence of events', whereas for Fukuyama it was about 'History: that is, history understood as a single, coherent, evolutionary process, when taking into the account the experience of all peoples in all times' (Fukuyama, 1992, p. xii). Paradoxically, the article made its impact largely through its association with history at another level again: the origins, development and ultimate fate of ideologies, systems of economy and government, geopolitical relationships. A decade later, the questions it raised – about the forces that shape the historical process, the possibility of historic closures and new beginnings – have even greater force.

These questions, often linked explicitly to the phrase 'end of history', arose many times in Ireland during the 1990s in relation to the conflict in Northern Ireland, and more generally the conflict between Britain and Ireland (for example Aughey, 1995). The wider context stimulated such reflection, but it was encouraged by the language of the peace process and, in particular, that of the Downing Street Declaration of December 1993. The goal was not just a truce, or a temporary settlement, but a final and complete end to the centuries-old conflict. And if initially that seemed impossible, over time the combination of change on the ground – above all the ceasefires – and the wider sense of 'new times/new possibilities' nurtured the hope that perhaps the impossible might happen. When, after many delays and setbacks, the Belfast Agreement was finally signed on Good Friday, 10 April 1998, it seemed to many that this finally was the historic breakthrough, the end of a long, dark period in Irish history, and the beginning of something completely new.[1]

Throughout the period, there were of course more sober calculations of what was happening and what could be achieved. The more pessimistic refused to attribute any significance or potential to the peace process, portraying it as simply a new and malign twist in republican strategy.[2] Others, closer to the negotiations, were less cynical, but stressed the difficulties that lay ahead and the fragile nature of the process. More than a year after the signing of the Agreement, the mood is cautious and uncertain. The Democratic Unionist Party (DUP), with at least one third of the Protestant vote, remains unreconciled to the Agreement. A majority of republicans support the Agreement, but their support is conditional on progress towards republican goals. At the time of writing (July 1999) tensions are once again high over Orange marches; sectarianism is intense in some localities; and the further implementation of the Agreement is blocked by disagreement on decommissioning.

If we are truly at the 'end of Irish history', the birth of the new is proving protracted and painful. But are we at the end of Irish history in that sense? And if we are not, what is the state of the historic conflict as it has unfolded, particularly in Northern Ireland, over the past 30 years? In other words, what is the present conjuncture? The question is at once critically important and extremely difficult to answer. What had been for some time a relatively stable situation appears now to be in flux. But is it? Has there been fundamental change in the structures underlying the conflict, with political leaders now laying the foundations for new, non-conflictual relationships? Or does the older structural logic remain in force, with recent developments simply further twists and turns within it? Or are we in a situation of structural openness and indeterminacy where the future, whether conflictual or otherwise, will be decided by the choices now being made?

This chapter proposes answers to these questions in the form of three different readings of the present conjuncture. This is done not in the spirit of a postmodernist emphasis on multiple rather than single readings, but for two reasons: first, we are in the middle of a process whose outcome is still far from clear; second, it is possible that the conjuncture is constituted by contradictory forces which cannot be grasped in the logic of a single reading. The goal is to map the interpretative terrain in a manner which does justice to both its indeterminateness and complexity. Briefly stated, the first reading adopts the 'end of history' view: it sees the historic conflict as now unravelling and current problems as temporary difficulties in bringing it finally to a close. The second reading is less optimistic: it sees no fundamental change in the conditions of conflict; on the other hand it sees a shift taking place from a high to a low intensity phase in the conflict. The third reading is pessimistic: it sees no prospect of change in either the conditions of conflict or its intensity.

In the conclusion I consider whether the three readings should be viewed as complementary rather than competing, with each reading capturing one aspect of a contradictory reality. I then draw out their policy implications.

Each reading is based on the same theoretical understanding of the causes of the conflict, but makes different assumptions about current structural relationships and actor strategies. I begin with a statement of the theory of the conflict. In the present context 'theory' refers, not to the application of general theory to a particular case, but to the formalisation at a theoretical level of the historical and social forces at play in this particular instance (for a discussion of method, see Ruane and Todd, 1996, chapter 1). Note that the readings seek only to capture general tendencies; their usefulness does not stand or fall on the adequacy of each and every detail.

A THEORY OF THE CONFLICT

The origins of the conflict lie in the impact on Ireland of the new forces reshaping western Europe in the early modern period – agricultural capitalism, the Protestant reformation, political consolidation and centralisation, nation-building, imperial and colonial expansion.[3] Ireland was caught up in these developments in a conflictual and contradictory way. Sixteenth-century England was precociously capitalist, aggressively Protestant, determined both to secure control over the whole of the British Isles and to exploit the opportunities opened up by the discovery of the Americas. Ireland had been a peripheral lordship of the English crown since the twelfth century. It was economically backward and politically fragmented and was now subject to the logic of English political consolidation, religious standardisation, economic and imperial expansion (Kearney, 1989).

Irish resistance to those processes, particularly to the reformation, led to the adoption of increasingly harsh measures, and to the displacement of almost the entire Catholic ruling elite and their replacement by Protestant settlers from England and Scotland. As a result Ireland underwent the transformations of the modern period – political centralisation, reformation, the beginnings of economic expansion, nation-building – in a markedly colonial way. The colonial dimension would persist, though in complex interaction with other, non-colonial dimensions. Eighteenth-century Ireland was both colony and sister kingdom (Foster, 1988; Canny, 1989). The Act of Union was intended to settle the matter once and for all but, as Garvin points out, the British attempt in the nineteenth century to transform Ireland from colony to peripheral region unleashed tensions and contradictions that finished by undermining the union (Garvin, 1981, p. 213)

It is difficult to theorise so uneven a historical process and so ambiguous a political formation. The approach adopted here conceives of a 'system of relationships', forged by Ireland's conflictual integration into the British state, with three components: first, a set of overlapping cultural and ideological oppositions within Ireland based on religion (Catholic vs Protestant), ethnic origin (Gaelic–Irish and Old English vs New English and Ulster Scots), settler-native status and a set of antagonistic cultural stereotypes (barbarism vs civility, progressiveness vs backwardness); second, a structure of dominance, dependence and inequality in which the British state controlled Ireland through the Protestant minority whose loyalty was assured as long as the British government underwrote their dominance over Catholics; third, a tendency toward communal polarisation in Ireland around the differences of religion, ethnicity and culture. The effect of this system was to constitute the British state as the major power-holder in Ireland and Irish Catholics and Protestants as culturally distinct communities with sharply opposed interests and identities.

Once in place, the system showed remarkable resilience. It was maintained in part by intra-systemic processes. For example, the inscription of cultural and religious differences in differential relations of power and inequality led to the further elaboration of those differences; competition for resources and the sense of mutual threat encouraged each community to downplay its internal differences and to form a solidary bloc in opposition to the other; an irreconcilable sense of cultural 'otherness' intensified the struggle for communal power. It was maintained also because those to whom it allocated power – the British state and Irish Protestants – had a compelling interest in the status quo: for the British state securing Ireland was a strategic imperative; for Irish Protestants, surrounded by a hostile majority, dominance was the key to their survival. But Catholics too had resources, and as time passed more came their way. Together with a tendency towards stability, therefore, was a dynamic for change.

The dynamic came ultimately from wider processes of structural transformation (Cullen, 1981; Whelan, 1991). The transformations of the early modern period had created the conditions for the specific, quasi-colonial, form of Ireland's integration into the British state. Now the process of modernisation proper began to heighten the contradictions inherent in the system and to alter – and in part, erode – the conditions of its reproduction. As elsewhere, modernisation redistributed power and resources down the social scale; in the Irish context this meant a shift in the power balance from the dominant to the subordinate community. As Catholics acquired resources, they used them to extract concessions, which they then turned into resources to press for further concessions.

The process of Catholic recovery was slow. Their defeat had been comprehensive and the apparatus of power erected to consolidate the Protestant victory was formidable. Also the British response to Catholic pressure was to resist it for as long as possible, the effect in part of a conservative strategy of rule, in part of a fear of long term Catholic intentions and Protestant reactions. But from very early on the direction of change was clear enough and 'the Catholic question' – how to integrate Catholics into the political system without overturning it – was already the key political question in internal Irish and British–Irish relations in the late eighteenth century (Bartlett, 1990). The eventual answer, precipitated by the 1798 rebellion, was the Act of Union, conceived as a context in which Catholic grievances could be addressed without danger to British or Irish Protestant interests.

Union did not, however, dismantle or transform the system of relationships, though it gave it a new political twist. It did little directly to reduce Catholic grievances, and indeed soon became a source of grievance in its own right. Eighteenth century Catholic loyalism now gave way to nineteenth century Irish nationalism, while Protestants regrouped around the defence of the union (Boyce, 1982). The developing struggle between Catholic nationalism and Protestant unionism fed directly into the system of relationships: accentuating the cultural differences between the two communities (Catholics were 'Irish', and Protestants 'British'), reinforcing the alliance between the British state and Protestants, and strengthening the tendency towards communal polarisation.

By the closing decades of the nineteenth century the nationalist–unionist struggle had divided the British political establishment. Liberal attempts to introduce home rule provoked ever-increasing unionist opposition, particularly in east Ulster, where industrialisation had consolidated the Protestant position and given the union a stronger material basis. From 1912 Ulster unionists made clear their determination to resist home rule in Ulster by force of arms. In the crisis conditions of the First World War and after, Irish nationalism radicalised in both its goals and its methods. The stage was now set for partition.

Southern Irish secession and partition were the product of two forces: first, unresolved conflicts within the system of relationships which intensified the Catholic and nationalist sense of grievance; second, the balance of power as it then existed between Catholic and Protestant on the island of Ireland, and between Irish nationalists and the British state. The location of the border was the geographical measure of that power balance. Complete Irish independence would have dissolved the system of relationships; partition reconstituted it within the new territorial context. The old oppositions of religion, culture and identity continued as before, as did the alliance of the British state and Protestants – this time an alliance between the British government and the Protestants of Northern Ireland. Catholic subordination was now confined to Catholics north of the border, but was resented by Catholics throughout the island. Partition fractured the two island-wide Catholic and Protestant communities, but the Catholic one retained much of its solidarity and was committed to national reunification.

The reconstituted system was no less conflictual in its implications. Northern Protestants, fearful of finding themselves a marginalised minority in a reunified Ireland, felt compelled to secure their position by relying on British support and excluding Catholics from influence or power. Exclusion in turn confirmed Catholics in their disaffection, disloyalty and resentment of Protestant control. There was a continuity in another respect from the pre-partition period: the balance of power between Protestant and Catholic on the island continued to shift in the Catholic favour. Partition slowed it for a time by giving Protestants direct control over a state apparatus, but did not stop it. In time Northern Catholics recovered from the shock and disorganisation of partition and developed new, more effective, forms of political mobilisation. In contrast, the Protestant position though still powerful was weakening, as industrial decline increased economic and political dependence on Britain. The shift in the balance of power had profound consequences: it reduced the capacity of unionists to contain nationalist resistance, and undermined the structural basis of the 1921 settlement.

The Catholic challenge finally came in the 1960s in the form of a civil rights movement that left the constitutional issue to one side and demanded a broad range of economic and political reforms. The civil rights movement and the response of the Northern government to it exposed the oppressive and discriminatory nature of the Northern state and precipitated a full-scale political and security crisis. The British government was forced to intervene, thereby reopening the question of partition and the settlement of 1921. Both constitutional nationalists and republicans seized the opportunity to press their demands: at the very least, major reforms; if possible, the dismantling of the Stormont government. By 1972 it was clear to the British government that any hope of restoring political stability had gone. It prorogued the Northern government and established direct rule. In 1973 it made clear that while Northern Ireland would remain part of the United Kingdom for as long as a majority so decided, any future devolved government would have to have cross-community support; this meant some form of power-sharing and an Irish (i.e. North–South) dimension.

The securing of a new settlement was to prove longer, more difficult and more painful that anyone anticipated in 1972. For close to 20 years a majority within each community opposed absolutely the kind of compromise needed to make a settlement possible. Some did so through constitutional politics, others did so through violence. The conflict blighted the lives of a whole generation and cost more than 3000 lives. And yet compromise was resolutely resisted. Then, when it seemed that this truly was a conflict without a solution, republicans launched the 'peace process', offering an end to violence in return for comprehensive political negotiations and an agreed settlement. So deep was the distrust of republicans that in its initial stages the peace process met with widespread incredulity, suspicion and cynicism.[4] But as it brought results – in particular the Downing Street Declaration of 1993 and the IRA ceasefire of 1994 – it became the focal point of all political activity, until finally in April 1998 it yielded the Belfast Agreement.

There is no guarantee that the Agreement will succeed or even that it will be fully implemented. But one way or another it has changed profoundly the political landscape in Northern Ireland and throughout the two islands. The question is: into what?

The readings presented below offer three very different answers to that question. Reading I locates the Agreement within a wider process of change which has been acting upon the system of relationships, unravelling it and bringing the historic conflict to an end. Reading II holds that the system of relationships is still substantially intact and that the underlying conditions of conflict are still present. However, the Agreement, by effecting a realignment of communal structural and institutional power, is bringing the recent phase of high intensity conflict to an end. Reading III argues that little change has occurred either in the conditions of conflict, or its intensity; conflict will continue within the framework of the new institutions. The most that can be expected is a reduction in the level of violence associated with it.

THREE READINGS OF THE CURRENT CONJECTURE

Reading I

Reading I corresponds most closely to the notion of 'an end to (Irish) history'. It holds that the centuries-old conflict which has divided Catholic and Protestant in Ireland, and Ireland and Britain, is now coming to an end. It will take some time for the process to be complete, but it is beginning. The Belfast Agreement is at once a manifestation of that process and a means through which it will advance. The change comes from the impact of wider structural transformations on the system of relationships which have underlain the conflict since its inception. The system was formed in the early modern period, a product of the way in which Ireland was integrated into the expanding English/British state. The process of modernisation reshaped this system, redistributed power within it, heightened its tensions and contradictions, but left it intact. The intense conflict of the post-1969 period was a product of the particular form the system took in the post-partition period. However, as the century ends, the shift from modernity to postmodernity, in a context of intensified globalisation, has begun to erode the conditions of its reproduction.

It is happening in the following way. Secularism, liberalism and religious pluralism in the western world are generating a climate of greater religious tolerance. Critical reflection on colonialism and its aftermath has created concepts (for example, hybridity) which make possible a transcendence of the stark opposition of settler and native traditions (Bhabha, 1994). Postmodernism is challenging fixed notions of place and cultural authenticity, and challenging the modernist dichotomies of advanced/backward, modern/traditional (Carter et al., 1993; Vattimo, 1988). Post-nationalism is undermining notions of absolute sovereignty and impermeable national boundaries (Waters, 1995, chapter 5). European integration and the birth of a new, post-Cold War, US-led global order has taken western Europe beyond the nationalist and imperial rivalries of the past and their strategic imperatives. The cultural differentiations, social fragmentations and individualisation characteristic of postmodernity are reducing the intensity of internal communal solidarities (Crook et al., 1992). These are global-level changes which are also impacting on Northern Ireland. As they do so, they are moderating the conflictual tendencies of the system of relationships; over time they will undermine it altogether.

This process is now under way. Some of the most dramatic changes have been at the level of culture and ideology. The 1980s and 1990s have witnessed exceptionally rapid change in the religious culture of Irish Catholics: Irish Catholicism today is highly differentiated with strong liberal and pluralist currents, which have broken with the theological absoluteness and dogmatism of the past, and are open to dialogue with the Protestant tradition (Hardiman and Whelan, 1998; Ruane, 1998). The same period has also seen a wholesale re-examination of the traditional tenets of Irish nationalism, and a vigorous critique of past integralist tendencies. The dominant strands of Irish nationalism today are liberal and pluralist; there is respect for the achievements of the past, but also a willingness – indeed an eagerness – to 'move on'. One expression of the change is Irish nationalism's enthusiasm for European integration (Ruane, 1994). Another is the willingness to recognise the legitimacy of the unionist tradition in Ireland, and partition if that is the will of the majority in Northern Ireland. A third is the willingness to move away from the nationalist interpretation of Irish history and the imperial/colonial model of British–Irish relations.[5]

Ideological change has been most marked among nationalists, but liberal and pluralist currents are also emerging within unionism. They are particularly evident in the leadership of the Progressive Unionist Party (PUP), but also within sections of the Ulster Unionist Party (UUP). There has been a shift away from a strictly majoritarian notion of democracy, a recognition that minorities – even those which oppose the very existence of the state – have rights which have to be respected. The notion of a 'Protestant parliament for a Protestant people', so central to unionist thinking in the past, has been replaced, in David Trimble's phrase, by that of a 'pluralist parliament for a pluralist people' (Trimble, 1998). The antipathy of liberal and radical unionism to fundamentalist loyalism, covered over in the past, is now out in the open and vigorously expressed.

Change has also been taking place at the level of the structure of dominance, dependence and inequality. Here the crucial change has been in British policy towards Ireland. For centuries British policy towards Ireland has had two interrelated elements: maintaining control over Ireland for strategic reasons, and managing communal divisions in Ireland to secure those strategic ends. In practice, for most of Irish history this meant British support for the Protestant minority in return for their loyalty, though over time, as a Catholic recovery began, it became strategically necessary to conciliate Catholics. In that context, the Stormont period which saw the British government once again offer unconditional support for Protestant dominance, was a historic regression.

The situation today is radically different. European integration, advanced weaponry and NATO mean that Britain no longer has a strategic interest in remaining in Ireland; insofar as Ireland is important at all, British interests are best served through friendly relations with the Republic. Moreover, contemporary international norms of equality and justice rule out the strategic manipulation of communal divisions to achieve political ends, and the subordination of minorities to majorities. The shift in British policy towards a neutralist and reformist stance was already evident in 1972 when it was made clear that any new structures of government had to have the support of both communities (Cunningham, 1991, pp. 48ff.). The change was by no means evident at all levels of policy, and at times needed external pressure to sustain it, but two far-reaching developments in the 1980s – the Anglo-Irish Agreement of 1985 and the revised Fair Employment Act of 1989 – showed the increasingly egalitarian thrust of British policy.

The Downing Street Declaration of 1993 marked a further shift and made clear the way in which British government now conceived its role. It declared itself free of any 'selfish strategic' interest in the present, while accepting its responsibility to help resolve a conflict between traditions on the island of Ireland to which it had contributed. The Belfast Agreement of 1998 confirms this. The British government undertakes to withdraw from Northern Ireland if that is the wish of a majority of its people; in the meantime it is committed to establishing substantive equality between the Catholic and Protestant communities. Equality will not be achieved overnight, but already the process is under way. Since 1972 Catholics have made substantial progress on all fronts – demographic, economic, political and cultural – and the pace of change will now quicken (Ruane and Todd, 1996).

The shift in the British stance has implications for the entire system of relationships. British support for Protestant dominance in Ireland was the linchpin of the entire system. It reinforced the unwillingness of unionists to make any concessions to nationalists, strengthened nationalist hostility to Britain and Britishness and was used by republicans to justify their armed struggle. If the full effects of the change have still to become evident in Northern Ireland, their effect on British–Irish relations is already dramatic. Historic anti-British sentiment in Ireland was declining in the 1960s but was renewed and intensified in the 1970s by British political and security policies in Northern Ireland. Hostility to Britain was particularly strong in the early 1980s in response to the hunger strikes and Margaret Thatcher's summary dismissal of the proposals contained in the New Ireland Forum. The improvement in relations began with the Anglo–Irish Agreement of 1985, and are now at an all-time high (FitzGerald, 1999).

The improvement in British–Irish relations has helped in turn to improve communal relations within Ireland. It has made it easier for nationalists to accept a British dimension to Irish culture and to their own past, and to acknowledge the reality, integrity and legitimacy of a separate British tradition on the island. The magnitude of the shift was symbolised in November 1998 by the joint Irish–British, nationalist–unionist, commemoration at Messines Ridge of the Irish soldiers who died during the First World War battle. These changes have helped ease relations between the Southern government and pro-Agreement unionists. There is still tension and hostility in the relationship, but also much more understanding, trust and respect than in the past.

The third point at which change has been taking place in the system of relationships is at the level of community. The tendency of the system to produce polarised communities has been a key factor in the reproduction of the conflict. This tendency is now weakening. The effect has been particularly evident in the Protestant community which for the first time has split down the middle on a political settlement. The political significance of this cannot be overestimated: without it there would not have been an Agreement, not least because the peace process was founded on the notion of rebuilding nationalist unity after the divisions of the 1970s and 1980s. The peace process is, however, still far from completion, and once peace is consolidated, divisions may emerge here as well.

There can be no single explanation for the new willingness of Protestants to accept political division. The Protestant community has always been more differentiated internally than the Catholic one, and the political changes of recent decades – in particular direct rule and the British government's security and reform policies – have widened these differences (Coulter, 1996, p. 175). But the changes also owe something to the fragmenting and individualising effects of postmodernity. Protestant communal solidarity was built on a cross-class alliance that itself presupposed a stable (predominantly industrial) class structure with readily identifiable class interests. That coherent class structure no longer exists, no more than it does in any other advanced society.[6] Similarly, the a-political, 'opting-out' syndrome so evident in the Protestant middle class, has clear parallels in the politics of other advanced societies, and has as much to do with consumerist individualism as it does with the specificity of the Northern situation (Coulter, 1996; Beck, 1997).

Reading I brings a long historical view to bear on the conflict – the successions of social transformations from early modernity to postmodernity – and traces their implications for the system of relationships underlying the conflict. The system has its origins in the structural and cultural conditions of early modernity; modernisation consolidated it and intensified its contradictions; the conditions of postmodernity are dissolving it. They are working at all levels of the system, moderating difference, undoing the structure of dominance, dependence and inequality, and (on the Protestant side at least) weakening the tendency towards internally solidary oppositional communities. A virtuous circle of conflict reduction and resolution has now begun.

Reading II

Reading II is less optimistic. It locates recent progress towards a settlement within the unfolding dynamics of the traditional conflict, rather than as evidence that the conflict is coming to an end. For the coming period it anticipates at best a shift from a high to a low intensity phase in the conflict, which could return to a high intensity phase at some time in the future. It questions how much impact the wider changes described in Reading I are having on the system of relationships as it operates at the level of the communities in Northern Ireland. The key issue is the relations of power and inequality within Northern Ireland. Catholic resentment at their unequal position has been the single most destabilising element in Northern Ireland. Reading II acknowledges the improvements which have taken place in the past two decades, but stresses how much has still to be achieved and the difficulties that stand in the way of achieving it. It focuses on three issues.

First, the adoption by the British government of a neutral stance in relation to the communities does not mean that the total effect of its presence in Northern Ireland will be neutral. States are not simply policy making bodies: they are concentrations of structural, institutional and symbolic power which configure class, territorial and ethnic-cultural relations in distinctive ways. The United Kingdom is built around an ethnocultural hierarchy which, despite the new emphasis on multiculturalism, shows little sign of fading. It is enacted in the relations between the different nationalities which make up the United Kingdom; it is also encoded in the politics and culture of 'Britishness' which imposes itself as an overlay on all parts of the UK. Within this hierarchy, the English of the Home Counties are positioned at the summit, and the Northern Irish of both communities at the base. As far as the people of Great Britain are concerned, there is little to distinguish between either Northern community. However, the situation is quite different in Northern Ireland itself. There unionists, uniquely, lay claim to the identity 'British', and Britishness is a source of status and power. Moreover, this aspect of Britishness in Northern Ireland forms part of its appeal, consciously or unconsciously, to many unionists (Todd, 1988). The Belfast Agreement acknowledges the Irish identity of nationalists, and promises parity of esteem. But the central role of the state in shaping the public sphere means that as long as Northern Ireland remains so firmly part of the United Kingdom, there is no possibility of placing Irishness and Britishness on an equal footing (Ruane and Todd, 1996, chapter 8).

Second, communal inequality is structurally embedded in other ways, and there is a limit to how much equality policies can achieve in the short run. Economic inequality is bound up with class, region and locality, differential levels of education, and differential access to cultural capital (Eversley, 1989; Smith and Chambers, 1991). Cultural inequality is embedded in the landscape, place names, public buildings and official culture, and in the very existence of Northern Ireland as a cultural as well as a political formation (Ruane and Todd, 1996, chapter 7). The Belfast Agreement has made elaborate provision to promote equality (McCrudden, this volume, p. 103 ff.). But even if the legislation is used to the full and in an open and generous spirit, it will take time to have effect. There has been progress towards economic equality as measured by occupational change, but it is much more pronounced at the middle-class than at working-class levels, where there are still vast swathes of Catholic deprivation (Gallagher et al., 1995). Also, occupational data do not take account of accumulated personal and family wealth, or the social and cultural capital which accompany it, which will favour the Protestant community for a long time to come. On the cultural front, it is a relatively easy matter to give financial support to the Irish language, to grant the right to fly the Irish flag, or even to re-route Orange marches. It will be much more difficult to rid the culture of the stock of epithets and assumptions which devalue nationalists and Irish culture, and to give Catholics the sense of cultural ownership of, and 'at-homeness' in, Northern Ireland that Protestants have traditionally enjoyed (O'Connor, 1993)

Third, the extent and rate of progress towards equality will also depend on whether unionists actively support it. If they do, progress will be more rapid and the whole atmosphere in Northern Ireland will change. However, unionists face a serious structural dilemma in relation to the 'equality agenda'. The constitutional status of Northern Ireland is to be determined by the preference of the majority, which itself will depend crucially on the demographic mix of the population. The two communities are moving towards demographic equality, and perhaps a Catholic majority (Cormack et al., 1993). There is no guarantee that a Catholic majority would be a nationalist one, but there is a strong possibility that it would. The dilemma for unionists is that if the 'equality agenda' is successful, it is likely to strengthen further the Catholic demographic advance. They have three options. First, they can ignore the issue and let matters take their course: the danger here is of failing to make adequate provision for that eventuality should it arrive. Second, they can actively support Catholic equality in the hope that this will help reconcile the two communities, and persuade Catholics to support the union; the risk in doing so is that they may help Catholics into a position of strength from which they will then challenge the union. Third, they can adopt the traditional strategy of blocking or delaying the Catholic advance as far as possible: the risk here is that they might not succeed, while attempting it may further alienate Catholics and strengthen their nationalism. There are signs of a generous spirit among some unionists in the wake of the Agreement, and these may well select the second option. However, the close to 50 per cent of unionists who opposed the Agreement are more likely to select the third one.

All of this suggests that the issue of inequality – the Catholic struggle for equality and Protestant resistance to this – is likely to remain at the centre of politics in Northern Ireland and a source of communal division for a long time to come. This means that in spite of the shift in the British stance towards a neutralist and reformist position, little has changed thus far at the level of the two communities in Northern Ireland. Their interests remain opposed and power continues to be a crucial resource. But if this crucial aspect of the system of relationships remains intact, there is little likelihood of progress at the other levels. Postmodernising tendencies that in other situations (for example, Southern Ireland) might moderate cultural differences or differentiate communities will soon reach their limits here.

If the system of relationships is not in process of unravelling, what explains the peace process and the Belfast Agreement? Reading II locates the change within the system of relationships, in terms of a shift from a high intensity to a low intensity phase in the conflict. Phases of high and low intensity have been characteristic of this conflict since its inception. The high intensity phases are those of the final decades of eighteenth century, from the late 1820s to the early 1840s, the 1880s to the 1920s and most recently, from 1968 to the present. Within each of the major phases there were peaks and hollows. Between the major phases, conflict was always present in some degree, but reached serious levels only in particular localities where the contradictions were unusually intense.

The episodic nature of the conflict is often commented on, but rarely explained. Reading II addresses it in terms of the relationship between Catholic structural and institutional power. Structural power refers to demographic strength, control over economic resources, political and military strength, dominance in the cultural sphere. Institutional power refers to access to, and presence within, the major public and policy making institutions (Ruane and Todd, 1996, pp. 139–43). The relationship between structural and institutional power in any society is complex and interactive: there will be a tendency for institutional power to stay in line with structural power, but gaps can open up and institutional power can be used to defend or consolidate structural power. In the Irish case, the interaction has also been complex, but there has been a recurring tendency: where Catholic structural power has come to exceed their institutional power, they have exerted pressure to bring institutions into line. The effect has been an intensification of conflict as Catholic pressure met Protestant and/or British resistance. Conflict has remained intense until a settlement has been achieved – until, in effect, institutional power has been brought back into line with structural power.

How long the conflict lasts in such circumstances, and how intense it becomes, depends in part on perceptions and expectations. In any conflict it is easy for the participants to overestimate the extent of their power, to expect too much, and then to overstretch their resources. Moreover the struggle itself can generate new grievances, fears and expectations; it can also open up previously unperceived possibilities and dangers. Even when the broad parameters of an institutional adjustment are becoming clear, each side will have an interest in negotiating the best deal it can. Equally, how long the deal lasts depends on how long the balance of structural power and the new institutions remain in line. This depends in turn on the rate of change in the wider structural forces on which the communal power balance ultimately depends.

The crisis which erupted in Northern Ireland in the late 1960s was the result of the opening up of a gap between structural and institutional power in the decades after the foundation of the state. By the 1960s a crisis of some kind was inevitable. Its severity was the product of a number of factors. The decades of Stormont rule had created a deep well of grievance among Catholics; the attacks of loyalists and the harsh measures adopted by the security forces in response to the crisis added further to this. Protestants had lived for decades in fear of a nationalist rebellion which would try to force them into a united Ireland: they believed that this was now it. Neither side thought it could afford to compromise. Moreover, neither side could easily establish how much it might have to compromise: in the power vacuum that followed the collapse of Stormont, it was difficult for any participant to establish the extent of its power.

As time went on the nature of the power balance became clearer, as did the cost of pursuing goals that could not be achieved. With the resources now available to them, Catholics could not achieve more than some form of power-sharing within Northern Ireland coupled with a North–South dimension. The SDLP faced up to that fact in the 1970s; republicans resisted it until the 1990s. Once they accepted it, the basis for a republican compromise was in place. At that point it was up to the two governments to begin negotiations with republicans or to continue their efforts to marginalise and defeat them. They decided to negotiate and to try to persuade unionists to compromise also. The result – the Belfast Agreement – closes the gap between Catholic structural and institutional power that opened up during the Stormont period, and that widened further after 1972. There is now every reason to expect the high intensity conflict of the past 30 years to come to an end. The underlying conditions of conflict have not disappeared, but neither side now has an interest in maintaining the struggle at an intense level.

An episodic model of the conflict raises the spectre of a return to high intensity conflict sometime in the future. This cannot be ruled out. According to the model, it will happen if the gap between the structural and institutional power of the communities widens again. This is a distinct possibility. Over the past 25 years the Catholic community has grown in size, improved its position in the economy, strengthened its vote and increased its cultural self-confidence. This process seems set to continue. If some day Catholics become a demographic majority, demand deeper and more extensive contacts between North and South, and then push for unity, there is every likelihood of a return to serious conflict.

The Belfast Agreement has been deliberately crafted to allow change in the demographic and political balance between the communities to be reflected at the institutional and constitutional levels without precipitating a political crisis (see chapter 1, p. 21 ff.). But while institutional-level changes might be handled with relative ease, constitutional changes are of a different order. Some unionists have indicated their willingness, on point of democratic principle, to accept Irish unity if that is the will of the majority of the people of Northern Ireland; others have been less forthcoming; still others have made it clear that they will not accept Irish unity under any circumstances. That, however, is a matter for the future, and the worst case scenario may never arise. For the moment, the conditions are in place to bring the intense conflict of the past 30 years to a close.

Reading III

Reading III and Reading II are in agreement that the conditions of conflict persist and that the Belfast Agreement brings about a realignment of structural and institutional power. The readings differ over whether on this occasion realignment will bring intense conflict to an end. Reading III holds that it will not. First, the power balance between the communities is unlikely to remain stable for long. Second, the Agreement promises diametrically opposed things to the two sides, and political leaders will be under pressure from their supporters to deliver on those promises. Communal struggle will, therefore, continue within the new institutions. Tension and mistrust will remain high. Organised paramilitary violence may cease, but violence will persist in the form of confrontations at marches and sectarian attacks.

The closing of the gap between structural and institutional power inaugurates a period of low intensity conflict only if the communal power balance remains stable for some considerable time. If it does not – if a gap again opens up – the conditions for intense political struggle re-emerge. In the past, settlements have typically been followed by a stable – or at least, slowly changing – power balance. It is unlikely on this occasion for two principal reasons: the rapid rate of change in wider structures and relationships, and changes in the demographic balance in Northern Ireland.

The balance of communal power has always been inextricably linked to developments in wider structures and relationships. Since the conflict began in the early modern period, wider developments have worked on and reshaped the power balance, redefining interests and creating different conditions for political struggle. This did not mean, however, continuous struggle. There were long periods when change at the wider level, and therefore in the communal power balance, was slow and uneven. During these periods, assuming political institutions were broadly in line with the power balance, there was no basis for assertive communal politics. It returned only when developments at the wider level altered the power balance and provided the resources to make possible a renewed Catholic challenge

The difference today is that change is now occurring at an increasingly rapid rate and, if wider structures are in process of continuous transformation, there is little prospect of the communal power balance stabilising. It is possible that some of Northern Ireland's distinctive features – the conflict itself, a pronounced social conservatism, the peripheral relationship to Britain – will insulate it from these wider forces in some degree. For example, the conflict has made Northern Ireland unattractive to multinational industry and has given it a vastly expanded state sector (O'Dowd, 1995). This has made for a much more stable economic and cultural environment in Northern Ireland than, for example, in the Republic with its dynamic industrial and financial sectors (O'Hearn, 1998). But the currents of political change in Northern Ireland in the 1990s offer ample evidence of openness to wider global forces. The successful implementation of the Belfast Agreement is likely to increase its exposure to such forces, particularly in the economic domain.

How exactly this will impact on the power balance in Northern Ireland is difficult to predict. If the pattern of the Stormont period is repeated, the changes are likely to benefit Catholics. On the other hand a longer view reveals periods (for example, the late nineteenth century) when the impact of wider changes favoured Protestants (Boyce, 1992). There could also be multiple and contradictory effects which leave the balance of power unchanged. One way or another the impact of global forces and their resource implications are likely to create multiple points of contestation and conflict. Even the perception that the power balance may be changing will require each community to monitor closely what is happening. If it suspects that it is changing in its favour, it will be tempted to test this out. If it is confirmed, there will be a further temptation to translate this into institutional gains. Meanwhile, even the suspicion that the power balance is shifting against one or other community will raise questions in its mind about the merits of the Agreement.

The potential for conflict is further aggravated by the demographic issue. The gap is narrowing and some observers see a Catholic majority as imminent (Simon, 1999). Others argue that, while the gap will continue to close for a while, the rate of Catholic growth has already begun to slacken: there may be a Catholic majority in Northern Ireland some day, but it will not be for a long time (Compton, 1989). The issue is, however, enormously complicated by population flows. In the past Catholics have been more likely than Protestants to emigrate from Northern Ireland. Demographic convergence is due in large measure to the decline in that disparity (Cormack et al., 1993). The change also suggests that, as the Catholic position improves in Northern Ireland, they are more likely to remain. If that is so, future migration differentials could favour Catholics. In any event, even the possibility of demographic change has politically destabilising consequences. The fear of a Catholic majority is very real for many Protestants, while the support of many republicans for the Agreement is predicated on the notion that a Catholic majority is both inevitable and will come soon.

The emphasis which the Belfast Agreement places on equality, and the measures it puts in place to achieve this, are a further source of instability in the communal power balance. Past periods of stability have arisen when Catholics have had no obvious new resources on which they could draw to press their case. If the equality provisions of the Agreement are successful, such resources will become available to them on a continuing basis. If they succeed in harnessing these resources to political effect, they will have a powerful new political weapon. But identifying and using resources for communal advance – or defence – is an option open to both sides, and likely to be used by both.

If this happens, the most likely scenario for the future is not that of the communities addressing common problems and managing their differences in a peaceful and cooperative way, but using what resources they have, or can acquire, to continue the power struggle in which they have engaged over the past 30 years. This would not be 'in the spirit of the Agreement' as understood by its principal architects, but events since the Agreement was signed show how uncertain that spirit is. The Agreement sets down the rules to be observed in the conduct of such struggle; in particular it prohibits the use of violence or injustice as political weapons. But if political and communal struggle becomes intense, questions of justice will count for little, and there is every possibility of a spill-over into violence.

The second reason why the realignment of structural and institutional power will not initiate a phase of low intensity conflict arises from the nature of the Agreement itself: it rests on fundamentally contradictory expectations. Those unionists who supported the Agreement did so to achieve the end of the IRA's campaign and to secure the union. The nationalists and republicans who supported it did so to achieve equality and closer links with the South while advancing the process of Irish reunification in the longer term. The difficulty with the Agreement is that it does not – cannot – deliver all of these simultaneously. It has confirmed the end of the IRA's campaign, but it makes the union dependent on the will of the majority of the population, and the demographic balance is shifting. It offers nationalists the means to pursue equality, but does not guarantee it, still less in the time frame some nationalists expect; whether it will advance the cause of Irish unity is even less certain. In other words, at most one community can have its expectations fulfilled, and even that will happen only if it is active, vigilant and assertive.

In such circumstances, conflict is inevitable. The only question is how intense it will be. Some factors could help to moderate it. The most promising is that political elites across the parties will see a shared interest in making the Agreement work. They could endeavour to sideline the most divisive issues and concentrate on those where there is most common ground. This would be in the spirit of the consociationalist model of politics on which the Agreement in part rests (Ruane and Todd, this volume, p. 16). The articulation of moderate and reconciliatory sentiments by the leadership of the UUP and Sinn Féin over the past year suggests that an attempt will be made to do this.

The difficulty is that, as long as the structural conditions for conflict remain in place, it will be impossible to sideline the fundamental issues. Matters will repeatedly arise where the overall effect of the Agreement will appear in some way to be tested: movement in the demographic ratio, trends in Catholic and Protestant employment, the effectiveness of the new equality and human rights legislation, the composition and behaviour of the police, the presence and activities of the British army, the handling of Orange marches, support for Irish and Ulster-Scots cultural activities, the functioning of the North–South bodies. What happens in these areas has long been viewed as a test of what is happening in the situation overall. The party leaders on both sides might discover a common interest in pursuing a conciliatory line in the interests of overall stability; but their supporters are unlikely to be so indulgent. And if the party they support does not deliver, they will switch to another one which will – or will at least press the case more assertively.

On both sides political elites will find themselves with little room for manoeuvre. Each party sold the Agreement to its supporters on the basis that their fundamental concerns had been, and would be, met. The UUP, PUP and Ulster Democratic Party (UDP) assured unionists that the union was secure; the Social Democratic and Labour Party (SDLP) and Sinn Féin assured nationalists and republicans that the Agreement would secure equality and pave the way to a united Ireland. Very many of the unionists and nationalists who voted for the Agreement did so with doubts and misgivings, supporting it as much out of trust in the leadership as from personal conviction. If, in the years to come, that trust appears to have been misplaced, the party and its leadership will pay a heavy price. And both sides cannot simultaneously deliver what they promised.

In those circumstances, the only hope for a culture of give-and-take at elite level, is that one develops at the level of the society as a whole. As yet there is no sign of this happening. The balance of evidence suggests the opposite – that the communities are drifting farther apart. Hayes and McAllister (this volume, pp. 35–6) show the widening gap in political and cultural identities in the population as a whole. In the more militant sectors of both communities, the evidence is even more compelling: the difficulties surrounding the decommissioning of weapons, the activities of fringe paramilitaries who reject the ceasefires of the major paramilitary organisations, the controversies surrounding key marches, the sectarian attacks on individuals and families living in vulnerable areas.

One final matter bears on the question both of instability in the power balance and the capacity of pro-Agreement political elites to operate the new institutions in a consensual manner. Much of the anticipation of a reduction in the intensity of conflict during the coming period rests on the assumption that Irish unity has now been removed from the agenda for the foreseeable future, possibly forever (for example Ryder, 1999). According to this view, the pressure for unity came primarily from Sinn Féin and the IRA. Sinn Féin now places its emphasis on equality rather than unity; once the IRA yields its weapons it ceases to be a significant political force. By supporting the Agreement and participating in its institutions Sinn Féin is implicitly accepting the legitimacy of partition, even if it does not formally acknowledge this. Moreover, as time goes on, it will, like its predecessors, move farther and farther from its radical republican roots. The Agreement in effect consolidates partition; and in doing so it represents the triumph of pragmatism over unrealistic aspirationalism.

There are two difficulties with this argument. First, while Sinn Féin has been playing-down the question of unity and placing most of its emphasis on achieving equality within Northern Ireland, there is no evidence that it has abandoned the goal of Irish unity. On the contrary, it argues that equality is the means to unity. It may be mistaken in this, but if it is, it can revise its strategy. Second, the context in which unity presents itself as an option is changing. The assumption that Sinn Féin is retreating from the goal of unity rests in part on the view that the aspiration is essentially reactive, emotional and, in varying degrees, irrational. This was a sustainable argument in the 1980s when the Southern economy was in deep, apparently insurmountable, crisis. The very rapid economic growth of the 1990s alters this picture considerably. The Republic will never have British-level resources to carry Northern Ireland as an economic dependency, but the successful application of its model of development to the North would make this unnecessary. If present trends continue, the North may soon have a positive economic interest in unity (O'Hearn, 1998, pp. 69–70).

This would be much more important to nationalists than to unionists, most of whom would remain opposed to unity, even if it promised economic benefits. But the issue is further complicated by the rebirth of Scottish nationalism, and the possibility – some believe certainty – that Scotland will some day secede from the union. Ulster Protestants have a strong attachment to the British state, and in particular to the Crown; but their deepest cultural ties are with Scotland (Erskine and Lucy, 1997). If Scotland secedes from the union, it is not clear in what sense the state would still be 'British' as distinct from English, how attractive it would be to Ulster Protestants, or whether Northern Ireland would still be welcome within it. One way or another the question of the reunification of Ireland would arise, and in a context in which the nationalist hand was strengthened. Even if Sinn Féin wanted now to sideline the question of unity, it might not find it possible to do so.

For Reading III all this rules out the possibility that the conflict will once more settle down, stabilising around the consensual implementation of the Agreement within the existing constitutional framework. Instability and the possibility of radical change are now inherent in the situation; increasingly, each community will be operating in a 'divided-society' version of the 'risk society' characteristic of late modernity/postmodernity (Beck, 1992). Neither community will feel secure enough to relax its guard, to concentrate on the 'smaller' issues and allow the 'big' ones to sort themselves out in the longer term. Each will feel compelled to do what it has done for the past 30 years: monitor change, anticipate threats and dangers, build up its resources, and struggle to defend or advance its position.

DISCUSSION AND CONCLUSION

This chapter began with the question: are we at the 'end of Irish history'? Is the historic conflict of Catholic and Protestant in Ireland, and of Britain and Ireland, now coming to a close? We have seen that the question can be answered in the affirmative, backed with a theoretically informed reading of the present: Reading I argues that because of wider international changes, the system of relationships which has underlain the conflict since its inception is now unravelling. But it is not the only possible reading. Reading II argues that the underlying conditions of conflict persist – that the apparent end to the conflict is simply the shift to a low intensity phase. Reading III discounts even that: it sees the conflict continuing at more or less the same intensity, if in a less violent way.

Indeed, for Readings II and III, far from the conflict coming to an end, there is a strong possibility of yet another crisis in the future if nationalists become a majority in Northern Ireland and push for Irish unity. The Belfast Agreement provides a constitutional mechanism to ensure a smooth transition to unity; it also allows it to take place in a gradual way by policies of harmonisation and by expanding the scope and range of the North–South bodies. But if the past is a guide, the transition would be far from smooth at the level of communal politics; the only question is how great and how violent the crisis would be, and to what extent the conflictual relationships of the past – sedimented over centuries – would be reconstituted within the structures of post-partition Ireland.

There is, however, a further possible interpretation of the present. So far the readings have been treated as competing; they might also be viewed as complementary. The very fact that one can offer such contrasting readings of the same reality, each carrying at least some plausibility, raises the question of whether the reality is more complex than any one of the readings is able to grasp. The readings share the presupposition of a single set of forces combining to drive the conflict in just one direction, even if they differ on what those forces are. An alternative would be to envisage contradictory forces pushing and pulling the conflict in several directions at once. This would suggest that the readings might be viewed as complementary, partial approximations to a contradictory reality, each capturing some aspects of that reality but not others.

There are two reasons why the situation may be more contradictory now than in the past. One relates to the particularities of the moment. Thirty years of violent conflict have convinced at least some of the participants – in particular the two governments – to address issues in a radical way. The stability and coherence born of fixed, non-negotiable, positions has now come to an end; new possibilities, many of them contradictory, have now emerged on the scene. The second possibility is that something more profound has changed: that the differentiations and dislocations attendant on a shift within modernity, or beyond it to some form of postmodernity, have begun to restructure the underlying conditions of conflict. As a result, the cohesive, self-reproducing, overdetermining character of the system of relationships in the past is now giving way to something much more uneven, contradictory and fractious, but not necessarily any less conflictual in its implications.[7]

This raises the further question as to whether there is also now a greater degree of structural openness and indeterminacy than in the past, and the possibility of radical change. There have, in fact, been such periods in the past. There has been a strong element of structural determination in the Irish situation over the centuries. But there have also been critical conjunctures when, for a time, a 'realm of freedom' opened up, when radical change was possible, not simply conceptually but practically. One such period was at the end of the eighteenth century and culminated in the rebellion of the United Irishmen; a second was the early years of the union when British–Irish relations could have been reconstructed; a third was the decade immediately before and after partition. In all cases there were powerful structural forces working to maintain the conflictual status quo. These forces channelled and constrained choices, but they did not determine them in an absolute sense, while the choices made shaped the way in which these forces would then evolve. The present moment has many of the characteristics of such a critical conjuncture.

What are the implications for policy? They differ depending on whether one selects one particular reading or sees all three as complementary. Taken on its own, Reading I suggests that current problems (for example, the difficulties in implementing the Agreement, sectarian tensions) are transitional and that, one way or another, we are moving beyond the conflict of the past 30 years, and indeed of the past 300 years. The Agreement will advance that process, but even it will be a way-station rather than a final destination. The Agreement is conceived within the terms of the historic conflict, notably in its emphasis on the representation of the communal blocs. As the traditional system of relationships dissolves, this will be neither necessary nor productive and a new framework can then be set in place. Since the process is already underway, the task of policy makers is to support it, to prevent any temporary blockages or breakdowns, and if possible to speed it up with a multi-levelled strategy targeted at the different levels of the system of relationships (for specific examples of such a strategy see Ruane and Todd, 1996, chapter 11).

For Reading II, the matter is not so simple. The conditions of conflict are not dissolving. On the other hand, we are moving out of a phase of high intensity conflict. The first priority is to implement the Agreement and to ensure that communal relationships are as good as they can be in the new phase. There will be difficulties. The traditional divisions will remain; so too, at least for a time, will the bitterness and mistrust engendered by more than 25 years of violence; serious conflict may also continue in localities where the wider contradictions are unusually intense. The task of policy makers will be to manage and contain these tensions, while taking advantage of the real opportunities which will then exist for reconciliation. At that point, the possibility will open up to address the underlying causes of the conflict: the system of relationships. Here the policy implications converge with those of Reading I: a multi-levelled strategy targeted at the different levels of the system of relationships with a view to dismantling it. The important difference is that for Reading I the goal is to speed up the process; for Reading II it is the much more difficult task of getting it under way.

For Reading III the situation is more difficult again: not alone do the conditions of conflict persist, there is no hope of an immediate end to intense conflict. The priority is the same as for the other readings – to implement the Agreement – but for Reading III, even this will be difficult. There is no certainty that the obstacles to implementation of the Agreement will be overcome, or, if they are, that it will be animated by a spirit that reconciles rather than divides. Much of the policy effort will be geared to conflict containment and crisis management. Policy for the longer term will have to address the underlying conditions of conflict, but progress will be limited by the corrosive effects of continued struggle. The one glimmer of light in this otherwise dark picture – and it may turn out to be important – is that the instability inherent in the new situation may itself create opportunities for radical interventions. In certain circumstances, it might prove possible to harness the new instability, which at one level is conducive to conflict, and use it to erode the reproductive tendencies of the system of relationships.

If, on the other hand, the readings are seen as complementary approaches to a contradictory situation, the policy environment is much more open, complex, dynamic and unstable, full of potential but also of risk. The potential lies in the structurally determined 'realm of freedom' referred to above, and freedom is never risk free. All the positive tendencies described will be present, but also all the negative ones. This highlights the critical role of political leadership. Political leaders cannot create social forces ex nihilo; but they can mobilise and strengthen some, and contain and deflect others. The strategic challenge in this instance is to identify and to harness the positive forces, while containing the negative ones, and to do this in conditions that are both unstable and unpredictable. If it is done successfully, the situation can be transformed; but the failure to act, or the wrong decisions, could renew the conflict for another generation or more.

A final question: does the experience of the peace process, and of the implementation of the Agreement thus far, tend to confirm one or other of the readings, or point to the need to take account of all three? The dangers of a rush to judgement based on the circumstances of the moment are clear. The logic of Reading I might have appeared compelling in the euphoria that followed the signing of the Agreement; although the fudge on decommissioning needed to achieve agreement would have counselled caution. Writing more than a year later, at a time when local-level sectarianism appears to be growing and the decommissioning issue has still to be resolved, Reading III comes closest to mind. But a resolution of the decommissioning issue in the coming months might point to Reading II. On the other hand, the one consistent feature of the peace process since its inception has been change, contradiction, uncertainty and unpredictability. This suggests that a model based on the readings as complementary, partial approximations to a contradictory reality may offer the best account of the current conjuncture.

NOTES

[1] For example, Tony Blair's hope that 'the burden of history can at long last be lifted from our shoulders'. For other examples, see the contributions to *The Irish Times* for Saturday 11 April 1998.

[2] The prime exponent of this view was Dr Conor Cruise O'Brien.

[3] For a more detailed account and references see Ruane and Todd, 1996.

[4] See, in particular, columnists with Independent Newspapers in the period before the IRA ceasefire.

[5] The most dramatic retreat from the imperial/colonial model in the recent period has been by the republican movement.

[6] For arguments and counter-arguments about class in contemporary society, see Lee and Turner, 1996.

[7] For a different argument about the shift from modernity to post modernity and its implications for Northern Ireland, see McCall, 1999.

APPENDIX

AGREEMENT REACHED IN THE MULTI-PARTY NEGOTIATIONS

DECLARATION OF SUPPORT

1. We, the participants in the multi-party negotiations, believe that the agreement we have negotiated offers a truly historic opportunity for a new beginning.

2. The tragedies of the past have left a deep and profoundly regrettable legacy of suffering. We must never forget those who have died or been injured, and their families. But we can best honour them through a fresh start, in which we firmly dedicate ourselves to the achievement of reconciliation, tolerance, and mutual trust, and to the protection and vindication of the human rights of all.

3. We are committed to partnership, equality and mutual respect as the basis of relationships within Northern Ireland, between North and South, and between these islands.

4. We reaffirm our total and absolute commitment to exclusively democratic and peaceful means of resolving differences on political issues, and our opposition to any use or threat of force by others for any political purpose, whether in regard to this agreement or otherwise.

5. We acknowledge the substantial differences between our continuing, and equally legitimate, political aspirations. However, we will endeavour to strive in every practical way towards reconciliation and rapprochement within the framework of democratic and agreed arrangements. We pledge that we will, in good faith, work to ensure the success of each and every one of the arrangements to be established under this agreement. It is accepted that all of the institutional and constitutional arrangements – an Assembly in Northern Ireland, a North/South Ministerial Council, implementation bodies, a British-Irish Council and a British-Irish Intergovernmental Conference and any amendments to British Acts of Parliament and the Constitution of Ireland – are interlocking and interdependent and that in particular the functioning of the Assembly and the North/South Council are so closely inter-related that the success of each depends on that of the other.

6. Accordingly, in a spirit of concord, we strongly commend this agreement to the people, North and South, for their approval.

CONSTITUTIONAL ISSUES

1. The participants endorse the commitment made by the British and Irish Governments that, in a new British-Irish Agreement replacing the Anglo-Irish Agreement, they will:

    (i) recognise the legitimacy of whatever choice is freely exercised by a majority of the people of Northern Ireland with regard to its status, whether they prefer to continue to support the Union with Great Britain or a sovereign united Ireland;

    (ii) recognise that it is for the people of the island of Ireland alone, by agreement between the two parts respectively and without external impediment, to exercise their right of self-determination on the basis of consent, freely and concurrently given, North and South, to bring about a united Ireland, if that is their wish, accepting that this right must be achieved and exercised with and subject to the agreement and consent of a majority of the people of Northern Ireland;

    (iii) acknowledge that while a substantial section of the people in Northern Ireland share the legitimate wish of a majority of the people of the island of Ireland for a united Ireland, the present wish of a majority of the people of Northern Ireland, freely exercised and legitimate, is to maintain the Union and, accordingly, that Northern Ireland's status as part of the United Kingdom reflects and relies upon that wish; and that it would be wrong to make any change in the status of Northern Ireland save with the consent of a majority of its people;

    (iv) affirm that if, in the future, the people of the island of Ireland exercise their right of self-determination on the basis set out in sections (i) and (ii) above to bring about a united Ireland, it will be a binding obligation on both Governments to introduce and support in their respective Parliaments legislation to give effect to that wish;

    (v) affirm that whatever choice is freely exercised by a majority of the people of Northern Ireland, the power of the sovereign government with jurisdiction there shall be exercised with rigorous impartiality on behalf of all the people in the diversity of their identities and traditions and shall be founded on the principles of full respect for, and equality of, civil, political, social and cultural rights, of freedom from discrimination for all citizens, and of parity of esteem and of just and equal treatment for the identity, ethos, and aspirations of both communities;

    (vi) recognise the birthright of all the people of Northern Ireland to identify themselves and be accepted as Irish or British, or both, as they may so choose, and accordingly confirm that their right to hold both British and Irish citizenship is accepted by both Governments and would not be affected by any future change in the status of Northern Ireland.

2. The participants also note that the two Governments have accordingly undertaken in the context of this comprehensive political agreement, to propose and support changes in, respectively, the Constitution of Ireland and in British legislation relating to the constitutional status of Northern Ireland.

ANNEX A

DRAFT CLAUSES/SCHEDULES FOR INCORPORATION IN BRITISH LEGISLATION

1. (1) It is hereby declared that Northern Ireland in its entirety remains part of the United Kingdom and shall not cease to be so without the consent of a majority of the people of Northern Ireland voting in a poll held for the purposes of this section in accordance with Schedule 1.

   (2) But if the wish expressed by a majority in such a poll is that Northern Ireland should cease to be part of the United Kingdom and form part of a united Ireland, the Secretary of State shall lay before Parliament such proposals to give effect to that wish as may be agreed between Her Majesty's Government in the United Kingdom and the Government of Ireland.

2. The Government of Ireland Act 1920 is repealed; and this Act shall

have effect notwithstanding any other previous enactment.

Schedule 1

Polls for the purpose of section 1

1. The Secretary of State may by order direct the holding of a poll for the purposes of section 1 on a date specified in the order.

2. Subject to paragraph 3, the Secretary of State shall exercise the power under paragraph 1 if at any time it appears likely to him that a majority of those voting would express a wish that Northern Ireland should cease to be part of the United Kingdom and form part of a united Ireland.

3. The Secretary of State shall not make an order under paragraph 1 earlier than seven years after the holding of a previous poll under this Schedule.

4. (Remaining paragraphs along the lines of paragraphs 2 and 3 of existing Schedule 1 to 1973 Act.)

ANNEX B

IRISH GOVERNMENT DRAFT LEGISLATION TO AMEND THE CONSTITUTION

Add to Article 29 the following section: 7.

1°. The State may consent to be bound by the British-Irish Agreement done at Belfast on the 10th day of April 1998, hereinafter called the Agreement.

2°. Any institution established by or under the Agreement may exercise the powers and functions thereby conferred on it in respect of all or any part of the island of Ireland notwithstanding any other provision of this Constitution conferring a like power or function on any person or any organ of State appointed under or created or established by or under this Constitution. Any power or function conferred on such an institution in relation to the settlement or resolution of disputes or controversies may be in addition toor in substitution for any like power or function conferred by this Constitution on any such person or organ of State as aforesaid.

3°. If the Government declare that the State has become obliged, pursuant to the Agreement, to give effect to the amendment of this Constitution referred to therein, then, notwithstanding Article 46 hereof, this Constitution shall be amended as follows:

   i. the following Articles shall be substituted for Articles 2 and 3 of the Irish text: [Irish text omitted]

   ii. the following Articles shall be substituted for Articles 2 and 3 of the English text:

Article 2

It is the entitlement and birthright of every person born in the island of Ireland, which includes its islands and seas, to be part of the Irish nation. That is also the entitlement of all persons otherwise qualified in accordance with law to be citizens of Ireland. Furthermore, the Irish nation cherishes its special affinity with people of Irish ancestry living abroad who share its cultural identity and heritage.

Article 3

1. It is the firm will of the Irish nation, in harmony and friendship, to unite all the people who share the territory of the island of Ireland, in all the diversity of their identities and traditions, recognising that a united Ireland shall be brought about only by peaceful means with the consent of a majority of the people, democratically expressed, in both jurisdictions in the island. Until then, the laws enacted by the Parliament established by this Constitution shall have the like area and extent of application as the laws enacted by the Parliament that existed immediately before the coming into operation of this Constitution.

2. Institutions with executive powers and functions that are shared between those jurisdictions may be established by their respective responsible authorities for stated purposes and may exercise powers and functions in respect of all or any part of the island."

   iii. the following section shall be added to the Irish text of this Article: [Irish text omitted]

   iv. the following section shall be added to the English text of this Article:

      "8. The State may exercise extra-territorial jurisdiction in accordance with the generally recognised principles of international law."

4°. If a declaration under this section is made, this subsection and subsection 3, other than the amendment of this Constitution effected thereby, and subsection 5 of this section shall be omitted from every official text of this Constitution published thereafter, but notwithstanding such omission this section shall continue to have the force of law.

5°. If such a declaration is not made within twelve months of this section being added to this Constitution or such longer period as may be provided for by law, this section shall cease to have effect and shall be omitted from every official text of this Constitution published thereafter.

STRAND ONE

DEMOCRATIC INSTITUTIONS IN NORTHERN IRELAND

1. This agreement provides for a democratically elected Assembly in Northern Ireland which is inclusive in its membership, capable of exercising executive and legislative authority, and subject to safeguards to protect the rights and interests of all sides of the community.

The Assembly

2. A 108-member Assembly will be elected by PR(STV) from existing Westminster constituencies.

3. The Assembly will exercise full legislative and executive authority in respect of those matters currently within the responsibility of the six Northern Ireland Government Departments, with the possibility of taking on responsibility for other matters as detailed elsewhere in this agreement.

4. The Assembly – operating where appropriate on a cross-community basis – will be the prime source of authority in respect of all devolved responsibilities.

Safeguards

5. There will be safeguards to ensure that all sections of the community can participate and work together successfully in the operation of these institutions and that all sections of the community are protected, including:

   (a) allocations of Committee Chairs, Ministers and Committee membership in proportion to party strengths;

   (b) the European Convention on Human Rights (ECHR) and any Bill of Rights for Northern Ireland supplementing it, which neither the Assembly nor public bodies can infringe, together with a Human Rights Commission;

   (c) arrangements to provide that key decisions and legislation are proofed to ensure that they do not infringe the ECHR and any Bill of Rights for Northern Ireland;

   (d) arrangements to ensure key decisions are taken on a cross-community basis;

   (i) either parallel consent, i.e. a majority of those members present and voting, including a majority of the unionist and nationalist designations present and voting;

(ii) _or_   a weighted majority (60%) of members present and voting, including at least 40% of each of the nationalist and unionist designations present and voting.

Key decisions requiring cross-community support will be designated in advance, including election of the Chair of the Assembly, the First Minister and Deputy First Minister, standing orders and budget allocations. In other cases such decisions could be triggered by a petition of concern brought by a significant minority of Assembly members (30/108).

(e) an Equality Commission to monitor a statutory obligation to promote equality of opportunity in specified areas and parity of esteem between the two main communities, and to investigate individual complaints against public bodies.

Operation of the Assembly

6. At their first meeting, members of the Assembly will register a designation of identity – nationalist, unionist or other – for the purposes of measuring cross-community support in Assembly votes under the relevant provisions above.

7. The Chair and Deputy Chair of the Assembly will be elected on a cross-community basis, as set out in paragraph 5(d) above.

8. There will be a Committee for each of the main executive functions of the Northern Ireland Administration. The Chairs and Deputy Chairs of the Assembly Committees will be allocated proportionally, using the d'Hondt system. Membership of the Committees will be in broad proportion to party strengths in the Assembly to ensure that the opportunity of Committee places is available to all members.

9. The Committees will have a scrutiny, policy development and consultation role with respect to the Department with which each is associated, and will have a role in initiation of legislation. They will have the power to:

•   consider and advise on Departmental budgets and Annual Plans in the context of the overall budget allocation;

•   approve relevant secondary legislation and take the Committee stage of relevant primary legislation;

•   call for persons and papers;

•   initiate enquiries and make reports;

•   consider and advise on matters brought to the Committee by its Minister.

10. Standing Committees other than Departmental Committees may be established as may be required from time to time.

11. The Assembly may appoint a special Committee to examine

and report on whether a measure or proposal for legislation is in conformity with equality requirements, including the ECHR/Bill of Rights. The Committee shall have the power to call people and papers to assist in its consideration of the matter. The Assembly shall then consider the report of the Committee and can determine the matter in accordance with the cross-community consent procedure.

12. The above special procedure shall be followed when requested by the Executive Committee, or by the relevant Departmental Committee, voting on a cross-community basis.

13. When there is a petition of concern as in 5(d) above, the Assembly shall vote to determine whether the measure may proceed without reference to this special procedure. If this fails to achieve support on a cross-community basis, as in 5(d)(i) above, the special procedure shall be followed.

Executive Authority

14. Executive authority to be discharged on behalf of the Assembly by a First Minister and Deputy First Minister and up to ten Ministers with Departmental responsibilities.

15. The First Minister and Deputy First Minister shall be jointly elected into office by the Assembly voting on a cross-community basis, according to 5(d)(i) above.

16. Following the election of the First Minister and Deputy First Minister, the posts of Ministers will be allocated to parties on the basis of the d'Hondt system by reference to the number of seats each party has in the Assembly.

17. The Ministers will constitute an Executive Committee, which will be convened, and presided over, by the First Minister and Deputy First Minister.

18. The duties of the First Minister and Deputy First Minister will include, inter alia, dealing with and co-ordinating the work of the Executive Committee and the response of the Northern Ireland administration to external relationships.

19. The Executive Committee will provide a forum for the discussion of, and agreement on, issues which cut across the responsibilities of two or more Ministers, for prioritising executive and legislative proposals and for recommending a common position where necessary (e.g. in dealing with external relationships).

20. The Executive Committee will seek to agree each year, and review as necessary, a programme incorporating an agreed budget linked to policies and programmes, subject to approval by the Assembly, after scrutiny in Assembly Committees, on a cross-community basis.

21. A party may decline the opportunity to nominate a

person to serve as a Minister or may subsequently change its nominee.

22. All the Northern Ireland Departments will be headed by a Minister. All Ministers will liaise regularly with their respective Committee.

23. As a condition of appointment, Ministers, including the First Minister and Deputy First Minister, will affirm the terms of a Pledge of Office (Annex A) undertaking to discharge effectively and in good faith all the responsibilities attaching to their office.

24. Ministers will have full executive authority in their respective areas of responsibility, within any broad programme agreed by the Executive Committee and endorsed by the Assembly as a whole.

25. An individual may be removed from office following a decision of the Assembly taken on a cross-community basis, if (s)he loses the confidence of the Assembly, voting on a cross-community basis, for failure to meet his or her responsibilities including, inter alia, those set out in the Pledge of Office. Those who hold office should use only democratic, non-violent means, and those who do not should be excluded or removed from office under these provisions.

Legislation

26. The Assembly will have authority to pass primary legislation for Northern Ireland in devolved areas, subject to:

(a) the ECHR and any Bill of Rights for Northern Ireland supplementing it which, if the courts found to be breached, would render the relevant legislation null and void;

(b) decisions by simple majority of members voting, except when decision on a cross-community basis is required;

(c) detailed scrutiny and approval in the relevant Departmental Committee;

(d) mechanisms, based on arrangements proposed for the Scottish Parliament, to ensure suitable co-ordination, and avoid disputes, between the Assembly and the Westminster Parliament;

(e) option of the Assembly seeking to include Northern Ireland provisions in United Kingdom-wide legislation in the Westminster Parliament, especially on devolved issues where parity is normally maintained (e.g. social security, company law).

27. The Assembly will have authority to legislate in reserved areas with the approval of the Secretary of State and subject to Parliamentary control.

28. Disputes over legislative competence will be decided by the Courts.

29. Legislation could be initiated by an individual, a Committee or a Minister.

Relations with other institutions

30. Arrangements to represent the Assembly as a whole, at Summit level and in dealings with other institutions, will be in accordance with paragraph 18, and will be such as to ensure cross-community involvement.

31. Terms will be agreed between appropriate Assembly representatives and the Government of the United Kingdom to ensure effective co-ordination and input by Ministers to national policy-making, including on EU issues.

32. Role of Secretary of State:

    (a) to remain responsible for NIO matters not devolved to the Assembly, subject to regular consultation with the Assembly and Ministers;

    (b) to approve and lay before the Westminster Parliament any Assembly legislation on reserved matters;

    (c) to represent Northern Ireland interests in the United Kingdom Cabinet;

    (d) to have the right to attend the Assembly at their invitation.

33. The Westminster Parliament (whose power to make legislation for Northern Ireland would remain unaffected) will:

    (a) legislate for non-devolved issues, other than where the Assembly legislates with the approval of the Secretary of State and subject to the control of Parliament;

    (b) to legislate as necessary to ensure the United Kingdom's international obligations are met in respect of Northern Ireland;

    (c) scrutinise, including through the Northern Ireland Grand and Select Committees, the responsibilities of the Secretary of State.

34. A consultative Civic Forum will be established. It will comprise representatives of the business, trade union and voluntary sectors, and such other sectors as agreed by the First Minister and the Deputy First Minister. It will act as a consultative mechanism on social, economic and cultural issues. The First Minister and the Deputy First Minister will by agreement provide administrative support for the Civic Forum and establish guidelines for the selection of representatives to the Civic Forum.

Transitional Arrangements

35. The Assembly will meet first for the purpose of organisation, without legislative or executive powers, to resolve its standing orders and working practices and make preparations for the effective functioning of the Assembly, the British-Irish Council and the North/South Ministerial Council and associated implementation bodies. In this transitional period, those members of the Assembly serving as shadow Ministers shall affirm their commitment to non-violence and exclusively peaceful and democratic means and their

opposition to any use or threat of force by others for any political purpose; to work in good faith to bring the new arrangements into being; and to observe the spirit of the Pledge of Office applying to appointed Ministers.

Review

36. After a specified period there will be a review of these arrangements, including the details of electoral arrangements and of the Assembly's procedures, with a view to agreeing any adjustments necessary in the interests of efficiency and fairness.

ANNEX A

Pledge of Office

To pledge:

(a) to discharge in good faith all the duties of office;

(b) commitment to non-violence and exclusively peaceful and democratic means;

(c) to serve all the people of Northern Ireland equally, and to act in accordance with the general obligations on government to promote equality and prevent discrimination;

(d) to participate with colleagues in the preparation of a programme for government;

(e) to operate within the framework of that programme when agreed within the Executive Committee and endorsed by the Assembly;

(f) to support, and to act in accordance with, all decisions of the Executive Committee and Assembly;

(g) to comply with the Ministerial Code of Conduct.

Code of Conduct

Ministers must at all times:

- observe the highest standards of propriety and regularity involving impartiality, integrity and objectivity in relationship to the stewardship of public funds;

- be accountable to users of services, the community and, through the Assembly, for the activities within their responsibilities, their stewardship of public funds and the extent to which key performance targets and objectives have been met;

- ensure all reasonable requests for information from the Assembly, users of services and individual citizens are complied with; and that Departments and their staff conduct their dealings with the public in an open and responsible way;

- follow the seven principles of public life set out by the Committee on Standards in Public Life;

- comply with this code and with rules relating to the use of public funds;

- operate in a way conducive to promoting good community relations and equality of treatment;

- not use information gained in the course of their service for personal gain; nor seek to use the opportunity of public service to promote their private interests;

- ensure they comply with any rules on the acceptance of gifts and hospitality that might be offered;

- declare any personal or business interests which may conflict with their responsibilities. The Assembly will retain a Register of Interests. Individuals must ensure that any direct or indirect pecuniary interests which members of the public might reasonably think could influence their judgement are listed in the Register of Interests;

STRAND TWO

NORTH/SOUTH MINISTERIAL COUNCIL

1. Under a new British/Irish Agreement dealing with the totality of relationships, and related legislation at Westminster and in the Oireachtas, a North/South Ministerial Council to be established to bring together those with executive responsibilities in Northern Ireland and the Irish Government, to develop consultation, co-operation and action within the island of Ireland – including through implementation on an all-island and cross-border basis – on matters of mutual interest within the competence of the Administrations, North and South.

2. All Council decisions to be by agreement between the two sides. Northern Ireland to be represented by the First Minister, Deputy First Minister and any

relevant Ministers, the Irish Government by the Taoiseach and relevant Ministers, all operating in accordance with the rules for democratic authority and accountability in force in the Northern Ireland Assembly and the Oireachtas respectively. Participation in the Council to be one of the essential responsibilities attaching to relevant posts in the two Administrations. If a holder of a relevant post will not participate normally in the Council, the Taoiseach in the case of the Irish Government and the First and Deputy First Minister in the case of the Northern Ireland Administration to be able to make alternative arrangements.

3. The Council to meet in different formats:

   (i)   in plenary format twice a year, with Northern Ireland representation led by the First Minister and Deputy First Minister and the Irish Government led by the Taoiseach;

   (ii) in specific sectoral formats on a regular and frequent basis with each side represented by the appropriate Minister;

   (iii) in an appropriate format to consider institutional or cross-sectoral matters (including in relation to the EU) and to resolve disagreement.

4. Agendas for all meetings to be settled by prior agreement between the two sides, but it will be open to either to propose any matter for consideration or action.

5. The Council:

   (i) to exchange information, discuss and consult with a view to co-operating on matters of mutual interest within the competence of both Administrations, North and South;

   (ii) to use best endeavours to reach agreement on the adoption of common policies, in areas where there is a mutual cross-border and all-island benefit, and which are within the competence of both Administrations, North and South, making determined efforts to overcome any disagreements;

   (iii) to take decisions by agreement on policies for implementation separately in each jurisdiction, in relevant meaningful areas within the competence of both Administrations, North and South;

   (iv) to take decisions by agreement on policies and action at an all-island and cross-border level to be implemented by the bodies to be established as set out in paragraphs 8 and 9 below.

6. Each side to be in a position to take decisions in the Council within the defined authority of those attending, through the arrangements in place for co-ordination of executive functions within each jurisdiction. Each side to remain accountable to the Assembly and Oireachtas respectively, whose approval, through the arrangements in place on either side, would be required for decisions beyond the defined authority of those attending.

7. As soon as practically possible after elections to the Northern Ireland Assembly, inaugural meetings will take place of the Assembly, the British/Irish Council and the North/South Ministerial Council in their transitional forms. All three institutions will meet regularly and frequently on this basis during the period between the elections to the Assembly, and the transfer of powers to the Assembly, in order to establish their modus operandi.

8. During the transitional period between the elections to the Northern Ireland Assembly and the transfer of power to it, representatives of the Northern Ireland transitional Administration and the Irish Government operating in the North/South Ministerial Council will undertake a work programme, in consultation with the British Government, covering at least 12 subject areas, with a view to identifying and agreeing by 31 October 1998 areas where co-operation and implementation for mutual benefit will take place. Such areas may include matters in the list set out in the Annex.

9. As part of the work programme, the Council will identify and agree at least 6 matters for co-operation and implementation in each of the following categories:

   (i) Matters where existing bodies will be the appropriate mechanisms for co-operation in each separate jurisdiction;

(ii) Matters where the co-operation will take place through agreed implementation bodies on a cross-border or all-island level.

10. The two Governments will make necessary legislative and other enabling preparations to ensure, as an absolute commitment, that these bodies, which have been agreed as a result of the work programme, function at the time of the inception of the British-Irish Agreement and the transfer of powers, with legislative authority for these bodies transferred to the Assembly as soon as possible thereafter. Other arrangements for the agreed co-operation will also commence contemporaneously with the transfer of powers to the Assembly.

11. The implementation bodies will have a clear operational remit. They will implement on an all-island and cross-border basis policies agreed in the Council.

12. Any further development of these arrangements to be by agreement in the Council and with the specific endorsement of the Northern Ireland Assembly and Oireachtas, subject to the extent of the competences and responsibility of the two Administrations.

13. It is understood that the North/South Ministerial Council and the Northern Ireland Assembly are mutually inter-dependent, and that one cannot successfully function without the other.

14. Disagreements within the Council to be addressed in the format described at paragraph 3(iii) above or in the plenary format. By agreement between the two sides, experts could be appointed to consider a particular matter and report.

15. Funding to be provided by the two Administrations on the basis that the Council and the implementation bodies constitute a necessary public function.

16. The Council to be supported by a standing joint Secretariat, staffed by members of the Northern Ireland Civil Service and the Irish Civil Service.

17. The Council to consider the European Union dimension of relevant matters, including the implementation of EU policies and programmes and proposals under consideration in the EU framework. Arrangements to be made to ensure that the views of the Council are taken into account and represented appropriately at relevant EU meetings.

18. The Northern Ireland Assembly and the Oireachtas to consider developing a joint parliamentary forum, bringing together equal numbers from both institutions for discussion of matters of mutual interest and concern.

19. Consideration to be given to the establishment of an independent consultative forum appointed by the two Administrations, representative of civil society, comprising the social partners and other members with expertise in social, cultural, economic and other issues.

ANNEX

Areas for North-South co-operation and implementation may include the following:

1. Agriculture – animal and plant health.

2. Education – teacher qualifications and exchanges.

3. Transport – strategic transport planning.

4. Environment – environmental protection, pollution, water quality, and waste management.

5. Waterways – inland waterways.

6. Social Security / Social Welfare – entitlements of cross-border workers and fraud control.

7. Tourism – promotion, marketing, research, and product development.

8. Relevant EU Programmes such as SPPR, INTERREG, Leader II and their successors.

9. Inland Fisheries.

10. Aquaculture and marine matters

11. Health: accident and emergency services and other related cross-border issues.

12. Urban and rural development.

Others to be considered by the shadow North / South Council.

STRAND THREE

BRITISH-IRISH COUNCIL

1. A British-Irish Council (BIC) will be established under a new British-Irish Agreement to promote the harmonious and mutually beneficial development of the totality of relationships among the peoples of these islands.

2. Membership of the BIC will comprise representatives of the British and Irish Governments, devolved institutions in Northern Ireland, Scotland and Wales, when established, and, if appropriate, elsewhere in the United Kingdom, together with representatives of the Isle of Man and the Channel Islands.

3. The BIC will meet in different formats: at summit level, twice per year; in specific sectoral formats on a regular basis, with each side represented by the appropriate Minister; in an appropriate format to consider cross-sectoral matters.

4. Representatives of members will operate in accordance with whatever procedures for democratic authority and accountability are in force in their respective elected institutions.

5. The BIC will exchange information, discuss, consult and use best endeavours to reach agreement on co-operation on matters of mutual interest within the competence of the relevant Administrations. Suitable issues for early discussion in the BIC could include transport links, agricultural issues, environmental

issues, cultural issues, health issues, education issues and approaches to EU issues. Suitable arrangements to be made for practical co-operation on agreed policies.

6. It will be open to the BIC to agree common policies or common actions. Individual members may opt not to participate in such common policies and common action.

7. The BIC normally will operate by consensus. In relation to decisions on common policies or common actions, including their means of implementation, it will operate by agreement of all members participating in such policies or actions.

8. The members of the BIC, on a basis to be agreed between them, will provide such financial support as it may require.

9. A secretariat for the BIC will be provided by the British and Irish Governments in co-ordination with officials of each of the other members.

10. In addition to the structures provided for under this agreement, it will be open to two or more members to develop bilateral or multilateral arrangements between them. Such arrangements could include, subject to the agreement of the members concerned, mechanisms to enable consultation, co-operation and joint decision-making on matters of mutual interest; and mechanisms to implement any joint decisions they may reach. These arrangements will not require the prior approval of the BIC as a whole and will operate independently of it.

11. The elected institutions of the members will be encouraged to develop interparliamentary links, perhaps building on the British-Irish Interparliamentary Body.

12. The full membership of the BIC will keep under review the workings of the Council, including a formal published review at an appropriate time after the Agreement comes into effect, and will contribute as appropriate to any review of the overall political agreement arising from the multi-party negotiations.

BRITISH-IRISH INTERGOVERNMENTAL CONFERENCE

1. There will be a new British-Irish Agreement dealing with the totality of relationships. It will establish a standing British-Irish Intergovernmental Conference, which will subsume both the Anglo-Irish Intergovernmental Council and the Intergovernmental Conference established under the 1985 Agreement.

2. The Conference will bring together the British and Irish Governments to promote bilateral co-operation at all levels on all matters of mutual interest within the competence of both Governments.

3. The Conference will meet as required at Summit level (Prime Minister and Taoiseach). Otherwise, Governments will be

represented by appropriate Ministers. Advisers, including police and security advisers, will attend as appropriate.

4. All decisions will be by agreement between both Governments. The Governments will make determined efforts to resolve disagreements between them. There will be no derogation from the sovereignty of either Government.

5. In recognition of the Irish Government's special interest in Northern Ireland and of the extent to which issues of mutual concern arise in relation to Northern Ireland, there will be regular and frequent meetings of the Conference concerned with non-devolved Northern Ireland matters, on which the Irish Government may put forward views and proposals. These meetings, to be co-chaired by the Minister for Foreign Affairs and the Secretary of State for Northern Ireland, would also deal with all-island and cross-border co-operation on non-devolved issues.

6. Co-operation within the framework of the Conference will include facilitation of co-operation in security matters. The Conference also will address, in particular, the areas of rights, justice, prisons and policing in Northern Ireland (unless and until responsibility is devolved to a Northern Ireland administration) and will intensify co-operation between the two Governments on the all-island or cross-border aspects of these matters.

7. Relevant executive members of the Northern Ireland

Administration will be involved in meetings of the Conference, and in the reviews referred to in paragraph 9 below to discuss non-devolved Northern Ireland matters.

8. The Conference will be supported by officials of the British and Irish Governments, including by a standing joint Secretariat of officials dealing with non-devolved Northern Ireland matters.

9. The Conference will keep under review the workings of the new British-Irish Agreement and the machinery and institutions established under it, including a formal published review three years after the Agreement comes into effect. Representatives of the Northern Ireland Administration will be invited to express views to the Conference in this context. The Conference will contribute as appropriate to any review of the overall political agreement arising from the multi-party negotiations but will have no power to override the democratic arrangements set up by this Agreement.

RIGHTS, SAFEGUARDS AND EQUALITY OF OPPORTUNITY

Human Rights

1. The parties affirm their commitment to the mutual respect, the civil rights and the religious liberties of everyone in the community. Against the background of the recent history of communal conflict, the parties affirm in particular:

- the right of free political thought;

- the right to freedom and expression of religion;

- the right to pursue democratically national and political aspirations;

- the right to seek constitutional change by peaceful and legitimate means;

- the right to freely choose one's place of residence;

- the right to equal opportunity in all social and economic activity, regardless of class, creed, disability, gender or ethnicity;

- the right to freedom from sectarian harassment; and

- the right of women to full and equal political participation.

United Kingdom Legislation

2. The British Government will complete incorporation into Northern Ireland law of the European Convention on Human Rights (ECHR), with direct access to the courts, and remedies for breach of the Convention, including power for the courts to overrule Assembly legislation on grounds of inconsistency.

3. Subject to the outcome of public consultation underway, the British Government intends, as a particular priority, to create a statutory obligation on public authorities in Northern Ireland to carry out all their functions with due regard to the need to promote equality of opportunity in relation to religion and political opinion; gender; race; disability; age; marital status; dependants; and sexual orientation. Public bodies would be required to draw up statutory schemes showing how they would implement this obligation. Such schemes would cover arrangements for policy appraisal, including an assessment of impact on relevant categories, public consultation, public access to information and services, monitoring and timetables.

4. The new Northern Ireland Human Rights Commission (see paragraph 5 below) will be invited to consult and to advise on the scope for defining, in Westminster legislation, rights supplementary to those in the European Convention on Human Rights, to reflect the particular circumstances of Northern Ireland, drawing as appropriate on international instruments and experience. These additional rights to reflect the principles of mutual respect for the identity and ethos of both communities and parity of esteem, and – taken together with the ECHR – to constitute a Bill of Rights for Northern Ireland. Among the issues for consideration by the Commission will be:

- the formulation of a general obligation on government and public bodies fully to respect, on the basis of equality of treatment, the identity and ethos of both communities in Northern Ireland; and

- a clear formulation of the rights not to be discriminated

against and to equality of opportunity in both the public and private sectors.

New Institutions in Northern Ireland

5. A new Northern Ireland Human Rights Commission, with membership from Northern Ireland reflecting the community balance, will be established by Westminster legislation, independent of Government, with an extended and enhanced role beyond that currently exercised by the Standing Advisory Commission on Human Rights, to include keeping under review the adequacy and effectiveness of laws and practices, making recommendations to Government as necessary; providing information and promoting awareness of human rights; considering draft legislation referred to them by the new Assembly; and, in appropriate cases, bringing court proceedings or providing assistance to individuals doing so.

6. Subject to the outcome of public consultation currently underway, the British Government intends a new statutory Equality Commission to replace the Fair Employment Commission, the Equal Opportunities Commission (NI), the Commission for Racial Equality (NI) and the Disability Council. Such a unified Commission will advise on, validate and monitor the statutory obligation and will investigate complaints of default.

7. It would be open to a new Northern Ireland Assembly to consider bringing together its

responsibilities for these matters into a dedicated Department of Equality.

8. These improvements will build on existing protections in Westminster legislation in respect of the judiciary, the system of justice and policing.

Comparable Steps by the Irish Government

9. The Irish Government will also take steps to further strengthen the protection of human rights in its jurisdiction. The Government will, taking account of the work of the All-Party Oireachtas Committee on the Constitution and the Report of the Constitution Review Group, bring forward measures to strengthen and underpin the constitutional protection of human rights. These proposals will draw on the European Convention on Human Rights and other international legal instruments in the field of human rights and the question of the incorporation of the ECHR will be further examined in this context. The measures brought forward would ensure at least an equivalent level of protection of human rights as will pertain in Northern Ireland. In addition, the Irish Government will:

- establish a Human Rights Commission with a mandate and remit equivalent to that within Northern Ireland;

- proceed with arrangements as quickly as possible to ratify the Council of Europe Framework Convention on National Minorities (already ratified by the UK);

- implement enhanced employment equality legislation;

- introduce equal status legislation; and

- continue to take further active steps to demonstrate its respect for the different traditions in the island of Ireland.

A Joint Committee

10. It is envisaged that there would be a joint committee of representatives of the two Human Rights Commissions, North and South, as a forum for consideration of human rights issues in the island of Ireland. The joint committee will consider, among other matters, the possibility of establishing a charter, open to signature by all democratic political parties, reflecting and endorsing agreed measures for the protection of the fundamental rights of every-one living in the island of Ireland.

Reconciliation and Victims of Violence

11. The participants believe that it is essential to acknowledge and address the suffering of the victims of violence as a necessary element of reconciliation. They look forward to the results of the work of the Northern Ireland Victims Commission.

12. It is recognised that victims have a right to remember as well as to contribute to a changed society. The achievement of a peaceful and just society would be the true memorial to the victims of violence. The participants particularly recognise that young people from areas affected by the troubles face particular difficulties and will support the development of special community-based initiatives based on international best practice. The provision of services that are supportive and sensitive to the needs of victims will also be a critical element and that support will need to be channelled through both statutory and community-based voluntary organisations facilitating locally-based self-help and support networks. This will require the allocation of sufficient resources, including statutory funding as necessary, to meet the needs of victims and to provide for community-based support programmes.

13. The participants recognise and value the work being done by many organisations to develop reconciliation and mutual understanding and respect between and within communities and traditions, in Northern Ireland and between North and South, and they see such work as having a vital role in consolidating peace and political agreement. Accordingly, they pledge their continuing support to such organisations and will positively examine the case for enhanced financial assistance for the work of reconciliation. An essential aspect of the reconciliation process is the promotion of a culture of tolerance at every level of society, including initiatives to facilitate and encourage integrated education and mixed housing.

Economic, Social and Cultural Issues

1. Pending the devolution of powers to a new Northern Ireland Assembly, the British Government will pursue broad policies for sustained economic growth and stability in Northern Ireland and for promoting social inclusion, including in particular community development and the advancement of women in public life.

2. Subject to the public consultation currently under way, the British Government will make rapid progress with:

    (i)   a new regional development strategy for Northern Ireland, for consideration in due course by the Assembly, tackling the problems of a divided society and social cohesion in urban, rural and border areas, protecting and enhancing the environment, producing new approaches to transport issues, strengthening the physical infrastructure of the region, developing the advantages and resources of rural areas and rejuvenating major urban centres;

    (ii) a new economic development strategy for Northern Ireland, for consideration in due course by the Assembly, which would provide for short and medium term economic planning linked as appropriate to the regional development strategy; and

    (iii) measures on employment equality included in the recent White Paper

("Partnership for Equality") and covering the extension and strengthening of anti-discrimination legislation, a review of the national security aspects of the present fair employment legislation at the earliest possible time, a new more focused Targeting Social Need initiative and a range of measures aimed at combating unemployment and progressively eliminating the differential in unemployment rates between the two communities by targeting objective need.

3. All participants recognise the importance of respect, understanding and tolerance in relation to linguistic diversity, including in Northern Ireland, the Irish language, Ulster-Scots and the languages of the various ethnic communities, all of which are part of the cultural wealth of the island of Ireland.

4. In the context of active consideration currently being given to the UK signing the Council of Europe Charter for Regional or Minority Languages, the British Government will in particular in relation to the Irish language, where appropriate and where people so desire it:

    • take resolute action to promote the language;

    • facilitate and encourage the use of the language in speech and writing in public and private life where there is appropriate demand;

    • seek to remove, where possible, restrictions which

would discourage or work against the maintenance or development of the language;

- make provision for liaising with the Irish language community, representing their views to public authorities and investigating complaints;

- place a statutory duty on the Department of Education to encourage and facilitate Irish medium education in line with current provision for integrated education;

- explore urgently with the relevant British authorities, and in co-operation with the Irish broadcasting authorities, the scope for achieving more widespread availability of Teilifís na Gaeilge in Northern Ireland;

- seek more effective ways to encourage and provide financial support for Irish language film and television production in Northern Ireland; and

- encourage the parties to secure agreement that this commitment will be sustained by a new Assembly in a way which takes account of the desires and sensitivities of the community.

5. All participants acknowledge the sensitivity of the use of symbols and emblems for public purposes, and the need in particular in creating the new institutions to ensure that such symbols and emblems are used in a manner which promotes mutual respect rather than division.

Arrangements will be made to monitor this issue and consider what action might be required.

DECOMMISSIONING

1. Participants recall their agreement in the Procedural Motion adopted on 24 September 1997 "that the resolution of the decommissioning issue is an indispensable part of the process of negotiation", and also recall the provisions of paragraph 25 of Strand 1 above.

2. They note the progress made by the Independent International Commission on Decommissioning and the Governments in developing schemes which can represent a workable basis for achieving the decommissioning of illegally-held arms in the possession of paramilitary groups.

3. All participants accordingly reaffirm their commitment to the total disarmament of all paramilitary organisations. They also confirm their intention to continue to work constructively and in good faith with the Independent Commission, and to use any influence they may have, to achieve the decommissioning of all paramilitary arms within two years following endorsement in referendums North and South of the agreement and in the context of the implementation of the overall settlement.

4. The Independent Commission will monitor, review and verify progress on decommissioning of illegal arms, and will report to both Governments at regular intervals.

6. Both Governments will take all necessary steps to facilitate the decommissioning process to include bringing the relevant schemes into force by the end of June.

SECURITY

1. The participants note that the development of a peaceful environment on the basis of this agreement can and should mean a normalisation of security arrangements and practices.

2. The British Government will make progress towards the objective of as early a return as possible to normal security arrangements in Northern Ireland, consistent with the level of threat and with a published overall strategy, dealing with:

    (i) the reduction of the numbers and role of the Armed Forces deployed in Northern Ireland to levels compatible with a normal peaceful society;

    (ii) the removal of security installations;

    (iii) the removal of emergency powers in Northern Ireland; and

    (iv) other measures appropriate to and compatible with a normal peaceful society.

3. The Secretary of State will consult regularly on progress, and the response to any continuing paramilitary activity, with the Irish Government and the political parties, as appropriate.

4. The British Government will continue its consultation on firearms regulation and control on the basis of the document published on 2 April 1998.

5. The Irish Government will initiate a wide-ranging review of the Offences Against the State Acts 1939-85 with a view to both reform and dispensing with those elements no longer required as circumstances permit.

POLICING AND JUSTICE

1. The participants recognise that policing is a central issue in any society. They equally recognise that Northern Ireland's history of deep divisions has made it highly emotive, with great hurt suffered and sacrifices made by many individuals and their families, including those in the RUC and other public servants. They believe that the agreement provides the opportunity for a new beginning to policing in Northern Ireland with a police service capable of attracting and sustaining support from the community as a whole. They also believe that this agreement offers a unique opportunity to bring about a new political dispensation which will recognise the full and equal legitimacy and worth of the identities, senses of allegiance and ethos of all sections of the community in Northern Ireland. They consider that this opportunity should inform and underpin the development of a police service representative in terms of the make-up of the community as a whole and which, in a peaceful environment, should be routinely unarmed.

2. The participants believe it essential that policing structures and arrangements are such that the police service is professional, effective and efficient, fair and impartial, free from partisan political control; accountable, both under the law for its actions and to the community it serves; representative of the society it polices, and operates within a coherent and co-operative criminal justice system, which conforms with human rights norms. The participants also believe that those structures and arrangements must be capable of maintaining law and order including responding effectively to crime and to any terrorist threat and to public order problems. A police service which cannot do so will fail to win public confidence and acceptance. They believe that any such structures and arrangements should be capable of delivering a policing service, in constructive and inclusive partnerships with the community at all levels, and with the maximum delegation of authority and responsibility, consistent with the foregoing principles. These arrangements should be based on principles of protection of human rights and professional integrity and should be unambiguously accepted and actively supported by the entire community.

3. An independent Commission will be established to make recommendations for future policing arrangements in Northern Ireland including means of encouraging widespread community support for these arrangements within the agreed framework of principles reflected in the paragraphs above and in accordance with the terms of reference at Annex A. The Commission will be broadly representative with expert and international representation among its membership and will be asked to consult widely and to report no later than Summer 1999.

4. The participants believe that the aims of the criminal justice system are to:

   • deliver a fair and impartial system of justice to the community;

   • be responsive to the community's concerns, and encouraging community involvement where appropriate;

   • have the confidence of all parts of the community; and

   • deliver justice efficiently and effectively.

5. There will be a parallel wide-ranging review of criminal justice (other than policing and those aspects of the system relating to the emergency legislation) to be carried out by the British Government through a mechanism with an independent element, in consultation with the political parties and others. The review will commence as soon as possible, will include wide consultation, and a report will be made to the Secretary of State no later than Autumn 1999. Terms of Reference are attached at Annex B.

6. Implementation of the recommendations arising from both reviews will be discussed

with the political parties and with the Irish Government.

7. The participants also note that the British Government remains ready in principle, with the broad support of the political parties, and after consultation, as appropriate, with the Irish Government, in the context of ongoing implementation of the relevant recommendations, to devolve responsibility for policing and justice issues.

ANNEX A

COMMISSION ON POLICING FOR NORTHERN IRELAND

Terms of Reference

Taking account of the principles on policing as set out in the agreement, the Commission will inquire into policing in Northern Ireland and, on the basis of its findings, bring forward proposals for future policing structures and arrangements, including means of encouraging widespread community support for those arrangements.

Its proposals on policing should be designed to ensure that policing arrangements, including composition, recruitment, training, culture, ethos and symbols, are such that in a new approach Northern Ireland has a police service that can enjoy widespread support from, and is seen as an integral part of, the community as a whole.

Its proposals should include recommendations covering any issues such as re-training, job placement and educational and professional development required in the transition to policing in a peaceful society.

Its proposals should also be designed to ensure that:

– the police service is structured, managed and resourced so that it can be effective in discharging its full range of functions (including proposals on any necessary arrangements for the transition to policing in a normal peaceful society);

– the police service is delivered in constructive and inclusive partnerships with the community at all levels with the maximum delegation of authority and responsibility;

– the legislative and constitutional framework requires the impartial discharge of policing functions and conforms with internationally accepted norms in relation to policing standards;

– the police operate within a clear framework of accountability to the law and the community they serve, so:

• they are constrained by, accountable to and act only within the law;

• their powers and procedures, like the law they enforce, are clearly established and publicly available;

• there are open, accessible and independent means of investigating and adjudicating upon complaints against the police;

- there are clearly established arrangements enabling local people, and their political representatives, to articulate their views and concerns about policing and to establish publicly policing priorities and influence policing policies, subject to safeguards to ensure police impartiality and freedom from partisan political control;

- there are arrangements for accountability and for the effective, efficient and economic use of resources in achieving policing objectives;

- there are means to ensure independent professional scrutiny and inspection of the police service to ensure that proper professional standards are maintained;

- the scope for structured co-operation with the Garda Síochána and other police forces is addressed; and

- the management of public order events which can impose exceptional demands on policing resources is also addressed.

The Commission should focus on policing issues, but if it identifies other aspects of the criminal justice system relevant to its work on policing, including the role of the police in prosecution, then it should draw the attention of the Government to those matters.

The Commission should consult widely, including with non-governmental expert organisations, and through such focus groups as they consider it appropriate to establish.

The Government proposes to establish the Commission as soon as possible, with the aim of it starting work as soon as possible and publishing its final report by Summer 1999.

ANNEX B

REVIEW OF THE CRIMINAL JUSTICE SYSTEM

Terms of Reference

Taking account of the aims of the criminal justice system as set out in the Agreement, the review will address the structure, management and resourcing of publicly funded elements of the criminal justice system and will bring forward proposals for future criminal justice arrangements (other than policing and those aspects of the system relating to emergency legislation, which the Government is considering separately) covering such issues as:

- the arrangements for making appointments to the judiciary and magistracy, and safeguards for protecting their independence;

- the arrangements for the organisation and supervision of the prosecution process, and for safeguarding its independence;

- measures to improve the responsiveness and accountability of, and any lay participation in the criminal justice system;

- mechanisms for addressing law reform;

- the scope for structured co-operation between the criminal justice agencies on both parts of the island; and

- the structure and organisation of criminal justice functions that might be devolved to an Assembly, including the possibility of establishing a Department of Justice, while safeguarding the essential independence of many of the key functions in this area.

The Government proposes to commence the review as soon as possible, consulting with the political parties and others, including non-governmental expert organisations. The review will be completed by Autumn 1999.

PRISONERS

1. Both Governments will put in place mechanisms to provide for an accelerated programme for the release of prisoners, including transferred prisoners, convicted of scheduled offences in Northern Ireland or, in the case of those sentenced outside Northern Ireland, similar offences (referred to hereafter as qualifying prisoners). Any such arrangements will protect the rights of individual prisoners under national and international law.

2. Prisoners affiliated to organisations which have not established or are not maintaining a complete and unequivocal ceasefire will not benefit from the arrangements. The situation in this regard will be kept under review.

3. Both Governments will complete a review process within a fixed time frame and set prospective release dates for all qualifying prisoners. The review process would provide for the advance of the release dates of qualifying prisoners while allowing account to be taken of the seriousness of the offences for which the person was convicted and the need to protect the community. In addition, the intention would be that should the circumstances allow it, any qualifying prisoners who remained in custody two years after the commencement of the scheme would be released at that point.

4. The Governments will seek to enact the appropriate legislation to give effect to these arrangements by the end of June 1998.

5. The Governments continue to recognise the importance of measures to facilitate the reintegration of prisoners into the community by providing support both prior to and after release, including assistance directed towards availing of employment opportunities, re-training and/or re-skilling, and further education.

VALIDATION, IMPLEMENTATION AND REVIEW

Validation and Implementation

1. The two Governments will as soon as possible sign a new British-Irish Agreement replacing the 1985 Anglo-Irish Agreement, embodying understandings on constitutional issues and affirming their solemn commitment to support and, where appropriate, implement the agreement reached by the participants in the negotiations which shall be annexed to the British-Irish Agreement.

2. Each Government will organise a referendum on 22 May 1998. Subject to Parliamentary approval, a consultative referendum in Northern Ireland, organised under the terms of the Northern Ireland (Entry to Negotiations, etc.) Act 1996, will address the question: "Do you support the agreement reached in the multi-party talks on Northern Ireland and set out in Command Paper 3883?". The Irish Government will introduce and support in the Oireachtas a Bill to amend the Constitution as described in Annex B, as follows: (a) to amend Articles 2 and 3 and (b) to amend Article 29 to permit the Government to ratify the new British-Irish Agreement. On passage by the Oireachtas, the Bill will be put to referendum.

3. If majorities of those voting in each of the referendums support this agreement, the Governments will then introduce and support, in their respective Parliaments, such legislation as may be necessary to give effect to all aspects of this agreement, and will take whatever ancillary steps as may be required including the holding of elections on 25 June, subject to parliamentary approval, to the Assembly, which would meet initially in a "shadow" mode. The establishment of the North-South Ministerial Council, implementation bodies, the British-Irish Council and the British-Irish Intergovernmental Conference and the assumption by the Assembly of its legislative and executive powers will take place at the same time on the entry into force of the British-Irish Agreement.

4. In the interim, aspects of the implementation of the multi-party agreement will be reviewed at meetings of those parties relevant in the particular case (taking into account, once Assembly elections have been held, the results of those elections), under the chairmanship of the British Government or the two Governments, as may be appropriate; and representatives of the two Governments and all relevant parties may meet under independent chairmanship to review implementation of the agreement as a whole.

Review procedures following implementation

5. Each institution may, at any time, review any problems that may arise in its operation and, where no other institution is affected, take remedial action in consultation as necessary with the relevant Government or Governments. It will be for each institution to determine its own procedures for review.

6. If there are difficulties in the operation of a particular institution, which have implications for another institution, they may review their operations separately and jointly and agree on remedial action to be taken under their respective authorities.

7. If difficulties arise which require remedial action across the range of institutions, or otherwise require amendment of the British-Irish Agreement or relevant legislation, the process of review will fall to the two Governments in consultation with the parties in the Assembly. Each Government will be responsible for action in its own jurisdiction.

8. Notwithstanding the above, each institution will publish an annual report on its operations. In addition, the two Governments and the parties in the Assembly will convene a conference 4 years after the agreement comes into effect, to review and report on its operation.

AGREEMENT BETWEEN THE GOVERNMENT OF THE UNITED KINGDOM OF GREAT BRITAIN AND NORTHERN IRELAND AND THE GOVERNMENT OF IRELAND

The British and Irish Governments:

Welcoming the strong commitment to the Agreement reached on 10th April 1998 by themselves and other participants in the multi-party talks and set out in Annex 1 to this Agreement (hereinafter "the Multi-Party Agreement");

Considering that the Multi-Party Agreement offers an opportunity for a new beginning in relationships within Northern Ireland, within the island of Ireland and between the peoples of these islands;

Wishing to develop still further the unique relationship between their peoples and the close co-operation between their countries as friendly neighbours and as partners in the European Union;

Reaffirming their total commitment to the principles of democracy and non-violence which have been fundamental to the multi-party talks;

Reaffirming their commitment to the principles of partnership, equality and mutual respect and to the protection of civil, political, social, economic and cultural rights in their respective jurisdictions;

Have agreed as follows:

ARTICLE 1

The two Governments:

(i)   recognise the legitimacy of whatever choice is freely exercised by a majority of the people of Northern Ireland with regard to its status, whether they prefer to continue to support the Union with Great Britain or a sovereign united Ireland;

(ii) recognise that it is for the people of the island of Ireland alone, by agreement between the two parts respectively and without external impediment, to exercise their right of self-determination on the basis of consent, freely and concurrently given, North and South, to bring about a united Ireland, if that is their wish, accepting that this right must be achieved and exercised with and subject to the agreement and consent of a majority of the people of Northern Ireland;

(iii) acknowledge that while a substantial section of the people in Northern Ireland share the legitimate wish of a majority of the people of the island of Ireland for a united Ireland, the present wish of a majority of the people of Northern Ireland, freely exercised and legitimate, is to maintain the Union and accordingly, that Northern Ireland's status as part of the United Kingdom reflects and relies upon that wish; and that it would be wrong to make any change in the status of Northern Ireland save with the consent of a majority of its people;

(iv) affirm that, if in the future, the people of the island of Ireland exercise their right of self-determination on the basis set out in sections (i) and (ii) above to bring about a united Ireland, it will be a binding obligation on both Governments to introduce and support in their respective Parliaments legislation to give effect to that wish;

(v)   affirm that whatever choice is freely exercised by a majority of the people of Northern Ireland, the power of the sovereign government with jurisdiction there shall be exercised with rigorous impartiality on behalf of all the people in the diversity of their identities and traditions and shall be founded on the principles of full respect for, and equality of, civil, political, social and cultural rights, of freedom from discrimination for all citizens, and of parity of esteem and of just and equal treatment for the identity, ethos and aspirations of both communities;

(vi) recognise the birthright of all the people of Northern Ireland to identify themselves and be accepted as Irish or British, or both, as they may so choose, and accordingly confirm that their right to hold both British and Irish citizenship is accepted by both Governments and would not be affected by any future change in the status of Northern Ireland.

ARTICLE 2

The two Governments affirm their solemn commitment to support, and where appropriate implement, the provisions of the Multi-Party Agreement. In particular there shall be established in accordance with the provisions of the Multi-Party Agreement immediately on the entry into force of this Agreement, the following institutions:

(i)   a North/South Ministerial Council;

(ii) the implementation bodies referred to in paragraph 9 (ii) of the section entitled "Strand Two" of the Multi-Party Agreement;

(iii) a British-Irish Council;

(iv) a British-Irish Intergovernmental Conference.

ARTICLE 3

(1) This Agreement shall replace the Agreement between the British and Irish Governments done at Hillsborough on 15th November 1985 which shall cease to have effect on entry into force of this Agreement.

(2) The Intergovernmental Conference established by Article 2 of the aforementioned Agreement done on 15th November 1985 shall cease to exist on entry into force of this Agreement.

ARTICLE 4

(1) It shall be a requirement for entry into force of this Agreement that:

(a) British legislation shall have been enacted for the purpose of implementing the provisions of Annex A to the section entitled "Constitutional Issues" of the Multi-Party Agreement;

(b) the amendments to the Constitution of Ireland set out in Annex B to the section entitled "Constitutional Issues" of the Multi-Party Agreement shall have been approved by Referendum;

(c) such legislation shall have been enacted as may be required to establish the institutions referred to in Article 2 of this Agreement.

(2) Each Government shall notify the other in writing of the completion, so far as it is concerned, of the requirements for entry into force of this Agreement. This Agreement shall enter into force on the date of the receipt of the later of the two notifications.

(3) Immediately on entry into force of this Agreement, the Irish Government shall ensure that the amendments to the Constitution of Ireland set out in Annex B to the section entitled "Constitutional Issues" of the Multi-Party Agreement take effect.

In witness thereof the undersigned, being duly authorised thereto by the respective Governments, have signed this Agreement.

Done in two originals at Belfast on the 10th day of April 1998.

For the
Government
of the United
Kingdom of
Great Britain and
Northern Ireland

For the
Government
of Ireland

ANNEX 1

The Agreement Reached in the Multi-Party Talks

ANNEX 2

Declaration on the Provisions of Paragraph (vi) of Article 1 In Relationship to Citizenship

The British and Irish Governments declare that it is their joint understanding that the term "the people of Northern Ireland" in paragraph (vi) of Article 1 of this Agreement means, for the purposes of giving effect to this provision, all persons born in Northern Ireland and having, at the time of their birth, at least one parent who is a British citizen, an Irish citizen or is otherwise entitled to reside in Northern Ireland without any restriction on their period of residence.

BIBLIOGRAPHY

Adams, Gerry, 1986. *The Politics of Irish Freedom*. Dingle: Brandon.

Adams, Gerry, 1998a. Speech to Sinn Féin Ard Fheis, 18 April 1998. *The Irish Times*, 20 April 1998.

Adams, Gerry, 1998b. Speech to resumed Sinn Féin Ard Fheis, 10 May 1998. *The Irish Times*, 11 May 1998.

Adams, Gerry, 1999a. Speech, *Irish News Service*, 8 January 1999.

Adams, Gerry, 1999b. 'UUP has blocked establishment of institutions it agreed last Easter', *The Irish Times*, 12 March 1999.

Agreement Reached in the Multi-Party Negotiations, 1998.

Ahern, Bertie, 1998a. Speech at Trinity College Dublin, 3 February 1998.

Ahern, Bertie, 1998b. Statement of An Taoiseach, Mr Bertie Ahern TD on Northern Ireland, Dáil Éireann, 4 February 1998.

Akenson, Donald, 1991. *Small Differences: Irish Catholics and Irish Protestants 1815–1922*. Dublin: Gill & Macmillan.

Alter, Peter, 1994. *Nationalism*. London: Edward Arnold (2nd edition).

Alexander, Andrew, 1986. 'How Ulster could ruin Britain', *The Spectator*, 29 March 1986.

Anderson, Benedict, 1991. *Imagined Communities: Reflections on the Origin and Spread of Nationalism*. London: Verso (revised edition).

Arthur, Paul, 1983. 'Anglo-Irish relations since 1968: a "fever chart" interpretation', *Government and Opposition*, 18 (2): 157–74.

Arthur, Paul. 1987. 'Elite studies in a paranocracy: the Northern Ireland case', pp. 202–17 in George Moyser and Margaret Wagstaff, eds, *Research Methods for Elite Studies*. London: Allen & Unwin.

Arthur, Paul, 1990. 'Negotiating the Northern Ireland problem: Track One or Track Two diplomacy?', *Government and Opposition*, 25 (4): 403–18.

Arthur, Paul, 1991. 'Diasporan intervention in international affairs: Irish America as a case study', *Diaspora*, 1 (2): 143–62.

Arthur, Paul, 1997a. '"Reading" violence: Ireland', pp. 234–91 in David Apter, ed., *The Legitimization of Violence*. London: Macmillan.

Arthur, Paul, 1997b. 'American intervention in the Anglo-Irish peace process: incrementalism or interference?', *Cambridge Review of International Affairs*, 11 (1): 46–64.

Aughey, Arthur, 1989. *Under Siege: Ulster Unionism and the Anglo-Irish Agreement*. Belfast: Blackstaff.

Aughey, Arthur, 1995. 'The end of history, the end of the union', pp. 7–14 in Arthur Aughey, David Burnside, Eoghan Harris, Gavin Adams, and Jeffrey Donaldson, *Selling Unionism at Home and Away*. Belfast: Young Unionist Council.

Barnes, S., 1999. 'Spiriting away the joy of playing', *The Times*, 17 February 1999.

Barritt, Denis P., and Charles F. Carter, 1962. *The Northern Ireland Problem: A Study in Group Relations*. Oxford: Oxford University Press.

Bartlett, Thomas, 1990. 'The origins and progress of the Catholic question in Ireland', pp. 1–20 in T.P. Power and K. Whelan, eds, *Endurance and Emergence: Catholics in Ireland in the Eighteenth Century*. Dublin: Irish Academic Press.

Beck, Ulrich, 1992. *Risk Society: Towards a New Modernity*. London: Sage.

Beck, Ulrich, 1997. *The Reinvention of Politics: Rethinking Modernity in the Global Social Order*. Cambridge: Polity.

Berki, Robert N., 1981. *On Political Realism*. London: Dent.

Berlin, Isaiah, 1990. *The Crooked Timber of Humanity: Chapters in the History of Ideas*. London: John Murray.

Bew, Paul, 1998. 'Agreement clears the way for the rebirth of liberal unionism', *The Irish Times*, 15 May 1998.

Bew, Paul, 1999. 'Good Friday man?', *Times Literary Supplement*, 8 January 1999.

Bew, Paul and Gordon Gillespie, eds, 1993. *Northern Ireland: A Chronology of the Troubles 1968–1993*. Dublin: Gill & Macmillan.

Bhabha, Homi K., 1994. *The Location of Culture*. London: Routledge.

Bloomfield, David, 1998. *Political Dialogue in Northern Ireland: The Brooke Initiative, 1989–92*. London: St Martin's Press.

Blumenthal, Sidney, 1997. 'Along the Clinton-Blair axis', *The Times*, 5 May 1997.

Blumrosen, Alfred W., 1993. *Modern Law: The Law Transmission System and Equal Employment Opportunity*. Madison, Wisconsin: University of Wisconsin Press.

Boehringer, Gill et al., 1974. 'Stirling: the destructive application of group techniques to a conflict', *Journal of Conflict Resolution*, 17 (4).

Boyce, D.G., 1982. *Nationalism in Ireland*. London: Croom Helm.

Boyce, D.G., 1992. *Ireland 1828–1923: From Ascendancy to Democracy*. Oxford: Blackwell.

Breen, Richard. 1996. 'Who wants a United Ireland? Constitutional preferences among Catholics and Protestants', pp. 33–48 in Richard Breen, Paula Devine, and Lizanne Dowds, eds, *Social Attitudes in Northern Ireland: The Fifth Report*. Belfast: Appletree Press.

Bullock, Alan, 1998. *Hitler and Stalin: Parallel Lives*. London: Fontana.

Burton, Frank, 1978. *The Politics of Legitimacy: Struggles in a Belfast Community*. London: Routledge & Kegan Paul.

[Cameron], 1969. Disturbances in Northern Ireland: Report of the Commission appointed by the Governor of Northern Ireland (the Cameron Report). Belfast: HMSO: Cmd 532.

Canny, Nicholas, 1989. 'Early modern Ireland', pp. 104–60 in R. F. Foster, ed., *The Oxford Illustrated History of Ireland*. Oxford: Oxford University Press.

Carnegie Commission, 1997. *Preventing Deadly Conflict*. New York: Carnegie Commission on Preventing Deadly Conflict.

Carter, Erica, James Donald, and Judith Squires, eds, 1993. *Space and Place: Theories of Identity and Location*. London: Lawrence & Wishart.

Central Secretariat Circular, 1990. *Equal Opportunity Proofing: Guidelines*, January 1990.

Central Secretariat Circular, 1993. *Policy Appraisal and Fair Treatment*, May 1993.

Clohessy, Anthony, 1998. 'Continuity and discontinuity in the discourse of provisionalism', PhD Thesis, Department of Government, University of Essex.

[Commentary], 1997. Commentary on 'Mainstreaming fairness? – A discussion paper on policy appraisal and fair treatment' by Dr Christopher McCrudden and on 'Policy appraisal and fair treatment in Northern Ireland: a contribution to the debate on mainstreaming equality'. Belfast: Committee on the Administration of Justice.

Compton, Paul, 1989. 'The changing religious demography of Northern Ireland: some political considerations', *Studies*, (78) 312: 393–402.

Connor, Walker, 1972. 'The Politics of Ethnonationalism', *Journal of International Affairs*, 27 (1): 1–21.

Connor, Walker, 1978. 'A Nation is a Nation, is a State, is an Ethnic Group, is a . . . ', *Ethnic and Racial Studies*, 1 (4): 377–400.

Connor, Walker, 1993. *Ethnonationalism: The Quest for Understanding*. Princeton: Princeton University Press.

Coogan, Tim Pat, 1995. *The Troubles: Ireland's Ordeal 1966–1995 and the Search for Peace*. London: Hutchinson.

Cormack, R. J., A. M. Gallagher, and R. D. Osborne, 1993. *Fair Enough? Religion and the 1991 Population Census*. Belfast: Fair Employment Commission.

Coulter, Colin, 1994. 'The Character of Unionism', *Irish Political Studies*, 9: 1–24.

Coulter, Colin, 1996. 'Direct rule and the unionist middle classes', pp. 169–91 in Richard English and Graham Walker, eds, *Unionism in Modern Ireland: New Perspectives on Politics and Culture*. London: Macmillan.

Council of Europe, 1998. Rapporteur Group on Equality between Women and Men, Gender Mainstreaming, GR-EG (98), 1 March 26.

Crick, Bernard, 1990. 'The high price of peace', pp. 261–75 in Hermann Giliomee and Jannie Gagiano, eds, *The Elusive Search for Peace: South Africa, Israel, Northern Ireland*. Oxford: Oxford University Press.

Crocker, Chester A., 1992. *High Noon in Southern Africa: Making Peace in a Rough Neighborhood*. New York: W.W. Norton.

Crocker, Chester A., 1996. 'The varieties of intervention: conditions for success', in Chester A. Crocker and Fen Osler Hampson with Pamela Hall, eds, *Managing Global Chaos: Sources of and Responses to International Conflict*. Washington DC: USTP Press

Crook, Stephen, Jan Pakulski, and Malcolm Waters, 1992. *Postmodernization: Change in Advanced Society*. London: Sage.

Crotty, William, and David Schmitt, eds, 1998. *Ireland and the Politics of Change*. London: Longman.

Cullen, Louis, 1981. *The Emergence of Modern Ireland 1600–1900*. London: Batsford.

Cunningham, Michael, 1991. *British Government Policy in Northern Ireland 1969–89: Its Nature and Execution*. Manchester: Manchester University Press.

Cunningham, Michael, 1997. 'The political language of John Hume', *Irish Political Studies*, 12: 13–23.

Darby, John, 1976. *Conflict in Northern Ireland*. Dublin: Gill & Macmillan.

Darby, John, 1986. *Intimidation and the Control of Conflict in Northern Ireland*. Dublin: Gill & Macmillan.

Darby, John, 1997. *Scorpions in a Bottle: Conflicting Cultures in Northern Ireland*. London: Minority Rights Publications.

Democratic Dialogue, 1996. *Reconstituting Politics*. Belfast: Democratic Dialogue.

Democratic Dialogue, 1997. *Making Consent Mutual*. Belfast: Democratic Dialogue.

Department of Economic Development, 1986. *Equality of Opportunity in Northern Ireland: Future Strategy Options*. Belfast: HMSO.

Department of Health and Social Services, 1997. *Policy Development and Review Unit, Review of Charging Policy for Non-Residential Personal Social Services*. Belfast: HMSO.

Deutsch, Karl W., 1953. *Nationalism and Social Communication*. New York: John Wiley.

Doherty, Pat, 1999. Speech at Noraid dinner, *Irish News Service*, 28 January 1999.

Doob, William, and William Foltz, 1973. 'The Belfast workshop: an application of group techniques to a destructive conflict', *Journal of Conflict Resolution*, 17 (3).

Dubs, Alfred, 1998. House of Lords, Official Report, 11 November 1998, column 810.

Duffy, Mary, and Geoff Evans, 1997. 'Class, community polarisation and politics', pp. 102–37 in Lizanne Dowds, Paula Devine and Richard Breen, eds, *Social Attitudes in Northern Ireland: The Sixth Report*. Belfast: Appletree.

Dunn, Seamus, 1995. 'The conflict as a set of problems', pp. 3–14 in Seamus Dunn, ed., *Facets of the Conflict in Northern Ireland*. New York: St. Martin's Press.

Egeland, Jan, 1994. 'Norway as international peacemaker', paper read at Royal Geographic Society, London, 5 October 1994.

Elliott, Sydney, 1997. 'The Northern Ireland Forum/Entry to negotiations election 1996', *Irish Political Studies*, 12: 111–22.

Enloe, Cynthia, 1983. *Ethnic Conflict and Political Development*. Boston: Little Brown.

Erskine, John, and Gordon Lucy, eds, *Cultural Traditions in Northern Ireland: Varieties of Scottishness. Exploring the Ulster-Scottish Connection.* Belfast: Institute of Irish Studies.

European Commission, 1997. *Equal Opportunities for Women and Men in the European Union 1996.*

Evans, Peter, Dietrich Rueschemeyer, and Theda Skocpol, eds, 1985. *Bringing the State Back In.* Cambridge: Cambridge University Press.

Eversley, David, 1989. *Religion and Employment in Northern Ireland.* London: Sage.

Fine, Robert, and Shirin Rai, eds, 1997. *Civil Society: Democratic Perspectives.* London: Frank Cass.

FitzGerald, Garret, 1991. *All in a Life: An Autobiography.* London: Macmillan.

FitzGerald, Garret, 1999. 'Anglo-Irish bond proves its strength', *The Irish Times*, 3 July 1999.

Fletcher, Martin, 1998. 'Mitchell fears collapse of deal within 18 months', *The Times*, 13 April 1998.

Folberg, Jay, and Alison Taylor, 1986. *Mediation: A Comparative Guide to Resolving Conflicts without Litigation.* Jossey Bass.

Forum for Peace and Reconciliation, 1995. *Paths to a Political Settlement in Ireland: Policy Papers submitted to the Forum for Peace and Reconciliation.* Belfast: Blackstaff.

Foster, R. F. , 1988. *Modern Ireland 1600–1972.* London: Allen Lane, Penguin Press.

Franco, Paul, 1990. *The Political Philosophy of Michael Oakeshott.* New Haven and London: Yale University Press.

Fukuyama, Francis, 1989. 'The end of History', *The National Interest*, 16 (summer): 3–18.

Fukuyama, Francis, 1992. *The End of History and the Last Man.* London: Hamish Hamilton.

Gallagher, A.M., R. D. Osborne, and R. J. Cormack, 1995. *Fair Shares? Employment, Unemployment and Economic Status.* Belfast: Fair Employment Commission.

Garvin, Tom, 1981. *The Evolution of Irish Nationalist Politics.* Dublin: Macmillan.

Garvin, Tom, 1987. *Nationalist Revolutionaries in Ireland 1858–1928.* Oxford: Clarendon.

Gellner, Ernest, 1996. *Conditions of Liberty: Civil Society and its Rivals.* London: Penguin.

Giliomee, Hermann and Jannie Gagiano, eds,1990. *The Elusive Search for Peace: South Africa, Israel, Northern Ireland.* Oxford: Oxford University Press.

Gillis, John R., ed., 1996. *Commemorations: The Politics of National Identity.* Princeton: Princeton University Press.

Gurr, Ted Robert, and Barbara Harff, 1994. *Ethnic Conflict in World Politics.* Boulder: Westview.

Hall, Peter, 1985. *Governing the Economy.* Cambridge: Polity.

Hann, Chris and Elizabeth Dunn, eds, 1996. *Civil Society: Challenging Western Models.* London: Routledge.

Hardiman, Niamh and Chris Whelan, 1998. 'Changing Values', pp. 66–85 in William Crotty and David Schmitt, eds, 1998. *Ireland and the Politics of Change*. London: Longman.

Hayes, Bernadette C., and Ian McAllister, 1998. 'The Northern Ireland Agreement: an explication of a political milestone', *ZA-Information*, 43: 167–80.

Hayes, Maurice, 1995. *Minority Verdict: Experiences of a Catholic Public Servant*. Belfast: Blackstaff.

Haymes, Thomas, 1997. 'What is nationalism really? Understanding the limitations of rigid theories in dealing with the problems of nationalism and ethnonationalism', *Nations and Nationalism*, 3: 25–33.

Heskin, Ken, 1980. *Northern Ireland: A Psychological Analysis*. Dublin: Gill & Macmillan.

Holland, Jack, 1987. *The American Connection*. New York: Viking.

Holland, Mary, 1998. 'Latest plan to tackle inequality crucial to North peace', *The Irish Times*, 12 March 1998.

Hume, John, 1985. 'John Hume's Commencement Address at the University of Massachusetts', *Congressional Record: Proceedings and Debates of the 99th Congress*, First Session, Washington, Tuesday 21 May, 131 (67).

Hume, John, 1986. 'A new Ireland: the acceptance of diversity', *The Irish Times*, 13 September 1986.

Hume, John, 1988. Letter to Gerry Adams, Sinn Féin/SDLP talks, Belfast: Sinn Féin.

Hume, John, 1989, Interview with Frank Millar, *The Irish Times*, 13 January 1989.

Hume–Adams, 1993. Statements, April and September 1993, *The Irish Times*, 31 January 1994.

Hume, John, 1995. 'SDLP response to a New Framework for Agreement', pp. 103–5 in Judge Catherine McGuinness, introd., *Paths to a Political Settlement in Ireland: Policy Papers submitted to the Forum for Peace and Reconciliation*. Belfast: Blackstaff.

Hume, John, 1996. *John Hume: Personal Views*. Dublin: Town House.

Hutson, Nigel, 1996. *Policy Appraisal and Fair Treatment in Northern Ireland: A contribution to the debate on mainstreaming equality*. Belfast: Standing Advisory Commission on Human Rights.

IRA, 1998. Response to Good Friday Agreement, *Irish Republican News Service*, 30 April 1998.

IRA, 1999. New Year's statement, *Irish Republican News Service*, 7 January 1999.

Irish News, 26 April 1999, 'Park deal and the peace process is over'.

Irwin, Colin, 1998. 'The Search for a Settlement: The People's Choice', supplement to *Fortnight*, 368. Belfast: Fortnight Educational Trust.

Jackson, Robert, 1990. *Quasi-States: Sovereignty, International Relations, and the Third World*. New York: Cambridge University Press.

Keane, J., ed., 1988. *Civil Society and the State: New European Perspectives*. London: Verso.

Kearney, Hugh, 1989. *The British Isles: A History of Four Nations*. Cambridge: Cambridge University Press.

Kearney, Richard, 1997. *Postnationalist Ireland: Politics, Culture, Philosophy*. London: Routledge.

Kelly, Gerry, 1999. 'The victims issue: reconciliation or just new tactics', *Irish News*, 26 April 1999.

Kennedy, Geraldine, 1998. 'Belfast accord fundamentally alters nature of North's place in the union', *The Irish Times*, 8 May 1998.

Kennedy, Liam, 1994. *People and Population Change: A Comparative Study of Population Change in Northern Ireland and the Republic of Ireland*. Dublin: Cooperation North.

Kratochwil, F., 1986. 'Of systems, boundaries and territoriality: an enquiry into the formation of the state system', *World Politics*, 39 (1): 27–52.

Kurtzman, Joel, 1998. 'An Interview with W. Brian Arthur', *Strategy and Business*, 11: 103.

Ladd, Brian, 1997. *The Ghosts of Berlin: Confronting German History in the Urban Landscape*. Chicago: Chicago University Press.

Lee, David J., and Bryan S. Turner, 1996. *Conflicts about Class: Debating Inequality in Late Industrialisation*. London: Longman.

Linder, Wolf, 1994. *Swiss Democracy: Possible Solutions to Conflict in Multicultural Societies*. New York: St Martin's Press.

Longley, Edna, 1994. 'From Cathleen to Anorexia: the breakdown of Irelands', pp. 173–95 in *The Living Stream: Literature and Revisionism in Ireland*. Newcastle upon Tyne: Bloodaxe.

Lustick, Ian S., 1993. *Unsettled States, Disputed Lands: Britain and Ireland, France and Algeria, Israel and the West Bank–Gaza*. London: Cornell University Press.

MacIntyre, Alasdair, 1988. *Whose Justice? Which Rationality?*. London: Duckworth.

Mallie, Eamon, 1999. 'The Long Good Friday', Channel 4, 2 April 1999.

Mansergh, Martin, 1996. 'Manufacturing Consent', *Fortnight*, 350: 13–15.

Mansergh, Martin, 1998. 'The challenges of the Good Friday Agreement – and the consolidation of peace', Address to the Irish Association, Glenview Hotel, Glen of the Downs, Co Wicklow, 22 November 1998, reprinted in *Céide*, 5: 5–8.

McAleese, Mary, 1999. 'President praises culture of consensus', *The Irish Times*, 21 April 1999.

McAllister, Ian, 1982. 'The Devil, miracles and the afterlife: the political sociology of religion in Northern Ireland', *British Journal of Sociology*, 33 (3): 330–47.

McCall, Cathal, 1999. *Identity in Northern Ireland: Communities, Politics, Change*. London: Macmillan.

McCann, Eamonn, 1999. 'Quest for a deal', *Belfast Telegraph*, 30 June 1999.

McCartney, Robert, 1998. 'Agreement unlikely to bring early end to violence', *The Irish Times*, 11 April 1998.

McCrone, David, 1998. *The Sociology of Nationalism*. London: Routledge.

McCrudden, Christopher. 1991. 'The evolution of the Fair Employment (Northern Ireland) Act 1989 in Parliament', in R.J. Cormack and R.D. Osborne (eds), *Discrimination and Public Policy in Northern Ireland*. Oxford: Oxford University Press.

McCrudden, Christopher, 1996. Committee on the Administration of Justice, 'Mainstreaming fairness? A discussion paper on "Policy appraisal and fair treatment"'. Belfast: Committee on the Administration of Justice.

McCrudden, Christopher, 1998a. 'Replacing "Equality" with "Equity" shows the difference a word can make', *The Irish Times*, 22 January 1998.

McCrudden, Christopher, 1998b. Committee on the Administration of Justice, 'Benchmarks for change: mainstreaming fairness in the governance of Northern Ireland'. Belfast: Committee on the Administration of Justice.

McCrudden, Christopher, 1998c. Committee on the Administration of Justice, 'Equality: A proposal in the light of Multi-party Talks Agreement'. Belfast: Committee on the Administration of Justice.

McCrudden, Christopher, 1999a. 'Mainstreaming Equality in the Governance of Northern Ireland', *Fordham International Law Journal*, 22 (4): 1696–775.

McCrudden, Christopher, 1999b. 'Human Rights Codes for Transnational Corporations: What Can the Sullivan and MacBride Principles Tell Us?', *Oxford Journal of Legal Studies*, 19: 167–201.

McGarry, John and Brendan O'Leary, eds, 1990. *The Future of Northern Ireland*. Oxford: Oxford University Press.

McGarry, John and Brendan O'Leary, 1995. *Explaining Northern Ireland: Broken Images*. Oxford: Basil Blackwell.

McGuinness, Martin, 1999. 'We never agreed to deliver IRA weapons' *Irish News*, 19 April 1999.

McIntyre, Anthony, 1995. 'Modern Irish republicanism: the product of British state strategies', *Irish Political Studies*, 10: 97–122.

McLaughlin, Mitchell, 1998. 'The republican ideal', pp. 62–84 in Norman Porter, ed., *The Republican Ideal: Current Perspectives*. Belfast: Blackstaff.

McLaughlin, Mitchell, 1999. 'Sinn Fein unease over EU integration', *Irish News*, 28 April 1999.

Miller, David, 1995. *On Nationality*. Oxford: Clarendon.

Mitchell Document, 1998. <http://www.nuzhound.com/articles/mitdraft.htm>

[Montfleur], 1996. *The Montfleur Project*. Centre for Generative Leadership, LLC.

Montville, Joseph, 1986. *Track two Diplomacy: The Development of Non-Governmental Peace Promoting Relationships*. Dublin: Irish Peace Institute.

Mouffe, Chantal, 1993. *The Return of the Political*. London: Verso.

Mowlam, Marjorie, 1997. 'Towards genuine consent in Ulster', *Independent*, 25 February 1997.

Murphy, Paul, 1998. House of Commons, Official Report, 18 November 1998: columns 1068–1069.

Murray, Gerard, 1998. *John Hume and the SDLP*. Dublin: Irish Academic Press.

Nairn, Tom, 1973. *The Break-Up of Britain: Crisis and Neo-Nationalism*. London: Verso (2nd edition, 1981).

Nairn, Tom, 1996. 'Internationalism and the second coming', pp. 267–80 in Gopal Balakrishnan, ed., *Mapping the Nation*. London: Verso.

New Ireland Forum, 1984 Report. Dublin: Stationery Office.

Northern Ireland Information Service, 1987. 'Secretary of State takes Direct Responsibility for Community Relations Matters', 8 September 1987.

Northern Ireland Information Service, 1998. 'Secretary of State Announces Equality White Paper Decisions', 10 July 1998.

Oakeshott, Michael, 1975. *On Human Conduct.* Oxford: Clarendon.

Oakeshott, Michael, 1991. *Rationalism in Politics and Other Essays.* Indianapolis: Liberty Fund.

O'Clery, Conor, 1997. *The Greening of the White House.* Dublin: Gill & Macmillan.

O'Connor, Fionnuala, 1993. *In Search of a State: Catholics in Northern Ireland.* Belfast: Blackstaff.

O'Dowd, Liam, 1995. 'Development or dependency? State, economy and society in Northern Ireland', pp. 132–77 in P. Clancy, S. Drudy, K. Lynch, and L. O'Dowd, eds, *Irish Society: Sociological Perspectives.* Dublin: Institute of Public Administration.

O'Dowd, Niall, 1998. 'Delicate balance has been upset by paper's pro-unionist slant', *The Irish Times,* 17 January 1998.

O'Duffy, Brendan, 1996. 'The price of containment: deaths and debate on Northern Ireland in the House of Commons, 1968–94', pp. 102–28 in Peter Caterall and Sean McDougall, eds, *The Northern Ireland Question in British Politics.* London: Macmillan.

O'Hearn, Denis, 1998. *Inside the Celtic Tiger: The Irish Economy and the Asian Model.* London: Pluto.

O'Leary, Brendan, 1999. 'Assessing the British-Irish Agreement', *New Left Review,* 233: 66–96.

O'Leary, Brendan and John McGarry, 1993. *The Politics of Antagonism: Understanding Northern Ireland.* London: Athlone Press.

O'Leary, Cornelius, Sidney Elliott, and Rick Wilford, 1988. *The Northern Ireland Assembly, 1982–86: A Constitutional Experiment.* London: Christopher Hurst.

O'Neill, S., 1994. 'Pluralist justice and its limits: the case of Northern Ireland', *Political Studies,* 42 (3): 363–77.

Osborne, Robert, Anthony Gallagher, and Robert Cormack, with Sally Shortall, 1996. 'The implementation of the policy appraisal and fair treatment guidelines in Northern Ireland', pp. 127–52 in Eithne McLaughlin and Padraic Quirk, eds, *Policy Aspects of Employment Equality in Northern Ireland* [Employment Equality in Northern Ireland Series, vol. 2]. Belfast: Standing Advisory Commission on Human Rights.

O'Sullivan, Noel, 1992. *Santayana (Thinkers of Our Time).* London: The Claridge Press.

Patterson, Henry, 1989. *The Politics of Illusion: Republicanism and Socialism in Modern Ireland.* London: Hutchinson.

Pearse, Patrick, 1966. *Political Writings and Speeches.* Dublin: Talbot.

Pollack, Andy, ed., 1993. *A Citizen's inquiry: The Opsahl Report on Northern Ireland.* Dublin: Lilliput.

Porter, Elisabeth, 1998. 'Identity, location, plurality: women, nationalism and Northern Ireland', pp. 36–61 in Rick Wilford and Robert L. Miller, eds, *Women, Ethnicity and Nationalism: The Politics of Transition*. London: Routledge.

Porter, Norman, 1996. *Rethinking Unionism: An Alternative Vision for Northern Ireland*. Belfast: Blackstaff .

Porter, Norman, 1998. *Rethinking Unionism: An Alternative Vision for Northern Ireland*. Belfast: Blackstaff (2nd edition).

Powell, Enoch, 1983. 'Dev and Devolution', *The Spectator*, 8 January 1983.

Razavi, Shahra and Carol Miller, 1995. *Gender Mainstreaming: A Study of Efforts by the UNDP, the World Bank and the ILO to Institutionalize Gender Issues*. Geneva: United Nations Research Institute for Social Development.

Richie, Alexandra, 1998. *Faust's Metropolis: A History of Berlin*. London: HarperCollins.

Rose, Richard, 1971. *Governing Without Consensus: An Irish Perspective*. London: Faber & Faber.

Rothstein, Robert, ed., 1996. 'After the peace. The political economy of reconciliation'. Inaugural Rebecca Meyerhoff memorial lecture, Harry S. Truman Institute, Hebrew University, Jerusalem, May 1996.

Ruane, Joseph, 1994. 'Ireland, European integration and the dialectic of nationalism and post-nationalism', *Etudes Irlandaises*, 19 (1): 183–93.

Ruane, Joseph, 1998. 'Secularisation and ideology in the Republic of Ireland', pp. 239–54 in Paul Brennan, ed., *La Secularisation en Irlande*. Caen: Presses Universitaires de Caen.

Ruane, Joseph and Jennifer Todd, 1991. '"Why can't you get along with each other?" Culture, structure and the Northern Ireland conflict', pp. 27–43 in Eamonn Hughes, ed., *Culture and Politics in Northern Ireland, 1960–1990*. Milton Keynes: Open University Press.

Ruane, Joseph and Jennifer Todd, 1992. 'Diversity, division and the middle ground in Northern Ireland', *Irish Political Studies*, 7: 73–98.

Ruane, Joseph and Jennifer Todd, 1996. *The Dynamics of Conflict in Northern Ireland: Power, Conflict and Emancipation*. Cambridge: Cambridge University Press.

Ruane, Joseph and Jennifer Todd, 1998a. 'Peace processes and communalism in Northern Ireland', pp. 178–194 in William Crotty and David Schmitt, eds, *Ireland and the Politics of Change*. London: Longman.

Ruane, Joseph and Jennifer Todd, 1998b. 'Irish nationalism and the conflict in Northern Ireland', pp. 55–69 in David Miller, ed., *Rethinking Northern Ireland: Culture, Ideology and Colonialism*. London: Longman.

Ryder, Chris, 1999. 'Real genius of Belfast Agreement is it underpins partition', *The Irish Times*, 20 May 1999.

SACHR, 1987. *Religious and Political Discrimination and Equality of Opportunity in Northern Ireland: Report on Fair Employment*. London: HMSO: Cmd 237.

SACHR, 1997. *Employment Equality: Building for the Future*. London: HMSO: Cmd 3684.

Sahlins, Marshall, 1981. *Historical Metaphors and Mythical Realities: Structure in the Early History of the Sandwich Island Kingdom*. Ann Arbor: University of Michigan Press.

Santayana, George, 1951. *Dominations and Powers: Reflections on Liberty, Society, and Government*. New York: Charles Scribner's Sons.

Saunders, Harold H., 1996. 'Pre-negotiation and circumnegotiation: arenas of the peace process', in Chester A. Crocker and Fen Osler Hampson, eds, with Pamela Aall, *Managing Global Chaos: Sources of and Responses to International Conflict*. Washington, DC: United States Institute of Peace.

Schmitt, Carl, 1976. *The Concept of the Political*. New Brunswick: Rutgers University Press.

Schmitt, Carl, 1985a. *Political Theology*. Cambridge, Mass.: Harvard University Press.

Schmitt, Carl, 1985b. *The Crisis of Parliamentary Democracy*, Ellen Kennedy, trans. Cambridge: Harvard University Press.

Schulze, Kirsten E., 1997. 'The Northern Ireland political process: a viable approach to conflict resolution', *Irish Political Studies*, 12: 92–110.

Scruton, Roger, 1985. *Thinkers of the New Left*. Harlow: Longman.

Seligman, Adam, 1992. *The Idea of Civil Society*. New York: Free Press.

Shannon, W. V., 1986. 'The Anglo-Irish Agreement', *Foreign Affairs*, 64 (4): 849–70.

Shils, Edward, and Steven Grosby, eds, 1997. *The Virtue of Civility: Selected Essays on Liberalism, Tradition, and Civil Society*. Indianapolis: Liberty Fund.

Shirlow, Peter and Mark McGovern, eds, 1997. *Who Are 'The People'? Unionism, Protestantism and Loyalism in Northern Ireland*. London: Pluto.

Simon, Sion, 1999. 'Catholic birthrate chases Trimble down the hard road of compromise', *Irish Independent*, 8 July 1999.

Sinn Féin, 1995. 'The nature of the problem and the principles underlying its resolution', in Judge Catherine McGuinness, introd., *Paths to a Political Settlement in Ireland: Policy papers submitted to the Forum for Peace and Reconciliation*. Belfast: Blackstaff.

Sisk, Timothy D., 1996. *Power Sharing and International Mediation in Ethnic Conflicts*. Washington, DC: US Institute of Peace.

Smith, Anthony D., 1991. *National Identity*. London: Penguin.

Smith, Anthony D., 1992. 'Chosen Peoples: Why Ethnic Groups Survive', *Ethnic and Racial Studies*, 15: 436–56.

Smith, Anthony D., 1996. *Nations and Nationalism in a Global Era*. London: Polity.

Smith, Anthony D., 1998 *Nationalism and Modernism*. London: Routledge.

Smith, David and Gerald Chambers, 1991. *Inequality in Northern Ireland*. Oxford: Clarendon.

Sofer, Sasson, 1997. 'The diplomat as a stranger', *Diplomacy and Statecraft*, 8 (3): 179–86.

Tamir, Yael, 1993. *Liberal Nationalism*. Princeton: Princeton University Press.

Tamir, Yael, 1995. 'The enigma of nationalism', *World Politics*, 47 (3): 418–39.

Tester, Keith, 1992. *Civil Society*. London: Routledge.

Thatcher, Margaret, 1993. *The Downing Street Years*. London: HarperCollins.

Todd, Jennifer, 1988. 'The limits of Britishness', *Irish Review*, 5: 11–16.

Trew, Karen, 1994. 'What it means to be Irish seen from a Northern Perspective', *Irish Journal of Psychology*, 15: 288–299.

Trew, Karen, 1996. 'National Identity', pp. 140–152 in Richard Breen, Paula Devine, and Lizanne Dowds, eds, *Social Attitudes in Northern Ireland: the Fifth Report*. Belfast: Appletree Press.

Trimble, David, 1998. 'At long last Dublin recognises British territorial sovereignty', *The Irish Times*, 18 May 1998.

Trimble, David, 1998. Address by the First Minister on the visit of President Clinton, 3 September 1998.

United Nations, 1995. Report of the Fourth World Conference on Women, UN DOC A/Conf.177/20.

Vattimo, Giani, 1988. *The End of Modernity: Nihilism and Hermeneutics in Post-modern Culture*. London: Polity.

Waters, Malcolm, 1995. *Globalization*. London: Routledge.

Watkins, David, 1997. 'Comments', in Equal Opportunities Commission for Northern Ireland, *Working Towards Equality in the Twenty-First Century: Report of a Conference held on 23 October 1996*. Belfast: Equal Opportunities Commission for Northern Ireland.

Whelan, Kevin, 1991. 'Catholic mobilisation, 1750–1850', pp. 235–58 in Centre de Recherches Historiques, ed., *Culture et Pratiques Politiques en France et en Irlande XVIᵉ–XVIIIᵉ Siècle*. Paris: Centre de Recherches Historiques.

Whyte, John, 1990. *Interpreting Northern Ireland*. Oxford: Clarendon.

Wilford, Rick, 1999. 'Epilogue', pp. 285–303 in Paul Mitchell and Rick Wilford, eds, *Politics in Northern Ireland*. Colorado: Westview.

Wilson, Andrew J., 1997. 'From the beltway to Belfast: the Clinton adminstration, Sinn Féin and the Northern Ireland peace process', *New Hibernia*.

[Working Party], 1973. *Working Party on Discrimination in the Private Sector of Employment: Report and Recommendations* (the Van Straubenzee Report). Belfast: HMSO, Ministry of Health and Social Services.

Wright, Frank, 1987. *Northern Ireland: A Comparative Analysis*. Dublin: Gill & Macmillan.

INDEX

Act of Union (1800), 147–8, 149, 167
Adams, Gerry, 6, 56, 71
  Hume–Adams talks, 57, 82
  US visa, 80–3, 94
affirmative action, 112–13
African National Congress (ANC),
    75, 79, 83
Ahern, Bertie, 8, 12, 27, 142
Akenson, Donald, 134
Alderdice, Lord, 93
Algeria, 32
Alliance party, 9, 12, 93
  responses to GFA, 44–6
Americans for a New Irish Agenda, 81
Anglo-Irish Agreement, 1985, 2, 14,
    15, 32, 63, 70, 76–7, 85, 92,
    154
  effect on republicans, 5, 56
  effect on unionists, 5–6, 8
  replacement of, 11, 16
Angola, 74
Archer, Lord, 111, 113
Assembly, see Northern Ireland
    Assembly
Australia, 97

Balfour, Arthur, 124
Belfast Agreement, see Good Friday
    Agreement
Belfast Workshop, 1972, 84–5
Belfast workshop, 1995, 86, 87
Belgium, 31
'Benchmarks for Change', 105
Berki, Robert, 129–30
Berlin, Isaiah, 124

Blair, Tony, 9, 12, 18
Bloody Sunday, 1972, 2, 84
Britain, 32, 53
  Adams visa, 82–3
  Anglo-Irish diplomacy, 73–8
  decommissioning issue, 25–6
  demilitarisation, 24
  DSD, 6–7
  IRA contacts, 6
  Labour in power, 8–9
  'mainstreaming,' 99–100
  NI Bill, 1998, 110–13
  NI dependence on, 2
  policy change, 153–4
  security pledge, 15
  sovereignty, 62, 64
  talks process, 11–12
  and unionists, 40–1, 130, 156
British army, 15, 24, 163
British–Irish Agreement Act 1999, 24
British–Irish Council, 14–15, 16, 18, 41
  in text of GFA, 184–5
British–Irish Intergovernmental
    Conference, 11, 15, 16
  human rights role, 108
  in text of GFA, 185–6
Brooke talks, see multi-party talks
    1991–3

Camp David Agreement, 74
Canada, 31, 97
Carnegie Commission on Preventing
    Deadly Conflict, 71
Carrickfergus, Co. Antrim, 28
Catholic church, 8

Catholics, *see also* nationalists
  challenge to state, 150–1
  community values, 84
  cultural change, 152
  demographic change, 162
  economic inequality, 98, 157
  ethnic identity, 38–41
  historical recovery, 148–9
  structural power, 158–9
ceasefires, 4, 7, 8, 11, 34, 103, 151
Central Community Relations Unit,
  99, 100, 101, 103, 110–11
Central Intelligence Agency (CIA), 82
Centre for Conflict Analysis and
  Resolution, GMU, 86
Centre for the Study of Conflict, UU, 86
citizenship, 125–6, 129
  in text of GFA, 201
Civic Forum, 16, 27–8
  in text of GFA, 179
civil rights movement, 15, 19, 53, 97,
  150–1
civil service, 27 (*see also* Northern
  Ireland Office)
  and equality issues, 120
  equality monitoring, 109
  PAFT, 100
civility
  condition of, 123–32
  politics of, 29, 122–44
  politics of incivility, 132–8
class structure, 155
Clinton, President Bill, 12, 71
  Adams visa, 80–3, 94
  NI visit, 34
Code of Conduct for Ministers, 106–7
  (*see also* Pledge of Office)
  text of, 180–1
Cold War, 74, 75, 79, 152
colonialism, 32, 58, 79, 147–8
  and ethnonationalism, 33
  hybridity, 152
Commission for Racial Equality, 105,
  108, 113
Committee on the Administration of
  Justice (CAJ), 101, 102, 104,
  105, 106
  NI Bill, 111, 113
communism, 30, 79, 129–30
communitarianism, 136–8

community relations, *see also*
  sectarianism
  changes in, 2–3, 155
  conflicts of interest, 17–19, 22–3
  cross-community networks, 28
  polarised, 28
  separation, 164
Community Relations, Ministry of,
  83–4
Community Relations Commission, 84
conflict regulation, 3, 16–22, 72–3 *see
  also* mediation, Track 2 diplomacy
Congressional Ad Hoc Committee, 81
Connor, Walker, 30
Conservative Party, 7, 110
consociationalism, 16
constitutional issues, 10, 13–14,
  16, 41–2, 62–4, 160 (*see also*
  sovereignty)
  cross-community support, 45–6
  majority consent, 57, 62
  in text of GFA, 172–5
consumerism, 155
Council of Europe, 97
Council of the Isles, 11
Craigavon, Lord, 139
Craig-Collins Pact, 138
Crick, Bernard, 74
criminal justice system, 16
  in text of GFA,195–6
Crocker, C., 93–4
cross-border cooperation, *see*
  North–South links
Cuba, 74, 75
cultural issues, 163
  in text of GFA,190–1
Czechoslovakia, 31

Dáil Éireann, 24, 63
de Chastelain, General John, 9, 10
decommissioning, 12, 15–16, 23,
  41–3, 65, 143, 164, 169
  block to implementation of GFA,
  25–7, 146
  cross-community support, 45–7
  International Commission, 10, 24
  prerequisite, 7–8
  questions of legitimacy, 66
  responsibility, 142
  in text of GFA, 191–2

demilitarisation, 24, 60, 65
democracy
    and republicanism, 56
    subscription to, 141–2
Democratic Dialogue, 128, 134–5
Democratic Party, 81, 82
Democratic Unionist Party (DUP), 7,
    88, 93, 146
    and AIA, 6
    and GFA, 42, 44–6
    Assembly elections, 24
    and talks process, 8, 9
    and UUP, 133
demography, 2, 19, 21, 157, 160, 163
source of instability, 162
Denmark, 97
Des Moines workshop, 1991, 86, 87,
    93
Deutsch, Karl, 30
devolution, 8–9
d'Hondt mechanism, 14, 26, 41
diplomacy
    Anglo-Irish, 73–8
    'hurting stalemate', 78–80
    interstate conflict resolution, see
        Track One diplomacy
    unofficial diplomacy, see Track
        Two diplomacy
direct rule, 97, 150–1, 155
Disability Action, 111
Disraeli, Benjamin, 136
Dodd, Senator, 83
Donaldson, Jeffrey, 12
Doob, William, 84–5
Downing Street Declaration, 1993, 4,
    6–7, 13, 77, 82, 140, 145, 151,
    154
Drumcree, Co. Armagh, 9, 28, 143
Dubs, Lord, 110
Duisburg workshop, 1988, 85–6, 92
Dunmurry, Co. Antrim, 28

Economic Development, Department
    of, NI, 98
economic issues, 15
    in text of GFA, 190–1
education system, 28
elections
    Assembly, 24
    Forum, 7

emigration, 162
Enniskillen bomb, 1987, 5
Equal Opportunities Commission,
    105, 108, 113
equality, 9–10, 15, 17–19, 29, 32, 63,
    96–121, 154, 162
    'affirmative action', 112–13
    complaints procedure, 116–17
    cultural, 60, 163
    degree of change, 64–5
    delivering on GFA provisions,
        117–21
    developing anti-discrimination
        agenda, 97–9
    economic, 98, 157
    extent of inequality, 156–8
    implementing, 109–13
    innovative provisions, 117–19
    mainstreaming, 96–7, 100
    alternative models of, 102–3
    NI Act, 1998, 110–17
    PAFT, 99–103
    religious, 110
    in Republican ideology, 58–62
    in text of GFA, 186–9
    White Paper, 105–6, 108, 109–10
Equality Commission, 15, 24, 28,
    107, 109–10, 112
    and Assembly, 120–1
    role of, 113–17
equality duty, 111, 112–13, 114
equality schemes, 114–15
ethnonationalism
    and elite intervention, 30–1
    and GFA, 30–48, 41–3
    and NI conflict, 31–6
    responses to GFA, 43–6
    and state identity, 36–41
    typology, 33–4
European Commission, 97
European Community, 76
European Convention on Human
    Rights, 15, 106, 107, 108,
    114
European Parliament, 90
European Union, 2, 9, 10, 53, 114
    economic links, 63
    integration, 61, 152, 153
    NI and SEA, 89–91, 92
    and NI conflict, 31–6, 78

Executive, GFA, 16, 25, 47, 48
  attempts to form, 24–6, 41
  decommissioning impasse, 24–6, 29, 65
  equality issues, 111–12, 120
  fair representation, 106
  ministries, 24
  power-sharing, 18
  'shadow' form, 14

fair employment, 2
Fair Employment Act 1976, 98, 113
Fair Employment Act 1989, 99, 101, 154
Fair Employment Agency, 98
Fair Employment Commission, 105, 108, 113
Federal Bureau of Information (FBI), 75, 82
Fianna Fáil, 8, 13
Finland, 97
First World War, 149, 154
FitzGerald, Garret, 5, 77
Flanders, 97
Flynn, Bill, 82
Folz, William, 84–5
Forum for Peace and Reconciliation, 1995, 59
Framework Document (Joint British–Irish), 1995, 7, 11, 13, 77
Franco, Paul, 126
Frederick Naumann Foundation, 73–4
Friends of Ireland, 81
Fukuyama, Francis, 145

Garvin, Tom, 148
Good Friday Agreement, see also equality
  background to, 4–9
  election, 31
  and ethnonationalism, 41–3
  implementing, 1998–99, 24–9
  interpretations, 145–69
  logic of, 16–23
  nationalist and republican responses, 62–70
  politics of civility, 122–44, 138–42

public responses to, 43–6
  public support for principles, 48
  role of leaders, 3–4, 28–9, 95
  talks process, 9–13
  terms of, 13–16
  text of, 171–201
Government of Ireland Act 1920, 13, 16
Gramsci, Antonio, 131
Grenoble workshop (1990), 86–94

Habermas, Jurgen, 129–30
Harvard workshop, 1996, 86–7, 88
Haughey, Charles, 8
Hayes, Maurice, 84
Heads of Agreement paper, see Propositions on Heads of Agreement
healing process, 22–3, 55
Hegel, G.W.F., 126, 136
Henlein, Konrad, 140
Heskin, Ken, 75
Hillsborough Declaration, 1999, 25, 142, 143
Holkerri, Harry, 9
Holland, Mary, 104
human rights, 23, 29, 96 (see also equality)
  in text of GFA, 186–9
Human Rights Act 1998, 96
Human Rights Commission, 24, 28
Hume, John, 6, 13, 53, 64, 83
  concept of legitimacy, 59
  Hume–Adams talks, 57, 82
  ideological innovations, 51, 52, 53–8, 66, 69, 70
  unionist response to, 62
hunger strikes, 1981, 56, 154

Identity
  essentialist, 54
  ethnic, 33–6
  and GFA, 65
  Irish, 54–5
  national, 33–6
  relations between ethnic, national, state identity, 37–40
  syncretic, 54, 78
  unionist, 58
  variation in, 37–8

Ideology
  change in, 52
  and GFA, 65–70
  structure, 51–2
  system, 51–2, 69–70
  nationalist, 53–6
  republican, 56–62
Immigration Bill, USA, 81
Institute for a Democratic Alternative
    in South Africa (IDASA), 73–4,
    92
Iran, 75
Ireland Funds, 90
Irish America, 81
Irish Constitution, 1937
  Articles 2 and 3, 14, 18, 41–2
    in text of GFA, 173–5
  changes delayed, 24
Irish Immigrant Reform Movement, 81
Irish language, 15, 24, 60, 63, 157
Irish National Caucus, 81
Irish Republic, 5–7, 32, 97, 149–50
  Anglo-Irish diplomacy, 73–8,
    153–4
  constitutional issues, 13–14, 18,
    19, 46
  decommissioning issue, 25–6, 66
  economy, 161, 165
  equality issues, 104, 111
  Irish dimension, 54–5
  majority consent, 46
  'middle Ireland', 140
  minority rights, 21
  North–South links, 63–4
  referendums, 13
  social changes, 8
  talks process, 11–12
  and unionists, 6
Irish Republican Army (IRA), 1–2, 6,
    92, 135, 163, 164 (*see also*
    decommissioning)
  ceasefire, 1994, 7, 34, 151
  ceasefire, 1997, 8, 103
  military stalemate, 5
  policing by, 28
  US support, 75, 82
  war weariness, 79–80
Israel, 73, 74, 79

Joint Steering Group (British–Irish), 76

Kennedy, Senator Edward, 81, 82, 83
Kennedy School of Government,
    Harvard, 87
King, Tom, 99
Kornfeld, Paul, 125

Labour Party, UK, 7–8, 8–9, 103
  and equality, 104
  NI Bill, 1998, 110–13
Lake, Anthony, 82
Lebanon, 32
legitimacy, 23
  changing concepts of, 54, 58–9,
    66–7
  conflicts over, 19–21
Lester, Lord, 111, 113
Liberal Democrats, 111
liberalism, 128, 152, 153
  and nationalism, 50–1, 54–5
  of SDLP, 53–6
Libya, 75
loyalism, 2
  equality issues, 103–4
  paramilitary ceasefire, 1994, 7
  paramilitary decommissioning, 43
  and unionism, 153
Lynch, Jack, 71

McAleese, Mary, 144
MacBride Principles, 98
McCall, Cathal, 78
McCartney, Robert, 135
McGarry, John, 32, 36, 50
McGuinness, Martin, 24, 80
Machiavelli, Niccolo, 73
McIntyre, Anthony, 56–7
Macmillan, Harold, 136
McNamara, Kevin, 111
MacPherson, C.B., 131
mainstreaming, 96–7, 100
  alternative models of, 102–3
  effects of, 118–19
majoritarianism, 45–6, 153
Mallon, Seamus, 24, 26
Mandela, Nelson, 83, 93
Mayhew talks, *see* multi-party talks
mediation, 72–3
  potential for, 78–80
Messines Ridge commemoration, 154
Middle East, 74, 79

Mitchell, Senator George, 9, 26
  appointment of, 82–3
  talks deadline, 11–12
Mitchell Document, 12, 106, 108
modernisation, effects of, 148–9
Molyneaux, James, 7
Mouffe, Chantal, 131–2, 139, 141
Mowlam, Mo, 104, 111
  equality issues, 109–10
Moynihan, Senator Daniel, 81
multiculturalism, 128, 156
multinational investment, 161
multi-party talks, 1991–3, 6, 77, 137
multi-party talks, 1996–8, 8, 9–13,
  34
Murphy, Paul, 110, 111–12
Musil, Robert, 139

Nairn, Tom, 30
Namibia, 74
National Democratic Institute, 86
National Security Council, 82
nationalism, *see also*
      ethnonationalism
  approach to unionism, 68–9, 130–1,
    135
  change within, 53–6
  classic vs liberal, 5–2
  community interests, 17–19
  cultural change, 152–3
  definitions challenged, 78
  and GFA
      expectations of, 163
      gains from, 62–5
      ideological effects of, 65–9
  growing respectability of, 39–40
  growth of, 149–50
  Irish identity, 37–41, 54, 156
  and 'middle Ulster', 139–40
  of SDLP, 53–6
  of SF, 56–62
NATO, 153
Nelson, Rosemary, 28
Netherlands, 97
New Ireland Forum, 154
New York Times, 82
New Zealand, 97
Nicaragua, 75
Noraid, 81
North Korea, 75

Northern Ireland Act 1998, 24, 96,
  119
  equality debate, 110–13
  equality provisions, 113–17
Northern Ireland Assembly (1984), 32
Northern Ireland Assembly (GFA), 4,
  11, 24, 47, 48
  agreed, 14
  d'Hondt mechanism triggered, 26
  disagreement on, 10
  equality issues, 111–12, 114,
    116–17, 120–1
  fair representation, 106
  and North-South bodies, 12
  political divisions, 22–3
  regional development strategy,
    107
  in text of GFA, 175–80
  voting system, 18
Northern Ireland Centre in Europe
    (NICE), 86, 90–1
Northern Ireland Constitution Act
    1973, 97–8
Northern Ireland Council on Ethnic
    Minorities, 111
Northern Ireland Disability Council,
    105, 108, 113
Northern Ireland Forum, 1996, 7, 10,
    86
Northern Ireland Human Rights
    Commission, 15, 107
  in text of GFA, 167–8
Northern Ireland (NI), *see also*
      equality
  Anglo-Irish diplomacy, 73–8
  balance of power, 158–60, 161–3
  conflict
      causes of, 22–3, 147–51
      risk of renewal, 160–5
      theory of, 147–51
  current conjuncture, 151–69
  economy, 1–2
  ethnonationalism in, 31–6
  geopolitical significance, 74–6
  legitimacy of state, 19–20
  politics of civility, 122–44
  state identity, 36–41
  status in UK, 13, 16, 20
  system of relationships, 148–50,
    158–60

Northern Ireland Office (NIO), 91,
    103
  community relations, 99, 101
  equality issues, 110–11, 112
Northern Ireland Women's Coalition,
    9, 89, 104
North–South bodies, 20, 24, 65,
    163
  fair representation, 106
  relations with Assembly, 10, 12
  on text of GFA, 181–4
North–South links, 6, 9, 59, 60, 141,
    151, 159
  nationalist views of, 43
  and SDLP, 65–6
North–South Ministerial Council, 14,
    16, 18, 21, 24, 41, 63
  responses to, 43
  in text of GFA, 181–3

Oakeshott, Michael, 129, 131, 132,
    137, 139, 141
  on civility, 123, 125–7
O'Leary, Brendan, 16, 32, 36, 50
Omagh bomb, 28
O'Neill, Shane, 130–1
O'Neill, Terence, 31–2
Orange Order, 8, 9, 19, 23, 27, 84,
    146, 157, 163
  post-GFA violence, 28
Oslo Accord, 74, 79, 87–8
O'Sullivan, Noel, 129

Paisley, Rev. Ian, 44
Palestine Liberation Organisation
    (PLO), 75, 79
paranocracy, 75
parity of esteem, 41, 47, 156
Parliamentary Commissioner Act
    1967, 115
partition, 20, 149–50, 164–5, 167
  recognition of, 153
  republican views, 56–7
'Partnership for Equality' (White
    Paper), 105–6, 108, 109–10
Patten Commission, see Police
    Commission
peace process, 6–7, 57, 60, 151
  DSD, 6–7
  'parallel', 104

Pledge of Office, 14, 106 (see also
    Code of Conduct for Ministers)
  in text of GFA, 180
Policing, Commission on, 15–16, 24,
    43
  in text of GFA, 194–5
police reform, 29, 59, 60, 64–5
policing, 9–10, 23, 41, 93, 163
  paramilitaries, 28
  responses to, 46
  in text of GFA, 192–4
Policy Appraisal and Fair Treatment
    (PAFT), 99–103, 113, 119
  reform sought, 103, 104
  replacement, 105, 106
Policy Studies Institute, 98
political civility, 29, 122–44
  condition of civility, 123–32
  and GFA, 138–42
  politics of incivility, 132–8
  prospects for, 142–4
political parties, see also DUP, PUP,
    SDLP, SF, UDP, UUP
  demands of political civility,
    141–2
  hostility to, 128–9
  tied to GFA, 163–4
Portadown, Co. Armagh, 28
Porter, Norman, 136–8
Portugal, 97
postmodernism, 152, 155, 158, 167
post-nationalism, 152
  in John Hume's ideology, 53–5
Powell, J. Enoch, 75, 80
power-sharing, 21, 151, 159
  executive, 1974, 32
prisoners
  releases, 4, 16, 20, 24, 29, 41, 65
  responses to releases, 42, 46
  in text of GFA, 196
prisons, 9–10
Pro Mundi Vita, 76
Progressive Unionist Party (PUP), 42,
    153
  equality issues, 104
  talks process, 8, 9–13
  views of GFA, 164
proportional representation, 14, 16
Propositions on Heads of Agreement,
    11, 104

Protestants, *see also* unionists
  cultural inequality, 157
  economic inequality, 98
  ethnic identity, 38–41
  individual responsibility, 84
  political divisions, 155
  sense of Irishness, 55
public sector, 161
  definition of, 115–16
  equality issues, 120
  equality schemes, 114–17
punishment beatings, 28

Reagan, Ronald, 75, 81
referendums, 13
regional development, 107
Reid, Father Alex, 86
religion
  and causes of conflict, 147–8
  and ethnonationalism, 33
  and identity, 38
Republican Party (US), 81
republicanism
  anti-colonialism, 79
  changes within, 52, 56–62
  electoral strategy, 56
  and GFA
    gains from, 62–5
    ideological effects of, 65–9
    response to, 62–5
  ideology of, 56–62
  and nationalism, 39–40
  negotiation, 159–60
  principle of consent, 62
  tensions within, 67–8
Reynolds, Albert, 8
'risk society', 165
Robinson, Mary, 8
Rose, Richard, 133
Royal Ulster Constabulary (RUC),
  27, 28, 43 (*see also* police
  reform, policing, policing,
  Commission on)

Santayana, George, 128–9, 130, 138,
  140, 142
Saunders, Harold H., 73
Schmitt, Carl, 124, 131, 132–3
Schulze, K.E., 78–9
Scotland, 8, 9, 11

Assembly, 14–15
  nationalism, 165
sectarianism, 4, 21, 28, 134, 136,
  143, 146, 160, 164, 169
  assassinations, 11, 28, 42
secularism, 56, 152
security
  for unionists
    in text of GFA, 192
self-determination, 59, 140
  redefined, 54
self-interest, politics of, 140
Shannon, Bill, 77
Shils, Edward, 123–5, 139
Single European Act (SEA), 89–91,
  92
Sinn Féin, 6, 80, 86
  decommissioning issue, 25–7,
    42–3
  elections, 7, 24
  equality issues, 103–4
  and GFA
    responses to, 44
    responsibilities of, 142
    steps towards, 77
    views of, 164–5
  peace process, 9–13, 138–9
  politics of threat, 143
  and republican ideology, 58–60
  role of moderates, 163
  and SDLP, 5, 133
  unionist views of, 135
  UUP talks, 27
  workshops, 88, 92, 93
Smith, Jean Kennedy, 83
Social Democratic and Labour Party
  (SDLP), 159
  effects of GFA, 65–6, 68
  elections, 7, 24
  and GFA
    responses to, 44–6
    views of, 164
  nationalism of, 39, 53–6
  NI Bill, 1998, 111
  pro-European, 90
  and Sinn Féin, 5, 133
  talks process, 9–13
  unionist views of, 135
  and UUP, 27
  workshops, 92

social issues, 15
  conservatism, 161
  in text of GFA, 190–1
Soderberg, Nancy, 82
South Africa, 32, 58, 73–4, 79, 83
  workshop, 1994, 86–7, 92–3
  workshop, 1997, 86, 92–3
sovereignty, issue of, 62–3, 64,
    152
  and multiple identities, 78
Spreicher, Dr Eberhard, 85–6
Standing Advisory Commission on
    Human Rights (SACHR),
    98–9, 101, 102–3, 106, 107
Stormont parliament, 97, 122, 133,
    153, 159, 160
  exclusionary character, 150
  suspended, 97
Strand 1 (Northern Irish
    relationships), 6, 9, 14, 41
  contentious issues, 10
  in text of GFA, 175
Strand 2 (North–South relations), 6,
    9, 14, 41
  contentious issues, 10–11
  in text of GFA, 181–4
Strand 3 (British–Irish relations), 6,
    9, 12, 14–15, 41
  human rights, 108
  in text of GFA, 184–6
Strasbourg workshop, 1993, 86, 87,
    88
Sudeten syndrome, 140
Sunningdale Agreement, 1–2
Sweden, 97
Switzerland, 31

Taylor, A.J.P., 140
terrorism, international, 75
Thatcher, Margaret, 77, 154
Track One diplomacy, 71, 77, 89,
    91, 92, 94
Track Two diplomacy
  Adams visa, 80–3, 94
  definition of, 72–3
  importance of communication,
    77
  in NI, 71–95
  workshops, 83–93
tradition, role of, 52, 137

Trimble, David, 8, 12–13, 25, 26, 27,
    137, 138, 139
  decommissioning issue, 12
  first minister, 24

Ulster Democratic Party (UDP), 42
  talks process, 8, 9–13
  views of GFA, 164
Ulster Unionist Party (UUP), 136, 153
  and AIA, 6
  changes within, 137
  decommissioning issue, 25–7
  and DUP, 133
  elections, 7, 24
  equality issues, 104
  and GFA
    opposition to, 42
    responses to, 44–6, 164
  NI Bill, 1998, 111
  peace process, 8, 9–13, 138–9
  role of moderates, 163
  and SDLP, 27
  Trimble leads, 7
  workshops, 88
Ulster-Scots culture, 163
unemployment, 98, 107
Union, 17–19, 18, 19, 40–1
  British commitment to, 9
  and GFA, 164
  majority consent, 45–6
  reasons for defence, 130–1
unionism, 56, 136–8 (see also
    ethnonationalism)
  and AIA, 5–6
  British identity, 37–41, 156
  community interests, 17–19
  cultural change, 153
  decommissioning issue, 66, 143
  defending with reasons, 130–1
  emergence of, 149–50
  and 'equality agenda', 157–8
  and EU, 91, 92
  Forum boycott, 7
  and GFA
    conditional support for, 52
    expectations of, 163
    steps towards GFA, 77
  ideology, 62
  legitimacy recognised, 153
  'middle Ulster,' 139–40

nationalist views of, 54, 58
and new republicanism, 68–9
veto, 43, 45–6
views of nationalism, 135
Unison, 101, 102, 104, 111
united Ireland, 17, 18, 159, 160
   and GFA, 20, 43, 164–5
   majority decision, 13
   in republican ideology, 57, 58–9
   in republican strategy, 59–62
United Irishmen, 167
United Kingdom Unionist Party
      (UKUP), 8, 9, 88
   anti-GFA, 42
United Nations Development
      Programme, 97
United Nations Security Council, 75
United Nations World Conference on
      Women, 1995, 97
United States of America, 2, 5, 53,
      75–6
   equality issues, 100, 111
   Irish-American changes, 80–2
   MacBride Principles, 98
   'new world order,' 9, 152

and South Africa, 74
University of Stirling, 84–5

van Straubenzee committee, 98
vigilantism, 28
Virginia workshop, 1990, 86–92

Wack, Pierre, 73
Wales, 8, 11
   Assembly, 14–15
'Way Forward, The', 1999, 26
Williams, Lord, 110
women
   gender equality, 96–7
   political participation, 89
Women's Support Network, 104
workshops, 71, 83–93
   1990–96, 86–93
   assessment of, 94–5
   Duisburg, 1988, 85–6
   Scotland, 1972, 84–5
   'shared learning,' 91–2
World Bank, 97

Yugoslavia, 33